JOURNAL OF SPORT MANAGEMENT

JOURNAL OF SPORT MANAGEMENT

The *Journal of Sport Management* aims to publish innovative empirical, theoretical and review articles focused on the governance, management and marketing of sport organizations. Submissions are encouraged from a range of areas that inform theoretical advances for the management, marketing and consumption of sport in all its forms, and sport organizations generally. Review articles and studies using quantitative and/or qualitative approaches are welcomed.

The *Journal of Sport Management* publishes research and scholarly review articles; short reports on replications, test development, and data reanalysis; editorials that focus on significant issues pertaining to sport management; articles aimed at strengthening the link between sport management theory and sport management practice; journal abstracts ("Sport Management Digest"); and book reviews ("Off the Press").

Editor:

David Shilbury
International Faculty of Business & Law
Sport Management Program
Deakin Business School
Deakin University
221 Burwood Hwy
Burwood, Victoria 3125 Australia
E-mail: shilbury@deakin.edu.au

Human Kinetics staff:

Publisher: Human Kinetics, Inc.
Journals Division Director: Kathleen Burgener
Journals Division Associate Director: Casey A. Buchta
Graphic Designer: Human Kinetics staff
Fulfillment/Circulation Director: Shari Schultz

Human Kinetics contact information:

Human Kinetics, Inc.
P.O. Box 5076, 1607 N. Market St.
Champaign, IL 61825-5076 USA
Phone: 800-747-4457 (USA); 217-351-5076

Subsidiaries of Human Kinetics, Inc.:

Australia
Phone: (08) 8372 0999
E-mail: info@hkaustralia.com

Canada
Phone: 1-800-465-7301 (in Canada only)
Phone: 519-971-9500
E-mail: info@hkcanada.com

Europe (United Kingdom)
Phone: +44 (0) 113 255 5665
E-mail: journals@hkeurope.com

New Zealand
Phone: 0800 222 062
E-mail: info@hknewzealand.com

JOURNAL OF
SPORT
MANAGEMENT

Volume 31 • Number 1 • January 2017

Articles

Other

The *Journal of Sport Management* is the official journal of the
North American Society for Sport Management.

Journal of Sport Management, 2017, 31, 1-14
https://doi.org/10.1123/jsm.2015-0371
© 2017 Human Kinetics, Inc.

All Rivals Are Not Equal: Clarifying Misrepresentations and Discerning Three Core Properties of Rivalry

B. David Tyler

Western Carolina University

Joe Cobbs

Northern Kentucky University

Rivalry is ubiquitous across sports, yet the representation and specification of rivalry varies widely. Such discrepancy poses problems when distinguishing between multiple out-groups and when employing rivalry to explain related questions such as demand for sport consumption. In this paper, we critically examine the many differing conceptions of rivalry and to discern properties of rivalry across different sports. We survey college football fans ($N = 5,304$) to empirically test the exclusivity, scale, and symmetry of rivalry; then, we replicate the study twice in the context of professional sports (1,649 National Football League fans; 1,435 National Hockey League fans). Results consistently indicate that fans perceive multiple rivals (nonexclusive), rivalry intensity varies among rivals (continuous in scale), and opposing fans rarely share equivalent perceptions of the rivalry (bidirectional). Accordingly, we develop and test a parsimonious 100-point rivalry allocation measure that specifies these three properties of rivalry.

Keywords: rivalry, demand, attendance, sport marketing, social identity, team identification

Green Bay is by far Chicago's biggest rival. Allocating over seven times the amount of [rivalry] to them over the second [rival] accurately represents my feelings. (Respondent 9521)

Ohio [State] will always be the biggest rival, with Notre Dame a distant second. MSU wants to be our rival, but hey, Little Brothers always want to live up to their big brothers. (Respondent 1084)

Those who split up rivalries among different schools don't really get what "rivalry" means. (Respondent 1)

Perhaps the very ubiquity of "rivalry" in sport parlance has contributed much to its muddied understanding. Were the idea of a "rival team" merely the centerpiece of barroom banter and media punditry, agreement on what properties compose a rivalry would be little more than pedantry. However, the implications of understanding which out-groups rise to the level of "rivalry" extend much further. Sport rivalry helps explicate player motivations (Kilduff, Elfenbein, & Staw, 2010), evaluation of

sponsors (Bee & Dalakas, 2015; Bergkvist, 2012), league alignment (Havard, Wann, & Ryan, 2013; Koos, 2014), tournament seeding (Cox & Clark, 2014), and broadcast scheduling (Nathan, 2010). Rivalry is a frequent variable within models of demand estimation for attendance and television ratings. Such information is vital for a variety of stakeholders, including a team's administrators, sport sponsors, broadcast outlets, event managers, and government entities (Borland & MacDonald, 2003), yet the rivalry construct has not been consistently specified. Individual researchers have employed their own approaches to determining what constitutes a rivalry, thereby formulating a construct that lacks consistent application.

Our purpose in this paper is to examine differing conceptions of out-groups that rise to the level of rival; then discern and empirically test key properties of rivalry across different sports; and finally, propose a measure of rivalry that accurately captures these properties. We start by highlighting social identity theory (SIT) and critically reviewing previous designations of rivalry. To do so, we outline scholars' understanding of multiple out-groups and how rivalry has been empirically specified in analysis of game demand. Next, we present a study of fan perceptions across three sports contexts that uncovers three key properties of rivalry often violated by past representations; accordingly, we offer a parsimonious alternative measure for researchers to employ when specifying the effect of

B. David Tyler is with the College of Business, Western Carolina University, Cullowhee, NC. Joe Cobbs is with the Department of Marketing, Economics and Sports Business, Northern Kentucky University, Highland Heights, KY. Address author correspondence to B. David Tyler at dtyler@wcu.edu.

a rivalry. Finally, ideas for future research directions are suggested. If researchers can better distinguish between out-groups and represent rivalry with consistency, demand models will be more accurate, thereby improving the prediction of event attendees and the television audience. Furthermore, the broad phenomenon of rivalry in the context of various out-groups can be dissected with greater consistency across future studies, which is necessary to further advance knowledge of the nature of rivalry, including its various antecedents and outcomes.

Out-groups, Opponents, and Rivalry

Rivalry is often understood through the lens of SIT (Havard, 2014; Tyler & Cobbs, 2015). According to SIT, individuals' identities are formed through the process of self-categorization whereby individuals align themselves to social groups in which they view the members as sharing common characteristics (Dimmock, Grove, & Eklund, 2005; Stets & Burke, 2000; Tajfel & Turner, 1986). These "psychological groups" (Turner, 1982) are viewed as collections of individuals sharing an emotional involvement in the group and defining themselves, to some degree, in terms of the same category of membership as others (Ashforth & Mael, 1989; Tajfel & Turner, 1986). Individuals use these group memberships as a classification technique to place others within the same group(s) as oneself to comprise an in-group, while alternative groups represent out-groups (Hogg, 2006; Stets & Burke, 2000).

When identifying with a group, an individual internalizes in-group accomplishments and failures while seeking positive distinction from out-groups (Ashforth & Mael, 1989; Madrigal & Chen, 2008). Conceptualized in-groups are diverse in nature, spanning from nationalities to consumer brands to sports teams (e.g., Goertz & Diehl, 1993; Heere & James, 2007; Muñiz & O'Guinn, 2001). In the case of sport teams, these teams may serve as representations of other components of one's collective identity, such as one's university or home city (Heere & James, 2007; Lock, Taylor, & Darcy, 2011). Yet, each in-group manifestation is often perpetuated as much by its oppositional group(s) as its internally shared qualities (Brewer, 1979). As a result, individuals emphasize differences with out-groups, particularly when the distinction is perceived as positive toward the in-group (Hogg & Terry, 2000; Jetten, Spears, & Manstead, 1998). Such classifications facilitate the fitting of others into "us" and "them" categories. Rivalry then surfaces when competition raises the salience of an out-group whose comparison with the in-group becomes problematic for in-group members' self-concept (Tyler & Cobbs, 2015).

A challenge, however, is knowing which out-groups an in-group perceives as *rivals* as opposed to being mere competitors or possible opponents. When considered in terms of collective identity, a rival is not simply a grueling competitor as defined by the management literature (cf. Chen, 1996; Porter, 1980) but is "a highly salient outgroup that poses acute threat to ingroup identity and/

or esteem" (adapted from Tyler & Cobbs, 2015, p. 230). In the case of the sport fan identity, individuals may welcome that threat for the enhanced opportunity it creates to make positive comparisons to particular out-groups (Berendt & Uhrich, 2016). That is, success against a rival enhances the view of oneself more than success against a similarly competent competitor.

Existing research on rivalry has identified rivalry's antecedents (Kilduff et al., 2010; Tyler & Cobbs, 2015) and explored its outcomes (Havard, 2014; Kilduff, Galinksy, Gallo, & Reade, 2016). Lacking from our current theory is an agreed-upon understanding and empirical testing of universal characteristics inherent to rivalry itself. Social identity scholars have accepted that certain out-groups pose increased threat to group esteem (Riek, Mania, & Gaertner, 2006), which has also been seen in sport fan studies (Wann & Grieve, 2005), but there is inconsistent identification of which out-groups qualify as *rivals* for each particular in-group, especially within the sport landscape. This inconsistency is perhaps best illustrated by the wide disparity in how rivalry is represented as a predictor of consumer interest in specific matches.

Rivalry in Short-Run Demand Estimation

A common way for researchers to analyze demand for specific sporting contests is through "short-run" (game-by-game) regression modeling (Hill, Madura, & Zuber, 1982). The basic model regresses a dependent variable, typically either stadium attendance or television audience, against a series of hypothesized predictors (the independent variables). Perceived rivalry, which is assumed to enhance the attractiveness of the contest, is regularly included as one of these independent variables. Researchers who account for rivalry tend to use a proxy for rivalry, based on league structural factors or geographic proximity, or subjectively identify specific games/teams where rivalry is assumed. Aside from the issue of rivalry's inconsistent specification, each of these approaches has inherent shortcomings as ways of measuring fans' rivalrous feelings.

A rivalry proxy based on teams within the same division (e.g., Butler, 2002; Paul, 2003; Tainsky & Jasielec, 2014) assumes that all divisional opponents are rivals. This assertion seems implausible, particularly in leagues where close to half of the annual schedule is composed of intradivision games (e.g., Lemke, Leonard, & Tlhokwane, 2010). The intradivisional proxy fails to capture teams that are often considered rivals but do not play in the same division, such as Major League Baseball's Chicago White Sox and Chicago Cubs (Bauman, 2004) or the National Basketball Association's Los Angeles Lakers and Boston Celtics (Spears, 2007). In addition, this proxy may be capturing other, unintended phenomena, such as geographic proximity or access to postseason play. Unsurprisingly, the statistical significance of a divisional proxy as a representation of rivalry has varied widely—at times demonstrating a high degree of significance (Butler, 2002; McDonald & Rascher, 2000; Tainsky & Jasielec,

2014), at other times mild significance (Paul, 2003), and occasionally no significance (Tainsky & McEvoy, 2011; Tainsky & Stodolska, 2010; Welki & Zlatoper, 1994).

Other research assumes rivalry is rooted in locational proximity and employs a geographic-based rivalry proxy. This proxy might view as rivals any teams separated by less than a certain distance (e.g., Falter, Pérignon, & Vercruysse, 2008; Paton & Cooke, 2005; Peel & Thomas, 1988, 1992) or teams whose regions share a border (Baimbridge, 1997; Morley & Thomas, 2007). An alternative geographic approach assumes an inverse relationship between the strength of rivalry and the distance between teams (e.g., Baimbridge, Cameron, & Dawson, 1995; Forrest, Simmons, & Feehan, 2002; García & Rodríguez, 2002); this method creates a continuous proxy variable, which differs from the binary-variable approaches used by all the other aforementioned methods. A geographic proxy seems logical, especially since it is frequently identified as an element of rivalry (Havard, Gray, Gould, Sharp, & Schaffer, 2013; Quintanar, Deck, Reyes, & Sarangi, 2015; Tyler & Cobbs, 2015). However, a short distance between teams represents neither "a sufficient or even necessary condition to be included [as a rival]" (Forrest & Simmons, 2006, p. 253), and using distance in the absence of a separate, dedicated rivalry term eliminates any distinction between the effects of cost of attendance and rivalry intensity (Knowles, Sherony, & Haupert, 1992).

The use of divisional or geographic proxies offers a convenient and relatively objective attempt to specify rivalries, but the noted flaws with this blanket objectivity has led some researchers to subjectively pick games to be designated as rivalries. This judgment may be accomplished through the authors' own evaluations (e.g., Forrest, Simmons, & Buraimo, 2005; García & Rodríguez, 2002; Wilson & Sim, 1995) or a panel of perceived experts who evaluate what constitutes a rivalry (Boyd & Krehbiel, 2003; Lemke et al., 2010; Pacey & Wickham, 1985). Handpicking rivalries avoids some of the issues that come with proxies, but in this approach the researchers (or their panels) are imposing their own biases on the fans being studied, which could result in an under- or overspecification of the rivalry term in the estimation equation. Even if subjective identification of specific rivalries offers increased face validity, the potential pitfalls of bias and inconsistency across studies spell the need for enhanced clarity around the definition.

The Conceptualization of Three Core Properties of Rivalry

The inconsistent operationalization of rivalry clearly demonstrates the lack of consensus regarding the conceptualization of the rival relationship. Conflicting representations arise, in part, from researchers' ongoing disagreement with respect to the characteristics of rivalry. The review below addresses key areas of contention and hypothesizes three core properties of rivalry: rivalry is nonexclusive, continuous in scale, and bidirectional.

H1: Nonexclusivity—A Team Can Have More Than One Rival

Research in the fields of social psychology (Hogg & Abrams, 1988), interorganizational competition (Baum & Korn, 1996), and sport fandom (Havard, Wann, et al., 2013) shows that in-group members can perceive multiple out-groups. Accordingly, existing operationalization of rivalry within sport research typically allows for multiple rivals (e.g., Kilduff et al., 2010; Quintanar et al., 2015; Wann et al., 2016). Despite this, there have been few empirical efforts that evaluate fans' views of multiple out-groups potentially qualifying as rivals, and the idea of rival nonexclusivity is not universally accepted by scholars, fans, or the media (cf. Hudnell, 2015; Leonard & Van Long, 2008; Schwartz & McGarry, 2014).

Our first research hypothesis, based on the preponderance of scholars' conceptions of rivalry, is that fans perceive more than one team (out-group) to be a rival to their favorite team:

H1: $c \geq 1$

where c is the count (i.e., number) of perceived rivals for an entity.

This view allows for fans to perceive a singular rival or multiple rivals. While there is no disagreement that in-group members can perceive multiple out-groups, confirmation of H1 would offer an empirically grounded quantity of the perceived number out-groups seen as *rivals*. More important to the current research is that the acceptance of H1 lays the necessary groundwork for additional hypotheses, starting with the question of whether the multiple rivals are perceived with equivalent intensity.

H2: Continuous in Scale—Degrees of Rivalry Exist Among Multiple Rival Teams

Demand estimation research captures rivalry using a binary variable, except when distance between teams has been used as a continuous proxy variable. By using a value of 1, researchers assume that all designated opponents generate the same level of rivalry. However, this assumption may be flawed, as discussed above when examining division as a proxy. Just as not all competitors are considered rivals, not all teams seen as rivals may generate the same impact on a focal team's fans. That is, the rivalrous feelings associated with one opponent are not necessarily of the same magnitude as those associated with another rival ($\mu_i \neq \mu_j$, where μ is the average rivalry feelings, and i and j are rivalry positions). In Sanford and Scott's (2014) study of college football fans' willingness to pay, which featured rivalry as the dependent variable, fans would spend more on tickets for games against certain rivals compared with other identified rivals, which implies that fans' feelings toward rival opponents are not always equivalent.

For ease of consideration, let us assume that 100 represents the total "rivalry points" that one could allocate toward all teams considered to be rivals. If rivalry were a binary construct and the feeling toward all rivals were the same, a team with two rivals would have a "rivalry score" of 50 toward one rival and 50 toward the other rival. If five rivals, scores of 20 would be allocated toward each rival. This common operationalization in research assumes rivalrous feelings to be evenly distributed among the number of perceived rivals, which is a highly questionable representation. Therefore, research hypothesis H2 posits that rivalrous feelings are not evenly distributed among multiple rivals:

H2: $\mu_{AB} \neq 100 \,/\, c$

where μ_{AB} is the average degree to which Entity A perceives Entity B to be a rival, 100 is the amount of "rivalry feelings," and c is the number of perceived rivals for Entity A.

H3: Bidirectional—Rivalry Is Perspective-Based and Not Necessarily Shared by Opponents

As discussed above, the dominant perspective in the literature claims that a matchup *is* or *is not* a rivalry through researchers' use of a dummy variable where one indicates a rivalry and zero indicates absence of a rivalry. This binary approach presents a problem not only in ignoring variations in magnitude (H2) but also by assuming a match is considered a rivalry by both teams. Humphreys (2003) noted the potential for asymmetry within NCAA football: "North Carolina State is the rival for East Carolina . . . but North Carolina is State's rival. Navy is the rival for Air Force but Army is Navy's rival" (p. 9). Recall that a rival is conceptualized as an out-group that poses an acute threat (Tyler & Cobbs, 2015) and differences in factors such as opponent success and status may create variance in the perception of rivalry (Kilduff et al., 2010). While some rivalries or derbies may be perceived equally from both sides, many more contests considered by fans as rivalries are likely to be bidirectional and asymmetrical, where the perception of rivalry is highly dependent on the perspective or associated in-group (Quintanar et al., 2015). Therefore, in research hypothesis H3 we suggest that the difference between rivalry perceptions on each side of rivalry dyads will not equal 0:

H3: $\left| \mu_{AB} - \mu_{BA} \right| \neq 0$

where μ_{AB} is the average degree to which Entity A perceives Entity B to be a rival and μ_{BA} is the average degree to which Entity B perceives Entity A to be a rival.

Method

We surveyed college football fans ($N = 5{,}304$) from 122 Football Bowl Subdivision (or Division I-A) teams using an online questionnaire (via Qualtrics) posted on 194 fan message boards. The initial collection yielded 7,369 responses; researchers reviewed each response, discarding those that were partially or improperly completed,

for a completion rate of 72.0%. This study sought to understand the views of highly identified fans; thus, message board participants are an appropriate population (Havard, Reams, & Gray, 2013). Results from a 7-point identification scale included in the survey (adopted from Mael & Ashforth, 1992) supported this decision ($M = 5.2$, $SD = 1.0$), and a 7-point single-item identification measure (Postmes, Haslam, & Jans, 2013) also showed high identification ($M = 6.0$, $SD = 1.0$). Consumption among respondents was high with 83.9% attending one or more games per year. Almost all respondents lived in the United States (99.1%), geographically dispersed across 50 states (and Washington, DC, and Puerto Rico). Respondents were predominantly male (95.7%), the average age was 36.8, and 85.1% reported their highest level of education completed as college or higher; 77.6% attended the college of their favorite team (alumnus/a, current student, former student).

The plurality (H1) and variability (H2, H3) of rivalry intensity are open research questions. Thus, the survey left the decision of how rivalry is perceived to the respondents. The survey provided each respondent 100 "rivalry points" to allocate across one or more opponents of his or her favorite team.

A limit of numeric measures is understanding respondents' rationale when answering the questions (Morgan & Smircich, 1980), which is particularly relevant in the current study given the general confusion around rivalry's fundamental properties. Therefore, to allow for further insight beyond the quantitative scoring, we also collected open-ended textual data. The survey provided respondents with the option of detailing their rationale for rivalry point allocation. Researchers reviewed responses to this question ($N = 1{,}266$; average words = 34.4, $SD = 38.4$), as well as the responses to a general "any other comments" question at the end of the survey ($N = 949$; average words = 35.3, $SD = 48.0$). Upon completion of the quantitative analysis, we returned to the open-ended text and highlighted the respondents' comments that best provided a contextual illustration of any of the three topics addressed in our quantitative results. While these examples are included with the statistical findings below, it is important to note that our study is designed as a broad quantitative test of the research questions; respondents' quotes are offered as illustrations of these quantitative conclusions and not as a qualitative inquiry.

The median time to complete the survey was 12 min, and respondents spent a median 1.37 min assigning rivalry points. Additional survey questions asked about factors underpinning the rivalries and further demographic questions, which were not analyzed as part of the current study.

Replication in Different Sport Leagues: National Football League and National Hockey League

The phenomenon of rivalry is present across sports. Common antecedents to rivalry appear within sports around the world (cf. Tyler & Cobbs, 2015, Study 1), and rivalry researchers suggest their findings are applicable to sports beyond those in their studies' populations (e.g., Havard, Gray, et al., 2013; Luellen & Wann, 2010; Tainsky & McEvoy, 2011). Yet, those same rivalry researchers also highlight the need for replication across different sports when acknowledging their studies' limitations. Given our research goal of explicating properties foundational to the rivalry construct and consistent across sporting context, our study must reach beyond any single sport.

To examine broader generalizability of these hypotheses, further data were collected using the same method described above. The survey was modified slightly to be appropriate in the professional sport context, and fans of National Football League (NFL) and National Hockey League (NHL) teams were solicited via message board posts. A summary of the profile of these respondents is shown in Table 1. Each sporting context was analyzed separately because of the myriad of differences between college and professional sports, and the NFL and NHL, including season duration, frequency of competition, division/conference structure, geographic concentration, acquisition of players, and fans' points of attachment.

Results and Discussion

As will be shown throughout the results, there were no substantial differences in the findings among the three leagues. Therefore, for the sake of readability, the focus of our reporting is on the college football results, the largest of our data sets. The replicated studies within the NFL and NHL contexts resulted in statistically similar findings, but to reduce redundancy, the presentation of that data is not expounded in the same detail as the college football analysis.

H1: Nonexclusivity—A Team Can Have More Than One Rival

H1 sought to confirm the view that fans perceive more than one rival among numerous out-groups. We found support for this hypothesis by examining the frequency with which a certain number of rivals were identified (see Table 2). Within college football, the most common number of rivals listed was 3 ($N = 1,748$, 33.0% of respondents), with 92.4% of the respondents ($N = 4,903$) identifying more than one rival to their favorite team. Three was also the most common number of rivals identified by NHL ($N = 415$, 28.9% of respondents) and NFL ($N = 560$, 34.0% of respondents) fans, who named multiple rivals with even greater frequency than the college football fans (96.7% of NHL fans and 95.5% of NFL fans listed 2–10 rivals).

Inferential statistics also confirmed the research hypothesis. A one-sample t test was run to compare the sample mean number of rivals identified ($M = 3.578$ in college football) to the population mean $\mu = 1$, as null hypothesized in H1. The results rejected the null hypothesis, $t(5303) = 104.063$ ($p < .001$); that is, we reject the claim that fans perceive only one rival. Inferential statistics on the NHL ($M = 3.797$), $t(1434) = 65.913$ ($p < .001$), and NFL ($M = 3.864$), $t(1648) = 71.740$ ($p < .001$), showed similar significant results. The statistically significant differences further support the notion of multiple rivals per team, confirming the multiple rival conceptualization employed by most, but not all, previous scholars. Furthermore, the empirical evidence of the nonexclusivity of rivalry demonstrates the theory of multiple out-groups and provides some practical guidance by quantifying a mean number of perceived rivals (3) according to fans in three sports.

Table 1 Profile of College Football, National Football League (NFL), and National Hockey League (NHL) Respondents

Metric	College football	NFL	NHL
Respondent numbers			
Total responses	7,369	2,111	1,863
Usable responses	5,304	1,649	1,435
Completion rate	72.0%	78.1%	77.0%
Identification scores (on 7-point scales)			
Multi-item—M (SD)	5.2 (1.0)	5.0 (1.1)	4.9 (1.1)
Single-item—M (SD)	6.0 (1.0)	6.1 (1.0)	6.3 (1.0)
Demographics			
Live in United States (N)	99.1% (4,705)	93.6% (1,339)	72.6% (1,215)
Male (N)	95.7% (4,545)	95.4% (1,278)	87.8% (1,067)
Completed college (N)	85.1% (4,042)	57.7% (772)	57.0% (693)
Average age (SD)	36.8 (13.0)	26.7 (8.3)	25.8 (7.2)

Table 2 Frequency of Identifying a Given Number of Rivals and Rivalry Points Descriptive Statistics

Metric	1	2	3	4	5	6	7	8	9	10
College football										
Count of rivals identified (N)	401	948	1,748	1,053	539	279	121	58	24	133
Percent of sample	7.6	17.9	33.0	19.9	10.2	5.3	2.3	1.1	0.5	2.5
Mean rivalry points assigned to rivalry position	62.4	23.7	12.8	8.4	6.6	5.2	4.3	4.0	3.5	3.2
Median rivalry points assigned to rivalry position	60	25	10	10	5	5	5	5	3	2
National Football League										
Count (N)	74	145	560	443	223	103	53	12	4	32
Percent of sample	4.5	8.8	34.0	26.9	13.5	6.2	3.2	0.7	0.2	1.9
Mean rivalry points assigned to rivalry position	57.4	24.4	14.4	8.2	6.1	4.8	3.6	2.9	2.4	2.1
Median rivalry points assigned to rivalry position	50	25	15	9.5	5	5	4	2	1.5	1
National Hockey League										
Count (N)	47	219	415	386	204	87	38	11	2	26
Percent of sample	3.3	15.3	28.9	26.9	14.2	6.1	2.6	0.8	0.1	1.8
Mean rivalry points assigned to rivalry position	57.8	25.0	13.4	8.6	6.3	5.1	4.0	3.3	2.5	2.0
Median rivalry points assigned to rivalry position	51	25	10	10	5	5	5	3	2	1

H2: Continuous in Scale—Degrees of Rivalry Exist Among Multiple Rival Teams

With the exception of studies that approximated rivalry using distance between opponents (e.g., Baimbridge et al., 1995; Forrest et al., 2002; García & Rodríguez, 2002), all demand estimation research employed a binary term to capture a rivalry—1 for a "rivalry game," 0 for other games. Based on our results, we suggest such indiscriminate representation of rivalry to be inaccurate. Starting with descriptive statistics, Table 2 shows the points allocated to multiple rivals differs considerably. That is, the mean points allocated to the first rival listed (62.4, in the college football example) is remarkably different from the points allocated to the second rival listed ($M = 23.7$), which also varies widely from the points allocated to the third rival ($M = 12.8$), and so on through those listing up to a tenth rival ($M = 3.2$).

Though the means in Table 2 are intuitively informative, we can test H2 in a more robust fashion by making point distribution comparisons across respondents who named the same number of rivals. Recall that each respondent was free to identify a different number of rivals, and H2 asked about the degree of rivalry across all rivals. This means that a 50–50 distribution across two rivals is akin to a 25–25–25–25 distribution across four rivals; in both cases, the intensity among rivals is equivalent and represents a 1–0 comparison with nonrival team. Yet, comparing respondents' distribution of points when naming two rivals to those respondents naming four would be invalid. Therefore, we examine rivalry point allocations within the nine possible subsets of multiple rivals selected.

To statistically test H2, we segmented respondents by total rivals selected and compared the means of the points allocated to each rival listed within segments (see Table 3). That is, we ran separate inferential statistical analyses for respondents who selected two rivals ($N =$ 948), three rivals ($N = 1,748$), and so on. We conducted a series of one-way repeated-measures analyses of variance (ANOVAs)[1] for segments of respondents who selected three or more rivals; for the group selecting only two rivals, a paired-sample t test was used since ANOVA is intended for comparing three or more conditions. The null hypothesis in these tests was that the means of the points allocated to each rival listed are equal, and a rejection of the null would suggest that the mean points are not the same across all listed rivals. To use an example from the college football data, we see that respondents identifying four rivals ($N = 1,053$) allocated 55.2 points to the first rival listed, 23.4 to the second rival, 13.4 to the third rival, and 8.0 to the fourth rival, $F(1.334, 1403.551) =$ 3,534.664, $p < .001$. The ANOVA leads us to reject the null hypothesis; that is, we reject the idea that the points are allocated equivalently across each rival listed. The same conclusion holds true throughout each of the nine conditions, and for both the NHL and NFL data sets. These findings provide strong support for H2.

Respondents' written comments illustrated the idea of different rivalries having different intensity. Consider Respondent 1532, a Florida State (FSU) fan who listed Florida (45 points), Miami (40 points), and Clemson (15 points) as FSU's three rivals. He wrote, "The rivalry with Florida and Miami are 2 of the biggest in the nation. Clemson is a small rivalry that only exists because they are in the same conference as FSU." While that respondent pointed to divisional affiliation as influencing the rivalries, Respondent 1529, a Washington fan, noted the opponents' performance can impact the discrepancy in intensity: "The balance between oregon [sic] and Washington St. shifts based on their respective success, although if they were equally successful, I would still consider oregon [sic] the chief rival." An Alabama fan contributed a similar perspective, highlighting the supremacy of Auburn as a rival (50 points) while acknowledging the rivalry felt toward Louisiana State (LSU, 30 points) as well: "Auburn will always be our biggest rival hands down. I would of normally given them upwards of ~70pts but with them being down the last couple years, LSU rivalry growing I took the points to give the rising LSU rivalry" (Respondent 1461).

Similar comments were seen in the NFL data, such as a Chicago Bears fan who allocated 80 points to Green Bay, 11 to Detroit, and 9 to Minnesota: "Green Bay is by far Chicago's biggest rival. Allocating over seven times the amount of rival points to them over the second place team accurately represents my feelings" (Respondent 9521). A Los Angeles Kings fan (NHL) allocated 60 points to the Anaheim Ducks and 40 to the San Jose Sharks, stating that "they're both pretty strong rivals, but with the Ducks being considered more of a threat they tend to take the spotlight as far as the rivalry goes" (Respondent 7736). This fan expresses strong rivalrous feelings toward both teams but acknowledges that the rivalry with one team (Anaheim) is stronger than the rivalry with the other.

These data support the conception that fans perceive varying degrees of rivalry. We therefore conclude that rivalry should be treated as continuous in scale rather than binary. Binary specifications not only limit rivalry to an overly restrictive dichotomous scale but also imply that both sides of each rivalry dyad view the rivalry equally. Given the variability in rivalry scores, we proceed to test the hypothesis that actors in a rivalry may disagree on the other's relative importance.

H3: Bidirectional—Rivalry Is Perspective-Based and Not Necessarily Shared by Opponents

The construct of a rivalry is typically treated as symmetrical; that is, both actors in the dyad are assumed to view the other as an equally intense rival. In nearly all attendance estimation models, researchers identified "rivalry games" or "derbies" by assigning a value to the contest itself, regardless of where the game was being

Table 3 Inferential Statistic Tests for Differences Among Mean Rival Point Allocations in College Football

No. of total rivals assigned 1	Rival position									
	2	3	4	5	6	7	8	9	10	
1										
Avg. points	100									
Statistic	n/a, $N = 401$									
2										
Avg. points	73.6	26.4								
t test	$t(947) = 49.450^*, N = 948$									
3										
Avg. points	63.7	24.0	12.4							
ANOVA	$F(1.248, 2180.530) = 6,910.7^*, N = 1,748$									
4										
Avg. points	55.2	23.4	13.4	8.0						
ANOVA	$F(1.334, 1403.551) = 3,534.664^*, N = 1,053$									
5										
Avg. points	48.4	22.5	13.3	9.1	6.7					
ANOVA	$F(1.461, 786.168) = 1,741.474^*, N = 539$									
6										
Avg. points	46.3	20.8	12.8	8.8	6.4	5.0				
ANOVA	$F(1.376, 382.602) = 735.073^*, N = 279$									
7										
Avg. points	39.6	21.5	13.7	9.0	6.8	5.3	4.0			
ANOVA	$F(1.628, 195.365) = 361.413^*, N = 121$									
8										
Avg. points	42.1	19.8	12.0	7.5	5.9	5.1	4.0	3.6		
ANOVA	$F(1.353, 77.119) = 134.554^*, N = 58$									
9										
Avg. points	35.1	19.6	12.3	9.4	7.2	5.0	4.4	3.8	3.3	
ANOVA	$F(1.367, 31.442) = 58.394^*, N = 24$									
10										
Avg. points	35.3	18.1	10.7	8.0	6.9	5.5	4.6	4.1	3.6	3.2
ANOVA	$F(1.544, 203.765) = 233.705^*, N = 133$									

Note. n/a = not applicable; avg. = average; ANOVA = analysis of variance.

$^*p < .001$.

played and the associated hometown fans' perspective. To test the assumption that rivalry is viewed equivalently from both sides of the dyad (i.e., with shared intensity), we calculated the absolute difference of the mean rivalry scores within each dyad. For example, if fans of Team A allocated an average of 70 points to Team B, and Team B fans allocated an average of 55 points to Team A, the absolute difference of the means was 15 points.

We used a one-sample t test to compare the mean of the differences within each dyad to the population mean μ = 0, as hypothesized in H3. An analysis of the full college football data set dispelled the notion that rivalry sentiment was same in both directions of the dyad, $t(1000) = 17.195$ ($p < .001$). However, the mean difference was relatively small at 5.829 ($N = 1,001$ dyads). We considered this mean difference in context of the mean rivalry points per position (recall Table 2), which showed a considerable reduction in points after the first few listed rivals. This comparison led us to question whether the mild difference between rival scores might be attributable to differences among rivals in later listings where few points were allocated, thereby limiting variability.[2]

We reran the analysis with a sample limited to only those rivalries where both teams' fans generally agreed that the other is a rival, as determined by at least half of the respondents listing the other team in the first or second rivalry position. The focused analysis showed a larger mean difference ($M = 22.831$, $N = 55$ dyads) that was significantly different from zero, $t(54) = 10.979$ ($p < .001$). The 23-point difference between the means in this set of dyads provides clear evidence of a difference in perceived rivalry between the two sides of rivalry dyads. We used a similarly restrictive approach on the NFL and NHL data sets (see Table 4), which corroborated the findings. Thus, even when focusing on mutually agreed upon rivalries, there is still a considerable discrepancy in fans' view of the rivalry.

Textual comments illustrate that some fans recognize the potential for bidirectionality in rivalry. This realization was perhaps best exemplified by respondents who gave minimal points to an opponent, describing that opponent as the "little brother," while that opponent's fans gave significant points to the "big brother." This familial term is part of the college football fan's lexicon, reinforced in 2007 when Michigan's star running back Mike Hart used the term in a press conference to refer to Michigan State (MSU; Snyder, 2014). Not surprisingly, the term was frequent among Michigan and MSU respondents.[3] Wrote one Michigan fan, "Ohio [State] will always be the biggest rival, with Notre Dame a distant second. MSU wants to be our rival, but hey, Little Brothers always want to live up to their big brothers" (Respondent 1084). Another wrote, "Mike Hart's infamous 'Little Brother' quote really does fit Michigan State so well, or at least how Michigan fans look on the rivalry. It is usually a Michigan win (series record 68–32–5) and its impact on the [conference]

isn't as easy to see because it happens mid-season" (Respondent 1618).

Notice in the quote above that the respondent brings up Michigan's 65% win rate against MSU in an effort to reinforce the perception of superiority by the big brother team. The big brother respondents often attempt to make it clear that they do not perceive the little brother to be a threat; if seen as a threat, that would acknowledge the opponent to be a legitimate rival (Tyler & Cobbs, 2015), and giving too many points to such an opponent would provide validation to the little brother. For example, a Tennessee fan "gave the little brother [Vanderbilt] 1 point just to feel good about himself even though he's not really a rival" (Respondent 1102), while a North Carolina fan described North Carolina State (NC State) thus:

> It's somewhat of the "Little Brother" syndrome. They believe us to be fierce rivals while the student body (myself included) are increasingly writing them off. There's not much of left of the rivalry on our side when we view ourselves as superior in nearly all aspects. (Respondent 1415)

Similarly, a Calgary Flames (NHL) fan asserted the superiority of his team while dismissing the opponent by stating, "Strength of rivalry depends on the strength of the rival team; you can't be rivals with a team that you constantly beat. If the Oilers ever get good, they would become more of a rival" (Respondent 7513).

Though the little brother language was not as prevalent outside of the college football sphere, it was still found in the NFL and NHL data sets. For example, a Cincinnati Bengals (NFL) fan wrote the following: "Cleveland is like the little brother in the division. Ya hate em, but you don't wish ill will against them. Usually they take care of that themselves. The Battle for Ohio is supposed to be our biggest rivalry game but eh. We know we are the best team in Ohio" (Respondent 10171). Likewise,

Table 4   Comparison of the Means Within Each Dyad

Metric	All dyads	Two-sided dyads
College football		
Mean difference in rivalry scores	5.829	22.831
Number of dyads (N)	1,001	55
Test of mean difference from 0	$t(1000) = 17.195$*	$t(54) = 10.979$*
National Football League		
Mean difference in rivalry scores	4.792	16.160
Number of dyads (N)	275	15
Test of mean difference from 0	$t(274) = 8.176$*	$t(14) = 6.183$*
National Hockey League		
Mean difference in rivalry scores	6.290	19.720
Number of dyads (N)	239	12
Test of mean difference from 0	$t(238) = 8.836$*	$t(11) = 5.762$*

*$p < .001$.

a Chicago Blackhawks (NHL) fan commented that the "[Nashville] Predators and [Minnesota] Wild are like little brother rivals in the Midwest" (Respondent 9179); not surprisingly, the Blackhawks had rivalry point disparities with these two teams of 45.9 and 19.4, respectively, with Blackhawks' fans giving neither team more than 5.5 rivalry points.

These quotes illustrate the existence of perceived *uneven* rivalries yet do not necessarily imply that such games are "lesser" contests. On the contrary, the comments show the considerable meaningfulness of the games for one side of the dyad while simultaneously recognizing that the opponent may not assign the same meaning to the games' outcome. Ours is not a qualitative study, and we cannot truly assess how fans construct meaning in rivalry games, but these contextual examples show the need to launch future in-depth inquiries.

The quantitative analysis and accompanying written statements provide considerable support for H3 and the notion that rivalry must not be viewed strictly as symmetrical. Rather than simply seeing "rivalry games," scholars and pundits must instead look at rivalry as a bidirectional construct to be evaluated from the perspective of each side.

Contributions

The results of this research provide several contributions for researchers. First, we have explicated three foundational properties of rivalry. Each of these characteristics had been debated by fans and the media, and relatively unexplored by scholars. Yet, we saw strong, consistent results across large samples of fans in three separate leagues showing that rivalry is a nonexclusive, bidirectional construct that is continuous in scale. Contrary to the dearth of formal exploration of rivalry before 2010, the last several years have seen a dozen or more scholarly articles focused on sport rivalry. While the recent surge in research has contributed much in terms of exploring fan reactions (Havard, Gray, et al., 2013; Havard, Reams, & Gray, 2013; Havard, Wann, et al., 2013), antecedents (Tyler & Cobbs, 2015), and sponsorship implications (Bee & Dalakas, 2015), further advancing our understanding of rivalry is dependent upon consistency across future studies in specifying the construct. As the inquiry into rivalry increases, acceptance of these foundational properties will provide scholars with empirically based guidelines that had been previously violated.

Second, this research builds on the existing theoretical understanding of SIT's role in sport fan behavior. SIT has been recognized as central to grasping the concept of sport rivalry (Havard, 2014; Tyler & Cobbs, 2015), and this research furthers our comprehension of multiple out-groups' threat to one's social identity as a sport fan. It is already known that an individual perceives multiple out-groups based on the salient aspects of one's social identity at a given time (Blanton, Crocker, & Miller, 2000; Havard, Wann, et al., 2013; Hogg & Terry, 2000).

By discovering empirical support for H1 and H2, we demonstrate that sport fans perceive varying degrees of acute threat from multiple out-groups while a particular identity (sport team fan) is salient. When attentive to one's collective identity, an individual often perceives multiple *rivals*, each with a differing level of intensity. Thus, future research on fan identity should consider the effects of multiple out-groups, particularly in examinations of rivalry and its impact.

The perception of rivalry exists within in-group members' construction of their social identity. Accordingly, to ascertain members' perspective, accurate evaluation of rivalry must be rooted in the views of individuals on each side of the dyad rather than objective characteristics about a particular match-up. Analysis of choices and behaviors by specific in-groups has delivered estimations of rivalrous feelings, such as by isolating rivalry within a willingness to pay for tickets (Sanford & Scott, 2014) or through behavioral economics experiments with fans (Mills, Tainsky, Green, & Leopkey, 2016), but the current study offers the broadest assessment of sport fans' perceptions of their rival out-groups.

The results for H2 demonstrated that fans perceive degrees of rivalry, contrary to the binary operationalization in the vast majority of demand estimation research. Thus, the third contribution of this research is the introduction and application of the 100-rivalry point allocation system. The 100-point approach needs further validation, but early trials demonstrate its promise as a parsimonious mechanism to determine fans' relative level of rivalrous feelings toward opponents. While we devoted considerable space to flaws in existing rivalry operationalization, that should not be interpreted as condemnation of past works; those scholars used what they judged as the best options available to represent rivalry. Now, in lieu of proxies or subjective judgments to identify rivalries, researchers have an alternative moving forward. They can implement the 100-point system in their own data collection, or pull the data from this and subsequent research at http://www.knowrivalry.com, an open website established expressly for sharing these findings with scholars and practitioners.

Limitations and Future Research

Replicating the findings across three different sports was imperative to generalize our results, yet we are still limited to North American team sports. Extending this research to other leagues, such as Australian Rules Football, German soccer, or Russian hockey, will help in understanding the cross-cultural robustness of these rivalry properties. Likewise, our focus is on team sports, but fan views may differ for rivalries in individual sports such as tennis (Evert vs. Navratilova) or golf (Palmer vs. Nicklaus), or in sports like Formula 1 or athletics. In addition, individuals identify with many social groups simultaneously (Heere & James, 2007; Lock & Funk, 2016), and there can be multiple out-groups for each identity. Future research should examine these core properties (especially H2 and H3) in other contexts, such as places of employment or nonsport brand communities.

Our study's findings are based only on quantitative analysis with respondents' comments chosen to illustrate these results. A qualitative study could achieve greater depth of individual fan insight regarding these properties of rivalry as well as potentially uncovering additional properties of the broader phenomenon. Such an inquiry could also build on Havard's (2014) qualitative findings in exploring how fans construct meaning within rivalry contests, something we cannot interpret using this article's chosen quotes but that would be of great value in understanding rivalry's importance to individuals. Some of our qualitative data also implied that perceptions of rivalry can change over time, yet our findings only represent fans' views at the time of data collection. Longitudinal work using the 100-point measure could provide a quantitative measure of the mutability of rival perceptions, particularly in instances of conference realignment (Havard, Wann, et al., 2013), as well as keeping these data current for future researchers.

Though the 100-point measure appears to represent rivalry well, further validation of this measure is needed. The next step may be to triangulate the findings with nonsurvey attempts at measuring rivalry (e.g., Mills et al., 2016; Quintanar et al., 2015; Sanford & Scott, 2014), or with survey efforts that have used a different approach (e.g., Havard, Reams, & Gray, 2013). Also useful would be the replication of previous demand estimation research but with replacement of the binary rivalry term with this continuous measure; the degree to which it improves the model's predictive ability will provide another indication of the 100-point mechanism's practical utility.

Finally, a limitation of the 100-point approach is that it cannot be used to accurately compare rivalry dyads outside of a single team's opponents. For example, we believe it works well to compare the relative feelings of Indianapolis Colts fans toward the New England Patriots (67.2 points) and the Houston Texans (55.7 points). However, the artificial rivalry ceiling of 100 points limits its effectiveness at comparing the Colts–Patriots rivalry to the rivalrous feelings that Chicago Bears fans have toward the Green Bay Packers (73.7 points). No researchers have suggested that fans have a consistent, limited amount of rivalrous feelings, so the intensity that Colts fans feel toward the Texans (their second listed rival) could very well exceed the rivalrous feelings of Bears fans toward their top rival.

Conclusion

While rivalry is one of the most discussed concepts in sports, clarity and consistency around the concept is lacking. Dissimilar representations of rivalry are not trivial concerns when researchers are attempting to build knowledge to better understand a phenomenon. Furthermore, inconsistent or misspecification of rivalry in demand

estimation could lead to inaccurate crowd forecasts or misallocation of marketing and event security resources. In this paper, we critically examine differing conceptions of rivalry among multiple out-groups, discern and empirically test key properties of rivalry across different sports, and propose a measure of rivalry that accurately captures these properties. We accomplished these purposes by cataloging representations of rivalry in demand estimation and surveying thousands of fans across collegiate and professional sports to test the exclusivity, scale, and symmetry of rivalry. Results indicated rivalry measures should allow for nonexclusivity, be continuous in scale, and permit asymmetry (bidirectionality) within the rivalry dyad. Accordingly, we propose a parsimonious 100-point rivalry allocation measure that meets these three properties of rivalry and encourages future researchers to test and build upon this foundation.

Acknowledgments

We recognize the diligent work of Tyler Mason, E. Connor Millay, Brad Bassinger, Kevin McCarty, and Michael Naraine in their help with data collection for this study. We also are grateful to Robert Bradford for the design and construction of the KnowRivalry.com website.

Notes

[1]Each repeated-measures ANOVA was completed using Greenhouse–Geisser corrections due to violations of sphericity.

[2]This issue becomes particularly apparent with dyads where only a few respondents allocated only a few points, thus creating small rivalry scores. For example, just 11.6% of Arizona State (ASU) fans ($N = 5$ respondents) identified Oregon as a rival (average position 4.2), and the mean points to Oregon across all ASU fans' rivalry points was 0.791. Likewise, 5.7% of Oregon fans ($N = 5$) identified ASU as a rival (average position 5.6) for a rivalry score of 0.276. None of the fans had the opposing team among the top two rivals. The absolute difference of rivalry scores was just 0.515, whose closeness to zero implies a symmetrical rivalry, but the miniscule number of points allocated challenges the face validity of either fan base as a whole accepting the opposing team as a rival.

[3]Michigan fans allocated 16.8 points to MSU, whereas MSU fans allocated 66.8 points to UM. Other examples of unequal points include NC State allocating 66.4 to North Carolina but getting only 39.8 in return, and Boston College allocating 74.2 points to Notre Dame but getting only 1.7 in return (the largest disparity in our college football sample).

References

Ashforth, B.E., & Mael, F. (1989). Social identity theory and the organization. *Academy of Management Review, 14,* 20–39.

Baimbridge, M. (1997). Match attendance at Euro 96: Was the crowd waving or drowning? *Applied Economics Letters, 4,* 555–558. doi:10.1080/135048597355014

Baimbridge, M., Cameron, S., & Dawson, P. (1995). Satellite broadcasting and match attendance: The case of Rugby League. *Applied Economics Letters, 2,* 343–346. doi:10.1080/758518985

Baum, J.A.C., & Korn, H.J. (1996). Competitive dynamics of interfirm rivalry. *Academy of Management Journal, 39,* 255–291. doi:10.2307/256781

Bauman, M. (2004, June 24). Baseball perspectives: In Chicago, no room for neutrality. *MLB.com.* Retrieved May 18, 2008, from http://cubs.mlb.com/news/article_perspectives.jsp?ymd=20040624&content_id=778986&vkey=perspectives&fext=.jsp&c_id=perspectives

Bee, C., & Dalakas, V. (2015). Rivalries and sponsor affiliation: Examining the effects of social identity and argument strength on responses to sponsorship-related advertising messages. *Journal of Marketing Communications, 21,* 408–424. doi:10.1080/13527266.2013.828768

Berendt, J., & Uhrich, S. (2016). Enemies with benefits: The dual role of rivalry in shaping sports fans' identity. *European Sport Management Quarterly, 16,* 613–634.

Bergkvist, L. (2012). The flipside of the sponsorship coin: Do you still buy beer when the brewer underwrites a rival team? *Journal of Advertising Research, 52,* 65–73. doi:10.2501/JAR-52-1-065-073

Blanton, H., Crocker, J., & Miller, D.T. (2000). The effects of ingroup versus out-group social comparison on self-esteem in the context of a negative stereotype. *Journal of Experimental Social Psychology, 36,* 519–530. doi:10.1006/jesp.2000.1425

Borland, J., & MacDonald, R. (2003). Demand for sport. *Oxford Review of Economic Policy, 19,* 478–502. doi:10.1093/oxrep/19.4.478

Boyd, T.C., & Krehbiel, T.C. (2003). Promotion timing in Major League Baseball and the stacking effects of factors that increase game attractiveness. *Sport Marketing Quarterly, 12,* 173–183.

Brewer, M.B. (1979). Ingroup bias in the minimal intergroup situation: A cognitive motivational analysis. *Psychological Bulletin, 86,* 307–324. doi:10.1037/0033-2909.86.2.307

Butler, M.R. (2002). Interleague play and baseball attendance. *Journal of Sports Economics, 3,* 320–334. doi:10.1177/152700202237498

Chen, M. (1996). Competitor analysis and interfirm rivalry: Toward a theoretical integration. *Academy of Management Review, 21,* 100–134.

Cox, J., & Clark, R. (2014). *Fightin' words: Kentucky vs. Louisville.* New York, NY: Sports.

Dimmock, J.A., Grove, R., & Eklund, R.C. (2005). Reconceptualizing team identification: New dimensions and their relationship to intergroup bias. *Group Dynamics, 9,* 75–86. doi:10.1037/1089-2699.9.2.75

Falter, J., Pérignon, C., & Vercruysse, O. (2008). Impact of overwhelming joy on consumer demand: The case of a soccer World Cup victory. *Journal of Sports Economics, 9*(20), 20–42.

Forrest, D., & Simmons, R. (2006). New issues in attendance demand: The case of the English Football League. *Journal of Sports Economics, 7,* 247–266. doi:10.1177/1527002504273392

Forrest, D., Simmons, R., & Buraimo, B. (2005). Outcome uncertainty and the couch potato audience. *Scottish Journal of Political Economy, 52,* 641–661. doi:10.1111/j.1467-9485.2005.00360.x

Forrest, D., Simmons, R., & Feehan, P. (2002). A spatial cross-sectional analysis of the elasticity of demand for soccer. *Scottish Journal of Political Economy, 49,* 336–356. doi:10.1111/1467-9485.00235

García, J., & Rodríguez, P. (2002). The determinants of football match attendance revisited: Empirical evidence from the Spanish football league. *Journal of Sports Economics, 3*(1), 18–38. doi:10.1177/152700250200300103

Goertz, G., & Diehl, P.F. (1993). Enduring rivalries: Theoretical constructs and empirical patterns. *International Studies Quarterly, 37,* 147–171. doi:10.2307/2600766

Havard, C.T. (2014). Glory out of reflected failure: The examination of how rivalry affects sport fans. *Sport Management Review, 17,* 243–253. doi:10.1016/j.smr.2013.09.002

Havard, C.T., Gray, D.P., Gould, J., Sharp, L.A., & Schaffer, J.J. (2013). Development and validation of the Sport Rivalry Fan Perception Scale (SRFPS). *Journal of Sport Behavior, 36,* 45–65.

Havard, C.T., Reams, L., & Gray, D.P. (2013). Perceptions of highly identified fans regarding rival teams in US intercollegiate football and men's basketball. *International Journal of Sport Management and Marketing, 14,* 116–132. doi:10.1504/IJSMM.2013.060628

Havard, C.T., Wann, D.L., & Ryan, T.D. (2013). Investigating the impact of conference realignment on rivalry in intercollegiate athletics. *Sport Marketing Quarterly, 22,* 224–234.

Heere, B., & James, J.D. (2007). Sports teams and their communities: Examining the influence of external group identities on team identity. *Journal of Sport Management, 21,* 319–337. doi:10.1123/jsm.21.3.319

Hill, J.R., Madura, J., & Zuber, R.A. (1982). The short run demand for Major League Baseball. *Atlantic Economic Journal, 10*(2), 31–35. doi:10.1007/BF02300065

Hogg, M.A. (2006). Social identity theory. In P.J. Burke (Ed.), *Contemporary social psychological theories* (pp. 111–136). Stanford, CA: Stanford University Press.

Hogg, M.A., & Abrams, D. (1988). *Social identifications: A social psychology of intergroup relations and group processes.* London, UK: Routledge.

Hogg, M.A., & Terry, D.J. (2000). Social identity and self-categorization processes in organizational contexts. *Academy of Management Review, 25,* 121–140.

Hudnell, L. (2015, May 31). Seriously, who is Penn State's chief rival? *Daily Local News.* Retrieved June 26, 2015, from http://www.dailylocal.com/sports/20150531/seriously-who-is-penn-states-chief-rival

Humphreys, B.R. (2003). *The relationship between big-time college football and state appropriations to higher education* (UMBC Economic Department Working Paper 03-102).

Jetten, J., Spears, R., & Manstead, A.S.R. (1998). Defining dimensions of distinctiveness: Group variability makes a difference to differentiation. *Journal of Personality and Social Psychology, 74,* 1481–1492. doi:10.1037/0022-3514.74.6.1481

Kilduff, G.J., Elfenbein, H.A., & Staw, B.M. (2010). The psychology of rivalry: A relationally dependent analysis of competition. *Academy of Management Journal, 53,* 943–969. doi:10.5465/AMJ.2010.54533171

Kilduff, G., Galinksy, A., Gallo, E., & Reade, J. (2016). Whatever it takes to win: Rivalry increases unethical behavior. *Academy of Management Journal, 59,* 1508–1534.

Knowles, G., Sherony, K., & Haupert, M. (1992). The demand for Major League Baseball: A test of the uncertainty of outcome hypothesis. *The American Economist, 36*(2), 72–80. doi:10.1177/056943459203600210

Koos, T. (2014, December 3). Conference priorities, money driving wedges between historic rivals. *Deseret News.* Retrieved January 7, 2015, from http://www.deseretnews.com/article/865616795/Conference-priorities-money-driving-wedges-between-historic-rivals.html?pg=all

Lemke, R.J., Leonard, M., & Tlhokwane, K. (2010). Estimating attendance at Major League Baseball games for the 2007 season. *Journal of Sports Economics, 11,* 316–348. doi:10.1177/1527002509337212

Leonard, D., & Van Long, N. (2008). *Is emulation good for you? The ups and downs of rivalry* (CIRANO Working Paper, 2008s-02).

Lock, D.J., & Funk, D.C. (2016). The multiple in-group identity framework. *Sport Management Review, 19,* 85–96. doi:10.1016/j.smr.2015.10.001

Lock, D., Taylor, T., & Darcy, S. (2011). In the absence of achievement: The formation of new team identification. *European Sport Management Quarterly, 11,* 171–192. doi:10.1080/16184742.2011.559135

Luellen, T.B., & Wann, D.L. (2010). Rival salience and sport team identification. *Sport Marketing Quarterly, 19,* 97–106.

Madrigal, R., & Chen, J. (2008). Moderating and mediating effects of team identification in regard to causal attributions and summary judgments following a game outcome. *Journal of Sport Management, 22,* 717–733. doi:10.1123/jsm.22.6.717

Mael, F., & Ashforth, B.E. (1992). Alumni and their alma mater: A partial test of the reformulated model of organizational identification. *Journal of Organizational Behavior, 13*(2), 103–123. doi:10.1002/job.4030130202

McDonald, M., & Rascher, D.A. (2000). Does bat day make cents? The effect of promotions on the demand for baseball. *Journal of Sport Management, 14,* 8–27. doi:10.1123/jsm.14.1.8

Mills, B., Tainsky, S., Green, B.C., & Leopkey, B. (2016, June). *From rivalry to reciprocity: Ultimatum game outcomes between college football rivals.* Research presented at the meeting of the North American Society for Sport Management (NASSM), Orlando, FL.

Morgan, G., & Smircich, L. (1980). The case for qualitative research. *Academy of Management Review, 5,* 491–500.

Morley, B., & Thomas, D. (2007). Attendance demand and core support: Evidence from limited-overs cricket. *Applied Economics, 39,* 2085–2097. doi:10.1080/00036840600707225

Muñiz, A.M., & O'Guinn, T.C. (2001). Brand community. *The Journal of Consumer Research, 27,* 412–432. doi:10.1086/319618

Nathan, D.A. (2010). "We were about winning": Larry Bird, Magic Johnson, and the rivalry that remade the NBA. In D.K. Wiggins & R.P. Rodgers (Eds.), *Rivals: Legendary matchups that made sports history* (pp. 69–108). Fayetteville: University of Arkansas Press.

Pacey, P.L., & Wickham, E.D. (1985). College football telecasts: Where are they going? *Economic Inquiry, 23,* 93–113. doi:10.1111/j.1465-7295.1985.tb01754.x

Paton, D., & Cooke, A. (2005). Attendance at county cricket: An economic analysis. *Journal of Sports Economics, 6*(1), 24–45. doi:10.1177/1527002503261487

Paul, R.J. (2003). Variations in NHL attendance: The impact of violence, scoring, and regional rivalries. *American Journal of Economics and Sociology, 62,* 345–364. doi:10.1111/1536-7150.t01-2-00003

Peel, D., & Thomas, D. (1988). Outcome uncertainty and the demand for football: An analysis of match attendances in the English Football League. *Scottish Journal of Political Economy, 35*(3), 242–249. doi:10.1111/j.1467-9485.1988.tb01049.x

Peel, D.A., & Thomas, D.A. (1992). The demand for football: Some evidence on outcome uncertainty. *Empirical Economics, 17,* 323–331. doi:10.1007/BF01206291

Porter, M.E. (1980). *Competitive strategy.* New York, NY: Free Press.

Postmes, T., Haslam, S.A., & Jans, L. (2013). A single-item measure of social identification: Reliability, validity, and utility. *British Journal of Social Psychology, 52*(4), 597–617. doi:10.1111/bjso.12006

Quintanar, S.M., Deck, C., Reyes, J.A., & Sarangi, S. (2015). You are close to your rival and everybody hates a winner: A study of rivalry in college football. *Economic Inquiry, 53,* 1908–1918. doi:10.1111/ecin.12215

Riek, B.M., Mania, E.W., & Gaertner, S.L. (2006). Intergroup threat and outgroup attitudes: A meta-analytic review. *Personality and Social Psychology Review, 10,* 336–353. doi:10.1207/s15327957pspr1004_4

Sanford, K., & Scott, F. (2014). Assessing the intensity of sports rivalries using data from secondary market transactions. *Journal of Sports Economics*; Advance online publication.

Schwartz, N., & McGarry, T. (2014, January 9). The 5 rivalries in sports that actually matter. *USA Today.* Retrieved January 13, 2014, from http://ftw.usatoday.com/2014/01/the-5-rivalries-in-sports-that-actually-matter

Snyder, M. (2014, October 25). Behind Mike Hart's 'Little brother' quote. *Detroit Free Press.* Retrieved October 13, 2015, from http://www.freep.com/story/sports/college/university-michigan/wolverines/2014/10/25/michigan-football-mike-hart-little-brother/17889659/

Spears, M.J. (2007, November 23). New generation embraces rivalry. *Boston Globe.* Retrieved May 18, 2008, from http://www.boston.com/sports/basketball/celtics/articles/2007/11/23/new_generation_embraces_rivalry/

Stets, J.E., & Burke, P.J. (2000). Identity theory and social identity theory. *Social Psychology Quarterly, 63,* 224–237. doi:10.2307/2695870

Tainsky, S., & Jasielec, M. (2014). Television viewership of out-of-market games in league markets: Traditional demand shifters and local team influence. *Journal of Sport Management, 28,* 94–108.

Tainsky, S., & McEvoy, C.D. (2011). Television broadcast demand in markets without local teams. *Journal of Sports Economics, 13,* 250–265. doi:10.1177/1527002511406129

Tainsky, S., & Stodolska, M. (2010). Population migration and team loyalty in professional sports. *Social Science Quarterly, 91,* 801–815. doi:10.1111/j.1540-6237.2010.00720.x

Tajfel, H., & Turner, J.C. (1986). The social identity theory of intergroup behavior. In S. Worchel & W.G. Austin (Eds.), *Psychology of intergroup relations* (2nd ed., pp. 7–24). Chicago, IL: Nelson-Hall.

Turner, J.C. (1982). Towards a cognitive redefinition of the social group. In H. Tajfel (Ed.), *Social identity and intergroup relations* (pp. 15–40). Cambridge, UK: Cambridge University Press.

Tyler, B.D., & Cobbs, J.B. (2015). Rival conceptions of rivalry: Why some competitions mean more than others. *European Sport Management Quarterly, 15,* 227–248. doi:10.1080/16184742.2015.1010558

Wann, D.L., & Grieve, F.G. (2005). Biased evaluations of ingroup and outgroup spectator behavior at sporting events: The importance of team identification and threats to social identity. *The Journal of Social Psychology, 145,* 531–545. doi:10.3200/SOCP.145.5.531-546

Wann, D.L., Havard, C.T., Grieve, G.F., Lante, J.R., Partridge, J.A., & Zapalac, R.K. (2016). Investigating sport rivals: Number, evaluations and relationship with team identification. *Journal of Fandom Studies, 4,* 71–88. doi:10.1386/jfs.4.1.71_1

Welki, A.M., & Zlatoper, T.J. (1994). US professional football: The demand for game-day attendance in 1991. *Managerial and Decision Economics, 15,* 489–495. doi:10.1002/mde.4090150510

Wilson, P., & Sim, B. (1995). The demand for semi-pro league football in Malaysia 1989–91: A panel data approach. *Applied Economics, 27*(1), 131–138. doi:10.1080/00036849500000015

Journal of Sport Management, 2017, 31, 15-26
https://doi.org/10.1123/jsm.2016-0089
© 2017 Human Kinetics, Inc.

Delivering Sports Participation Legacies at the Grassroots Level: The Voluntary Sports Clubs of Glasgow 2014

Eilidh H.R. Macrae
University of the West of Scotland

Voluntary sports clubs (VSCs) provide the primary opportunities for organized community sport in the UK and thus hold the responsibility for delivering on mega-event sports participation legacies. This study presents findings from open-ended questionnaires and interviews conducted in two phases (Phase 1—Spring, 2013; Phase 2—Summer, 2015) with representatives from a sample (*n* = 39) of VSCs to understand their ability to deliver on the participation legacy goals of London 2012 and the 2014 Commonwealth Games in Glasgow. Thematic analysis of the data outlined three themes where support for VSCs should be placed when planning future mega-events: building VSC capacity, retaining members in the long-term, and promoting general visibility of the VSC throughout the event. Bid teams who hope to use mega-events as catalysts for sports participation increases should direct funding and guidance toward VSCs to ensure they have the tools, knowledge, and capacity to deliver on national sports participation ambitions.

Keywords: community sport, mega-events legacy, Olympic Games, sport clubs, sports participation, volunteers

In the lead-up to the 2014 Commonwealth Games in Glasgow, Scotland (G2014), the Games' organizers held aspirations for positive post-Games legacies to be sustained in terms of national health, fitness, and sports participation rates. As with most mega-events of recent decades, the Scottish nation sought to make the most of their opportunities as hosts by securing an "active" legacy, as outlined by the Scottish Government Legacy Plan, which explicitly aimed to "increase physical activity and participation in sport" as a result of G2014 (Scottish Government, 2014, p. 64). In 2010 Glasgow City Council published the *Glasgow 2014 Commonwealth Games Sustainability Plan*, which set out the ways through which the council would attempt to ensure G2014 was managed sustainably to maximize the "potential positive impact" of the Games (Glasgow City Council, 2010). As part of this, the Council had a vision to enhance the health of the nation by using G2014 "as a catalyst to inspire people" to develop healthy and active lifestyles (Glasgow City Council, 2010). Glasgow has some of the worst figures in the UK for health and life expectancy (McCartney, Hanlon, & Bond, 2013). In particular, the subarea of Glasgow, Dalmarnock, which hosted the main events of

G2014, was shown by Shaw, Smith, and Dorling (2005) to have the lowest life expectancy in the UK. In 2010 the Office for National Statistics outlined that, for Scotland as a whole, men had an average life expectancy of 75.4 years and women had an expectancy of 80.1, but for Glasgow residents, the average life expectancy figures only reached 71.1 years for men and 77.5 years for women (Office for National Statistics, 2010). Glasgow's poor life expectancy rate has been linked by researchers to wide-ranging factors such as general socioeconomic deprivation, Vitamin D deficiencies, diet, and physical inactivity (Ahmed et al., 2011; Graham, 2009). Notably, Glasgow City Council's *Sustainability Plan* stressed that the "inspirational impact of the event itself," as well as the improved sports facilities on offer as a result of the regeneration put in place through the Games, would result in an improvement to the health of Glasgow's residents, particularly in relation to sports participation rates (Glasgow City Council, 2010).

Yet, with regard to this health legacy objective, this *Sustainability Plan* fails to account for the research (Weed et al., 2009) that has shown that a health and participation legacy cannot be guaranteed as a direct result of staging an event such as the Commonwealth Games. Rather, steps need to be taken by local voluntary sports clubs (VSCs) to ensure they make the most of the general rise in sport interest and capitalize on the opportunity it provides (Coalter, 2007; McCartney et al., 2013; McCartney, Palmer, et al., 2010; McCartney, Thomas, et al., 2010). There is thus often a reliance on VSCs to deliver

Eilidh H.R. Macrae is with the School of Science and Sport, University of the West of Scotland, Hamilton, South Lanarkshire, UK. Address author correspondence to Eilidh H.R. Macrae at eilidh.macrae@uws.ac.uk.

on these types of participation legacies, as it is they that are at the forefront of sport at the grassroots level in the UK. However, research has shown that VSCs can differ in their commitment and ability to deliver on—and also their knowledge of—policy-directed sports participation goals (May, Harris, & Collins, 2013). Therefore, this study investigated the experiences of VSCs in Glasgow, before, during, and after key mega-events, with a focus on the impact of both the 2012 London Olympics and, in particular, Glasgow 2014. Data were collected through a mixture of open-ended questionnaires and interviews conducted with key representatives from 39 semiformal VSCs, to understand their ability and commitment to deliver on the participation legacy goals of mega-events. The research findings identified key areas where focus should be placed when planning for any form of sports participation legacy from future mega-events, namely, VSC capacity, tools for retaining new members, and visibility of the VSCs.

In the UK, as Reid (2012) has stressed, most organized sport takes place through a VSC. These VSCs are accredited by or linked to their sport's national governing body (NGB): a nonprofit organization with responsibility for managing amateur and professional sports and the public funds allocated to these sports to encourage development (Pappous & Hayday, 2016). While informal participation, physical recreation, and private gym memberships are separate to the VSC system, all national and international sports—with recognized NGBs—have and need VSCs at their grassroots level to obtain and retain members locally and encourage progression and development to the elite level. Though some government funding is provided to the NGBs of the various sports in Britain and this can be disseminated to VSCs, they survive through membership payments and the use of primarily volunteer—rather than paid—staff at the local community clubs (Reid, 2012). What is more, as Taylor, Barrett, and Nichols (2009) note, due to being chiefly staffed by volunteers, British VSCs offer an extremely low-cost way of engaging in organized sport and are therefore some of the best ways to provide those in deprived localities with access to participation. Altering club membership levels are also a straightforward way to monitor the impact of mega-sporting events in terms of their ability to inspire a rise in participation for the sports they showcase. Following G2014, the national agency for sport in Scotland, SportScotland (2015), released figures showing that between 2011 and 2015 there was an 11% increase in overall memberships (junior and senior) of the 17 Commonwealth Games sports, with sports such as netball (58% rise), triathlon (49% rise), and gymnastics (37% rise) seeing clear improvements. Club memberships were used by SportScotland as a way of measuring and reporting impact on participation levels, thus justifying the focus on VSCs in the current study. However, given the importance of VSCs in helping encourage sport participation legacies, it is vital that there be a review of their ability to achieve this, and the areas that they feel they need support in to be able to deliver.

This study was initiated in Spring 2013, where the Phase 1 data were collected, with follow-up Phase 2 data collected in Summer 2015: The overall findings from both phases are presented here together. The research aims and objectives overlapped between Phase 1 and Phase 2, but there were specific themes linked to each of these stages that were investigated through open-ended questionnaires and interviews. Phase 1 of data collection—in Spring 2013—aimed to investigate what the impact of London 2012 was; whether Glasgow's clubs were able to cope with a similar spike in sports participation interest in the past; and how prepared Glasgow's sports clubs were capacity-wise for the possible "spike" that might follow G2014, and which had been witnessed at similar events (Brown, Massey, & Porter, 2004). Phase 2 of the data collection—in Summer 2015—looked into how G2014 affected clubs in terms of participation patterns, and the lessons learned from their experiences with regard to how to prepare for future mega-events. The results and recommendations will have relevance to sport policy makers who rely on the cooperation of VSCs to deliver their aims.

Literature Review

Over the past few decades there has been some limited research into the impact of mega-sporting events upon general sports participation rates. The evidence suggests that mega-sporting events produce little sustained increase in sports participation in the host nation or city; however, the exception would be the spike in participation rates, where a rise is witnessed but seldom sustained (Weed et al., 2009). The "trickle-down effect" is frequently referred to in discussions of the impact of mega-sporting events: It is used to describe the theory that extensive sports coverage in the media can "trickle down" to the general public and inspire them to get involved in sport (Hogan & Norton, 2000)—yet Weed et al. (2009) have shown that the evidence base for the existence of a trickle-down effect is extremely mixed. As Grix and Carmichael (2012) have argued, though governments view mega-events chiefly as a way of bolstering their international image in the "sporting arms race," enhanced domestic sport participation levels are still heralded as a primary output despite the evidence for this being fragmentary (Grix & Carmichael, 2012, p. 86). Hindson, Gidlow, and Peebles (1994) questioned the trickle-down effect through their case study of the Olympics and stressed that the effect was not clear or certain, but that if development strategies are forged to the event, a positive impact can, sometimes, be witnessed. Studies by Murphy and Bauman (2007) and Pappous (2011) recorded decreases in participation among certain groups following the Olympics in Sydney 2000 and Athens 2004, respectively. Craig and Bauman (2014) examined children's physical activity levels before and after the Vancouver Winter Olympics and saw no measurable impact on the exercise or sport participation of this group after the event. Other studies (Frawley & Cush, 2011; Veal, Toohey, & Frawley, 2012) have recorded positive impacts on sports participation rates following events, particularly rates among children. Thus, with the evidence for the trickle-down effect being patchy at best, the "festival" effect was proposed as an alternative model (Coalter, 2007; McCartney et al., 2013; Weed et al., 2009).

During mega-events we often witness the festival effect—where hosting a mega-sports event increases the festival atmosphere and profile of sport in the host nation—and if this is combined with appropriate marketing and strategic planning by VSCs, it can be used as a catalyst to increase overall sports participation (Weed et al., 2009). McCartney et al. (2013) also note that two further factors may encourage participation rates: the new facilities and infrastructure that develop as a result of staging the games, and sports participation legacy programs. It is the latter of these effects that is of most interest here, as a review of the research to date showed that if sports participation legacies were to be an aim of the event, then sports development legacy programs had to be in place to "catch" and retain the individuals inspired to take part in physical activity (Brown et al., 2004). Therefore, this suggests that the festival effect must be combined with marketing and club development strategies to encourage any sustained improvement in sports participation rates, and VSCs would play a large role in helping to achieve this. Of course, a major issue in relation to this is that of who is responsible for delivering sports targets on the ground and the quality of the sports infrastructure they engage with, as British sport is still largely built around a system of voluntarism at the grassroots club level.

Girginov and Hills (2008) have argued that achieving some form of participation legacy is possible but only if the government and event organizing bodies direct sport development appropriately through supplying funds and guidance. The participants in Frawley and Cush's (2011) study into the 2003 Rugby World Cup stressed that the rising registrations for rugby postevent could only be sustained through increased investment in development programs for the sport. Taks, Green, Misener, and Chalip (2014) evaluated the Pan American Junior Athletics Championships, and their findings only further stressed the need to examine the processes through which legacy can potentially be reached, to assess the efficacy of present structures and programs in achieving this task. Charlton's (2010) research into the potential impact of London 2012 stressed that community sports clubs would struggle to deliver on the participation legacies that had been set out. This was an area of focus for Pappous and Hayday (2016), who studied the impact of London 2012 on participation in fencing and judo in England and indicated that grassroots VSCs play a key role in encouraging postevent participation. They have argued that communication should be improved between the head office staff of the NGB and the local clubs to help them build in a way that will allow them to capitalize on the event—for example, through marketing and media (Pappous & Hayday, 2016). Therefore, when researching participation legacies, our attention should certainly be directed toward VSCs and their ability to

deliver on participation goals, and so this was the focus of this study.

Jarvie (2003) has stressed that when thinking about the possibilities for enhancing social capital and community engagement through sport, we must first deal with issues of ownership and "obligations" felt by those within this field. This is particularly the case when dealing with participation legacies and understanding who takes ownership for delivering policy objectives on the ground. The concept of community itself also requires definition. Krieger (2000) refers to "imagined" and "actual" communities, and Skinner, Zakus, and Cowell (2008) have suggested that communities need not refer to one geographical place but more to a collection of ties and social connections that bind people together or indeed, through the darker aspects of bonding social capital, restrict some others from joining the folds of these communities.

In the case of the sports clubs that were the focus in this research, all representatives tended to show a connection to their immediate geographical club area within the city, referring to the "east of the city" as their community (Club 1 interview, 2015) or noting their "community" to be the suburb their club operated out of (Club 2 interview, 2013). However, there was also recognition that people came from further afield to join the clubs and they were very welcome to do so. Thus, in these clubs this was more of an "imagined" community created by the ties and loyalty members had with the club and not necessarily their personal ties to the locality itself, suggesting potential for the development of bridging social capital (Skinner et al., 2008). Establishing whether this feeling of loyalty is to the club only or is open to the wider community as a whole is important here when dealing with issues of policy delivery and attempts at the ground level to enhance sports participation numbers in response to government aims. If a club has its own interests at heart but nevertheless does not want—or feels it is too much work—to grow its numbers, there is little hope for this club's contributing to the delivery of government objectives in terms of growing participation rates in sport. There is also little hope for developing the bridging form of social capital that helps to eradicate social exclusion by welcoming newcomers into community sport environments (Skinner et al., 2008). If clubs do not want to grow their numbers or become more inclusive, there is little chance of their contributing to the key government aim of bringing all members of communities closer together.

Community investment in sport development, and links between VSCs and their communities, are key themes for investigation here. Vail (2007) has argued in her research into community development that sustained impact and development occurs when a "community champion" (p. 575) is involved in directing the process rather than an independent sports development officer who may be viewed as an outsider parachuting in to make changes in the community. Vail argues that the community champion may be someone who is already a club committee member or a key volunteer within the club setting, and with that individual's approval and backing the project will take root sustainably. Similarly Hylton and Totten (2008) have suggested that when a community feels empowered to take on and personalize a project for their own local enhancement, this may have much more of an effect than a top-down approach. Thus, the strength of the links between VSCs and the communities they engage with are key components when investigating mega-event participation legacies, given the importance of VSCs in delivering on these types of legacy aims.

Studies by Doherty, Misener, and Cuskelly (2014) have outlined some of the key issues that VSCs are faced with when trying to build capacity, as well as best practice for building capacity, such as "shared values" of volunteers, the constant focus on recruitment as well as retention of volunteers, and succession of volunteers to ensure they can be replaced if they decide to leave. This research has enhanced our understanding of the pressures VSCs face, and though Millar and Doherty (2016) have proposed a model that they suggest can be used to "measure, predict and explain (in)effective capacity building" (p. 2), a key part of this is club willingness to grow and readiness to build their capacity. A focus of the current study was to investigate the need and willingness for capacity building in the sampled VSCs, building on the Canadian research by Doherty et al. (2014).

As Nichols, Padmore, Taylor, and Barrett (2012) have argued, any study that looks at delivery of policy objectives on the ground through club sport must establish the types of clubs under scrutiny—for example, their size, level of "formality," and how this impacts upon their desire and ability to work toward policy goals from above. Nichols et al. have shown that clubs can be clustered by level of formality, and this is a useful tool by which to decipher which clubs will be receptive to guidance from local or national government, and who will be willing to help progress policy aims, such as raising participation rates. In their study of policy delivery at the ground level in England, May et al. (2013) showed how the informal and semiformal sports clubs in their study often had little or no knowledge of current policy objectives though some of the more formal clubs had general ideas in terms of enhancing participation levels.

In the context of G2014 the semiformal clubs that were targeted for this research certainly had some awareness of the general aims that the Scottish Government had for health, participation, and urban regeneration legacies, but the clubs' support, and the degree to which they were willing to contribute to these policy aims, differed in accordance with their individual club aims and ambitions. The results were not clear-cut in that it was not the case that larger, more formal clubs were willing to develop the policy aims and smaller more traditional clubs were not; rather even some larger accredited clubs were still unwilling to become more inclusive and in turn enhance their potential membership pool. If the club itself did not want to develop—for example—a junior section, then there was little that could be done in terms of government marketing or encouragement to change this; fundamentally, it was a voluntary club, and it was

the club's choice. Thus, research to date has shown that participation legacies from mega-events can sometimes be achieved, but the best results come from having successful infrastructure, planning, and development at the grassroots level, and in the UK this means VSCs that have the capacity, tools, and knowledge to build their own legacy from the grassroots up. The focus of the current study was to investigate the ability of Glasgow's VSCs to deliver on this.

Method

This study consisted of two data collection phases. Phase 1 was conducted in Spring 2013, where open-ended questionnaires were distributed to 36 VSCs and semistructured interviews were carried out with representatives from 6 of these VSCs. Phase 2 was conducted in Summer 2015, where one face-to-face interview was carried out and five qualitative open-ended questionnaires were completed by VSC representatives. Three of the clubs were included in both Phase 1 and Phase 2, and so the experiences of a total of 39 VSCs informed the overall findings presented here.

The aims of the research overlapped throughout the two phases, but there were specific areas that were more prominent at each stage. Phase 1 aimed to look into whether VSCs in Glasgow were preparing for the 2014 Games, and where the gaps were in terms of club readiness and capacity for welcoming newcomers. Thus, Phase 1 looked into the impact of London 2012 on a sample of Glasgow's sport clubs to identify what the effects were when a similar (albeit significantly larger scale) mega-sporting event was held within Britain, levels of club awareness and preparation for the spike that might occur post-G2014, and club capacity levels for coping with a large influx of new members. At this stage—Spring 2013—basic analysis was conducted on preliminary findings, and recommendations were made to the local sport development team so they could produce an evidence-based pre-G2014 strategy—the "Get Ready Guide"—and distribute this to clubs in the city (Glasgow Sport, 2013). A more detailed analysis of these initial findings took place in 2015 as part of Phase 2 of the data collection and analysis. Phase 2 of the research occurred in Summer 2015 and involved the collection of qualitative data from 6 VSCs in the Glasgow area to establish the impact of G2014 and their clubs' experiences of the event in terms of the challenges in delivering a participation legacy.

Recruitment and Participants

As Nichols et al. (2012) have noted, larger, accredited (Clubmark) clubs are often overrepresented in research samples. Formal and semiformal clubs are usually more willing to engage with surveys and research because of having more manpower—and consequently more time to contribute—as well as usually having good relationships with local authorities who might encourage them to participate in such things. Less formal, isolated clubs that are not interested in expanding would understandably be less willing to take part in such research, and indeed this probably means that in any case they will be less inclined to deliver on policy objectives. For this study, clubs were purposively sampled in accordance with guidelines from Curtis, Gesler, Smith, and Washburn (2000) that encourage qualitative purposive sampling to ensure relevancy to the research questions to enhance the opportunity for generalization of the findings. Consequently, those clubs that were approached to complete questionnaires and/ or in-depth interviews were those that were relatively well established, were already known to the local sport development team, and were keen to progress. The sample therefore consisted of those that would in theory be the key clubs for developing government policy objectives on the ground through working to enhance their membership, and that would be most likely to take advantage of the opportunities presented to them by an event such as London 2012 or G2014.

For Phase 1, 36 clubs were recruited by the researcher through local sports development contacts and through contacting clubs directly using details on their websites; thus, all clubs were those who were at least semiformal as they had contacts with the local development team and/or an online presence. These clubs were sampled from the 17 Commonwealth Sports of 2014 although responses were not received from clubs offering wrestling, shooting or squash. A few Olympic, but non-Commonwealth, sports clubs (viz., rowing and tennis) were also included to gather further evidence of the impact of the 2012 Olympics on clubs in Glasgow, and to assess whether these clubs were expecting any impact from the 2014 Commonwealth Games or developing their clubs nonetheless despite not being one of the 17 sports. From these 36 clubs, representatives from 6 clubs were invited to take part in a semistructured interview examining the same themes from the questionnaire in more depth.

Phase 2 of the data collection was conducted post-G2014 in the summer of 2015 and involved one interview and five qualitative open-ended questionnaires with representatives (head coach or club chairperson) from VSCs. Three of the VSC representatives had already been involved in Phase 1, and the remaining three were new to the study in Phase 2. These three new clubs were purposively sampled through their contact details on their website: They were all semiformal VSCs that already had a connection to their local sport development team and were one of the key commonwealth sports of 2014. As already noted, these would in theory be the clubs most likely to have the ability and desire to deliver on policy-directed participation and legacy goals, and so this was the criteria against which they were selected. All club representatives completed informed consent forms before contributing to any aspect of the data collection process, and anonymity was agreed upon for each of the club representatives who contributed data to the questionnaires or interviews. Since the club representatives were all either the club chairperson or the head coach, the participants were key figures who had an awareness of membership trends and club development strategies.

Data Collection

For Phase 1, after club representatives had been recruited and informed consent secured, open-ended questionnaires were distributed and completed by the 36 sampled clubs. These questionnaires were distributed personally in hard copy to the club representatives and via personalized e-mails with a link to an online version of the questionnaire. Comments were collected through these questionnaires. Though the questionnaires were open-ended, many of the answers given by the VSCs were similar, and so this provided an opportunity for basic descriptive statistics to be generated to outline the general trends in responses. The questionnaires included 15 open-ended questions covering the clubs' general experiences of London 2012 (general positive or negative impact, membership impact, lessons learned); current club capacity levels; and club planning for G2014. The key theme of capacity issues emerged through the questionnaire responses, as will be seen in the Results section, and so this informed some of the focus of the subsequent Phase 1 semistructured interviews.

Phase 1 also included six semistructured interviews with club representatives that were conducted after the questionnaires were returned: One of these was conducted via telephone with the others being face-to-face interviews held in a private room at the VSC. The chosen interviewees were made up of a random sample of those club representatives who had completed the questionnaires and were available for interview. Interview questions followed the general themes of the initial questionnaires but allowed for more depth. The interviews were audio recorded and then transcribed verbatim. Initial themes were recorded at this stage, but the Phase 1 data were analyzed again after Phase 2 was conducted so that the evidence and overarching themes could be presented together, given that there was much overlap between themes from the two phases, as noted below.

Phase 2 of the data collection occurred in Summer 2015, a year after G2014. The VSC representatives were contacted via e-mail and asked to either engage in a face-to-face interview or complete an open-ended questionnaire where they could provide detailed responses. These open-ended questionnaires and interviews covered areas such as preparation or changes made by the club both in response to their London 2012 experience and in preparation for G2014, current club capacity levels and relevant gaps in capacity, and lessons learned from G2014. Ten VSC representatives responded positively; however, only five actually returned their questionnaires by the research deadline set, and only one participant agreed to an interview. Therefore, one interview and five questionnaires were completed in total. The interview was conducted at the representative's VSC facility, and the questionnaires were e-mailed to respondents with an agreed return date of 2 weeks' time via e-mail. A follow up e-mail was sent to encourage responses from those who did not meet the 2-week deadline, but this did not yield any further questionnaire returns or positive responses for interview.

There was an initial assumption by the researcher that the uptake for participation in the interviews would be higher, and this was a limitation of this aspect of the study that could not be rectified in the research period available to the researcher. Nonetheless, the responses via open-ended questionnaire were extremely detailed—with some single answers running to several paragraphs—and thus secured a substantial level of relevant data that could be analyzed in conjunction with the Phase 2 interview material and data collected from Phase 1.

Data Analysis

As with Phase 1, the Phase 2 face-to-face interview was audio recorded and transcribed verbatim. The data from Phase 1 and Phase 2 were analyzed together after all of the data collection had been carried out. The Phase 1 questionnaires uncovered some key areas and recurring themes: Despite their being open-ended, there was much overlap in the responses given by participants, and so some basic descriptive statistics could be generated at this stage to show common responses. The Phase 1 and Phase 2 interview transcripts and the detailed responses from the five Phase 2 open-ended questionnaires were then analyzed line by line through inductive thematic analysis (Braun & Clarke, 2006; Matthews & Ross, 2010). Initial concepts were identified, which were then reduced down and categorized into key themes. There was much overlap between the Phase 1 and Phase 2 data and, consequently, the overarching themes generated. Therefore, given this overlap between the themes in the two phases, in the following Results section the questionnaire and interview data from both phases will be presented together thematically. Within this the interviews and questionnaires can be identified as Phase 1 or Phase 2 by the year they were conducted: 2013 or 2015, respectively.

Results

The Need to Build VSC Capacity

Evidence points to a phenomenon of a spike in participation numbers for many sports immediately following certain mega-events (Weed et al., 2009). Following the London Olympics, in October 2012 the Sport and Recreation Alliance published results of a snapshot survey of volunteers at UK sports clubs. While 69% of surveyed clubs providing Olympic sports had witnessed an increase in people joining, 43% of these clubs stated that they were struggling to meet this increase in demand and thus were seeing a fall-off in numbers, or a "spike" in their participation figures (Sport and Recreation Alliance, 2012). Increased running costs, lack of affordable venues/facilities, and funding were noted as key reasons why these clubs were struggling to cope with increases in membership numbers. Similarly, in the Phase 1 questionnaires for this project, 50% of sampled VSCs (18/36 clubs) reported that they held "come and try" events to encourage newcomers after the Olympics, and 72% of

these clubs (13/18) saw newcomers wish to join their club as a result of this. Of those clubs that saw interest from potential new members, 85% (11/13) had the capacity for the new members, but 15% (2/13) reported that they were not able to welcome all of the newcomers because of space and coach shortages. While most of these clubs reported that they would be able to support a small number of new members, elsewhere in the questionnaire they were asked how their club would cope with a large influx of new members: 64% (23/36 clubs) stated that they would not have the capacity for a significant increase in newcomers to their club (the example given in the survey was up to 50 new members) because of shortages in facility space, volunteers, and coaches. One athletics club in the Phase 1 interview sample held a come and try taster event in August 2012 in an attempt to make the most of the publicity surrounding the Olympics. As their club chairperson notes below, this VSC had always held monthly induction evenings to welcome any potential new members, but this post-Olympics induction session—which they had publicized in the local community through their website and e-mail mailing list—attracted an unprecedented level of interest, which they struggled to cope with:

> A: [We had] a "come and try" type induction experience . . . separate from a training night . . . and we had 140 people, juniors, signing up to that on the night.
>
> Q: And at the usual taster sessions: how many would you usually get?
>
> A: Well I've got the figures, nothing like anything like that. An unusual night would be up to 30, and that would've been because something else had provoked interest. So there were 17 in February 2010, there were 30 in some cases. . . . And in the weeks subsequent to that it was quite challenging. Even in September [2012] there was 50 people at the induction again so there was a follow on. . . . We then had to start a waiting list which we have never in our history had. And it was because, well, we hadn't any forward planning, *didn't have enough coaches, didn't have a system for dealing with* [*those numbers*]. *Well, we didn't think it would be quite so overwhelming* [emphasis added]. (Club 2 interview, 2013)

This club was keen to welcome new members but was unprepared for such a high number. This meant that the VSC could not safely accommodate the 140 junior newcomers who attended the come and try session. As the high numbers were so unexpected, there was no contingency plan in place to ensure these newcomers had an alternative pathway to follow and did not simply fall away from the sport. The club could offer information and guidance at the end of the taster session, but they were unable to offer full membership to the club for everyone who attended, and they had to start a waiting list:

> I put out an email . . . a request saying, "Look guys, we're at the stage of the health and safety problems,

meaning that we can't take on any more people". The word of mouth message got through fairly quickly: that their wee sisters couldn't get into the club; that friends couldn't get into the club and so on and so on. So that spreads through a community, "[our club], they've got a waiting list for the first time." (Club 2 interview, 2013)

A cycling club interviewed for Phase 1 of the study also noted their capacity issues, not only in their own club but for the city as a whole: "We have lots of coaches and just as many volunteers, but the coaches are very busy and at the moment they are largely working to capacity, as are most of the clubs in Glasgow, many have waiting lists" (Club 4 interview, 2013). It should be stressed that these capacity issues were known about pre-Games, and throughout Scotland numbers of coaches rose dramatically throughout these years. SportScotland reported in 2015 that the number of United Kingdom Coaching Certificate (UKCC) awards had risen dramatically: In 2009/10 there were 764 UKCC Level Two coaches, but by 2014/15 this number had grown to 4,202, showing a 450% rise (SportScotland, 2015). Yet notably, these capacity issues were still experienced by some VSCs in the Phase 2 sample, and in the following data from another cycling club we can see that capacity issues meant that many newcomers inspired by G2014 had to be placed on a waiting list rather than being immediately welcomed into the club:

> We did prepare the club coaching staff and venue hire for an increase in interest in the club . . . and despite more coaches and increasing our membership we still had a waiting list of over 90 kids.
>
> In February 2015 we let another 65 kids join but sadly a large proportion of the waiting list has lost interest in joining, as we now have cleared it. If you can take as many kids straight away they may stay. People quickly lose interest on a waiting list. We didn't lose many kids to other cycling clubs as they are all full, but we haven't received feedback on where they went. (Club 3 questionnaire, 2015)

It is likely that by potential new members' being placed on a waiting list rather than being welcomed into the club membership, the initial enthusiasm sparked by the mega-event will be lost, thus perpetuating the spike phenomenon, and we see evidence for this from VSCs in both Phases 1 and 2. Learning from the missed opportunities of London 2012 and Manchester 2002 Commonwealth Games (M2002), an athletics VSC sampled in Phase 2 made a point of ensuring they avoided placing any newcomers on a waiting list during the post-G2014 period:

> A: We make sure we don't have a waiting list. Now the reason that we don't have a waiting list is, I'm a great believer of if a child comes down here tonight and he was say [someone with potential] and we say "sorry come back in three months", then they won't

come back again. Now there are all sorts of arguments over this. I don't know if some clubs think it is a status symbol to have a waiting list, but for us, we turn nobody away.

Q: Have you always been able to manage that then?

A: Yeah we do. Some night it's, well . . . we try and involve parents, okay? Parents as helpers to look after, and they can hold watches for us. And some nights it's scary, right, some nights it's scary, but I know for me personally, and the club, no we definitely have a policy where we're not turning anybody away, because we don't think they'll come back. But certain clubs would argue against that. (Club 1 interview, 2015)

Another Phase 2 club managed to avoid this potential pitfall by ensuring all newcomers at taster sessions were integrated: "We have had no 'drop offs'. All new members are immediately incorporated or welcomed into a specific session with a permanent, regular coach and if possible an assistant coach" (Club 6 questionnaire, 2015). Evidently capacity issues can easily become safety concerns for many VSCs, and so it can be difficult to avoid starting a waiting list when numbers peak, yet, it is worth noting that evidence from M2002, London 2012, and G2014 all showed that those clubs that could immediately welcome newcomers into a training program were able to retain these members in the long term. Therefore, here we can see some of the real-life barriers of delivering on participation legacies on the ground, and areas that should be targeted. Clubs must be made aware of the possibility for a sharp rise in numbers post-Games that could potentially be capitalized on, and the capacity issues that should be dealt with pre-Games so that this opportunity is not lost because of a shortage of resources. In 2013 the local sport development team provided Glasgow VSCs with a "Get Ready Guide" to flag up the spike phenomenon and the sources available for sport development guidance and funding so clubs could prepare to make the most of the Games, but we can see from the above evidence that some clubs still struggled with capacity issues post-Games.

Visibility of the VSC

A second theme drawn from the data pointed to the importance of club visibility during the mega-event to ensure potential new members can easily access them. Those clubs that were approached by high numbers of newcomers were those that had a visible presence at the event, either by hosting events themselves, having club members who were acting as volunteers and championing the club, or advertising their club throughout the host city. An athletics club noted their own visibility, through an event they staged themselves during the period of the 2014 Games: "As a celebration of the Games we organised a road race in support of [a local charity] which was so successful we have staged another race in 2015" (Club 2 questionnaire, 2015). Another semiformal club (100 members), which witnessed a 20% rise in their membership following the Games, stressed that their visibility at the Games played a large part in encouraging these new members: "As we were already working [with our sport development officers] we were invited to provide 'come and try' at their 'live' sites throughout the games themselves" (Club 6 questionnaire, 2015). Similarly a hockey club noted their communication with their NGB and direct involvement in the Games as key reasons for their club's seeing enhanced numbers:

> We supplied some helpers for the inflatable hockey pitch sessions which were organised, and I think we were lucky in terms of having very direct links into Glasgow 2014 and Scottish Hockey, so I think if we hadn't had that, we would have been needing more advice. I think I would advise clubs to seize on any options offered by their local sports organisation to get involved. I was a Clydesider [Games volunteer] as well at the hockey centre, so even doing something like that helped raise the profile of the sport and so the club. (Club 5 questionnaire, 2015)

Their results were clear:

> We picked up new members from outside our normal area—we usually get players from the local schools and graduating students, but this year we got lots of enquiries through our website who said they had seen the hockey at the Games and then looked for somewhere local to them. (Club 5 questionnaire, 2015)

In their study of the 2002 Manchester Commonwealth Games Brown et al. (2004) showed that capacity issues were certainly a concern in the aftermath of these Games, but there was also a lack of marketing from clubs themselves, and the visibility aspect was not there:

> If there was [sic] phone numbers around the track so people saying "I want to do this" could call, we wouldn't have been able to deal with them. . . . It wasn't easy to know what to do with the few that I did get calling anyway. . . . And I dread to think what some clubs would do if they suddenly had hundreds of potential new members knocking on their door. (Interview 19; Brown et al., 2004, p. 39)

Thus, these two themes of capacity and visibility must be coupled to ensure clubs are aware of how to plan, so they can rise to the challenge of delivering on a participation policy goal. Linked to this, clubs must be made aware of the spike phenomenon and trend for drop-offs and be informed of ways in which they can encourage sustained participation.

Retaining Members at VSCs

As well as working through capacity issues and ensuring they are visible to potential new members, the evidence shows that clubs also need to consider techniques to retain members to encourage a sustained rise in participation. A

rowing club in the Phase 1 sample noted their attempts to deal with this following London 2012:

> Following the Olympics—like every other club I would imagine—there was a huge surge in interest, and we had a taster session. When you run any sort of taster session there's always a fair bit of interest at the outset but that kind of tails away and it's a big demand for the clubs in terms of being able to host that in terms of having the numbers of volunteers and safety cover for these things. We've run two Learn to Row courses, so that's essentially another 24 people who had done a taster session. 40 people went through the taster session one weekend and of that we had about 24 who went on to the Learn to Row. Now, a few months on, there are about 12 people who have been retained so it has dropped, but this is still a good number. . . . At the end of the taster session today we'll tell them "the next Learn to Row course is in the Spring, a couple of months' time", which is long enough for us to get ready in terms of making sure we've got volunteers on the go, but also short enough that they're still going to be interested. If the gap is too big then it falls apart. (Club 5 interview, 2013)

Attempts to sustain the participation rise was something also noted by the hockey club in the 2015 sample:

> Before we entered the [new] team in the 2015 cup competition, we asked everybody who had come to these sessions if they were coming back in August, so we got seven positive replies and decided to enter the competition. Also we encouraged anybody who had come to winter training to play fun summer hockey—there are various summer teams loosely associated with our club, so we advertised this before the winter season ended. (Club 5 questionnaire, 2015)

Consequently, their numbers were retained as they prompted their newcomers to think about the future through having goals in mind and competitions to work toward: They were shown to be valued members of the club. It was also noted in Phase 1 that an important part of retaining newcomers is ensuring their experience at the club is positive so that they feel welcomed and want to stay, as noted in this extract from the Phase 1 data:

> I think we need to get our act in gear actually to try and organise for the deluge that will come. And things suffer if you just have everybody coming into the club [with no plan]. The kids who are performing athletes at age group level, we need to make sure that the experience for them remains good. (Club 2 interview, 2013)

This was something also stressed in the Phase 2 data:

> What we tend to do is people can come down [to the club], and we've already got a group [for them to join], and this group kind of welcome them and

encourage them. . . . You've got to make it fun, make it enjoyable. And I think with any sport, it's more than sport: you're developing the whole person. . . . Discipline in life, good friendship groups, good style of life, that's really what our coaching philosophy is about in the club. It's more than athletics. (Club 1 interview, 2015)

The emphasis here was on ensuring newcomers were immediately welcomed and shown an interest from the club, and this is advice that can be grouped with the points made earlier regarding avoiding waiting lists: "You've got to show a willingness of new members that come down, to tap into them right away. Because when the buzz is in the city, the excitement, you've got to really pull the people in" (Club 1 interview, 2015). Interestingly, this club witnessed a sustained membership rise in both the junior and senior athlete age groups:

We actually had an increase in our senior membership. We had a lot of adults who, I don't know if it was the games or just general fitness but we've had an increase in [those who] were moving from maybe sedentary lifestyle to a bit more active. We've certainly found that we've got a group of fast joggers, but not quite the elite athletes. We got more youngsters coming down definitely, and the interesting thing was that a lot of them stayed. That's what we found most interesting, because quite often what you do is you get transient members. (Club 1 interview, 2015)

The hockey club mentioned above also saw interest from older adults looking for general fitness, and they catered accordingly to this:

We identified from the enquiries to the website that there was a demand for starter sessions whether as re-introduction or complete beginners, so last September [2014] we started Back to Basics. We put this up on the website on the front page. We had around a dozen enquiries at the start of the season, and of the ones who came at first, three have moved up to regular training and playing in teams; then over the course of the season we had enquiries from another 12, and two of them are now playing in teams. (Club 5 questionnaire, 2015)

Discussion

The experiences of these VSCs aid our understanding of some of the key development issues to be faced when preparing to host major sports events. Policy makers continue to champion the idea that the trickle-down effect of hosting will encourage a rise in postevent sport participation rates, but the evidence suggests that there is a need for localized strategies and initiatives to be set in place to encourage any sustained positive impact on participation. The success stories in this sample came from those VSCs that were visible. These were VSCs whose

members acted as volunteers throughout the mega-event, had a good level of engagement with their NGB, had a strong community profile to begin with, and had programs in place to attract and retain members. This aligns with research by Frawley and Cush (2011), McCartney et al. (2013), Taks et al. (2014), and Pappous and Hayday (2016), who all stressed that infrastructure, planning, and development were the keys to success in this area, with communication between NGBs and VSCs being crucial. Mackintosh, Darko, and May-Wilkins (2016) noted that among their participants it was felt that there was an information barrier toward getting involved in sport post–London 2012, with not enough information being obviously available about where to go to participate. When conducting online searches for those lesser known sports, such as archery, families in their study found it difficult to gain information. They also mentioned their use of traditional sources to gain information—such as local newspapers—reminding us that there is a need to populate a variety of media sources. Given the findings presented here and through previous research, evidently during and around these events visibility of VSCs and communication between NGBs and local clubs must be prioritized. It is recommended that NGBs work toward mega-events well in advance, with clear strategies for building the profile of local VSCs during the event itself, as well as NGB strategies for capacity building that can be implemented at the local level where required. Some of the clubs in this sample knew that they needed to build their capacity preevent, and they did so, but postevent they still struggled to meet demand. NGBs must work with their own VSCs at the local level and improve the communication channels to their grassroots VSCs to understand where support should be directed. This study has shown that the need to build capacity tends to be an ongoing issue for VSCs, and so there is a clear need for NGBs and policy makers to support grassroots sports clubs in this process.

Frawley and Cush (2011) witnessed a higher number of junior members registering with rugby clubs after the 2003 Rugby World Cup in South Africa, and they suggested that it might primarily be youths who would be encouraged through an event. The evidence presented here shows that there was youth interest but also interest from older adults looking to develop their fitness in a more organized club environment. This was the case in athletics, cycling, hockey, and rowing clubs. While this would be unlikely to result in an increased pool of medal winners for the country, if it is increased sport participation and physical activity that is the policy goal, then we can see positive impacts. A key factor linked to this is the visibility of VSCs in the local community, as mentioned above. To enhance the opportunity for people to engage with a new sport postevent, the process has to be easy and, if potential members do make it to a VSC, they must be welcomed and not placed on a waiting list. Therefore, it is recommended that NGBs and VSCs ensure that local people can engage with a new sport easily if they have an inclination to do so. The process for doing this must be clear, easy, and visible throughout the event, with VSCs having a presence at the Games, in local media, and online.

The evidence from the experiences of these VSCs overwhelmingly shows that capacity remains a key theme. For participation growth to take place there is a primary need to build capacity of VSCs further and also a need for NGBs and policy makers to get this message across to those clubs that have the desire and ability to grow. Sixty-four percent of clubs in Phase 1 stated that they would not have the capacity for a significant increase in newcomers to their club, and they linked this to capacity issues in their facilities and numbers of volunteers. A cycling club (Club 3 questionnaire, 2015) noted that they had been aware of their capacity issues and had been building between London 2012 and G2014, but still they had to start a waiting list, meaning they lost some of the enthusiastic newcomers to their club post-G2014. Girginov and Hills (2008) stressed the need for governments to channel funds appropriately to encourage the right types of sport development if a participation legacy is sought. These findings indicate the key areas where successes and failings were made and thus where future efforts should be channeled, and helping clubs to build club capacity is an evident priority. Millar and Doherty (2016) have provided a process model of capacity building, but this only outlines themes of capacity building such as "readiness for capacity building" (p. 369). They stress that there is a need for the sharing of more case studies of practical strategies and best practice of capacity building in sport, and though the above evidence provides some detail on this, future research must develop it.

Conclusions and Future Study

Looking toward preparation for future mega-events, the evidence suggests that participation legacies can be witnessed in those NGBs and VSCs that ensure the routes into their sport are visible, and those that have development programs in place to catch and retain members. Clubs must also be ready to cope with any rise in participation levels, and this is where capacity building comes in. As Millar and Doherty (2016) have noted, organizational change theory shows that capacity building is stimulated as a result of some external environmental force, where the organization acts in response to an opportunity or a threat that stimulates change. As nations prepare to host future events, the upcoming mega-events should be used as catalysts for capacity building and planning. The clubs in this sample that had success were those that saw an opportunity in the upcoming event and built themselves up accordingly, using the event as a stimulant to attract and retain new volunteers and enhance their capacity as a club. However, it has been stressed that some VSCs still struggled with this capacity building, and strategic planning from their NGB in terms of national and local support for capacity building might have aided this process. More research is needed into the strategic processes

that VSCs should follow if they wish to see success in terms of capacity building and retaining new members postevent. A limitation here was the low participation in Phase 2 of the study due to lack of engagement from all suitable VSCs; thus, future research should work with a larger sample and track clubs from pre- to postevent to provide detailed models of best practice in terms of planning, capacity building, and post-Games programs to retain new members. Successful models and practical strategies of capacity building in sport must be shared more widely to aid our understanding of best practice. Future research should be directed here, and we must ensure findings are disseminated to the NGBs and VSCs to inform practice.

A further vital aspect lies in the issue of communication between NGBs and the VSCs at their grassroots. Pappous and Hayday (2016) stressed this in their research into fencing and judo, and the evidence from the current study also indicates the need for improved communication pathways, guidance, and training in the run-up to events, with NGBs being the obvious sources of leadership for this in the UK. However, this is best delivered as guidance and support from NGBs to allow VSCs to take ownership of their own development on their own terms. As Vail (2007) and Hylton and Totten (2008) have stressed, club development works best when it is directed at the grassroots through community ownership rather than from the top down. Policy makers and NGBs must appreciate the barriers faced by VSCs at the grassroots level and provide support, guidance, and funding where possible. Those interested in developing any form of sports participation legacy must provide VSCs with the knowledge and tools from which they can build their own capacity and develop where they need to. This is essentially classic sports development, but framed under the urgency of mega-event planning.

References

Ahmed, S.F., Franey, C., McDevitt, H., Somerville, L., Butler, S., Galloway, P., . . . Wallace, A.M. (2011). Recent trends and clinical features of childhood vitamin D deficiency presenting to a children's hospital in Glasgow. *Archives of Disease in Childhood, 96,* 694–696. doi:adc.2009.173195v1

Braun, V., & Clarke, V. (2006). Using thematic analysis in psychology. *Qualitative Research in Psychology, 3*(2), 77–101. doi:10.1191/1478088706qp063oa

Brown, A., Massey, J., & Porter, C. (2004). *The sports development impact of the 2002 Commonwealth Games: Post games report.* Manchester, UK: UK Sport.

Charlton, T. (2010). "Grow and Sustain": The role of community sports provision in promoting a participation legacy for the 2012 Olympic Games. *International Journal of Sport Policy and Politics, 2*(3), 347–366. doi:10.1080/1940694 0.2010.519340

Coalter, F. (2007). London Olympics 2012: The catalyst that inspires people to lead more active lives? *The Journal of the Royal Society for the Promotion of Health, 127,* 109–110. doi:10.1177/1466424007077342

Craig, C.L., & Bauman, A.E. (2014). The impact of the Vancouver Winter Olympics on population level physical activity and sport participation among Canadian children and adolescents: Population based study. *The International Journal of Behavioral Nutrition and Physical Activity, 11*(107), 1–9.

Curtis, S., Gesler, W., Smith, G., & Washburn, S. (2000). Approaches to sampling and case selection in qualitative research: Examples in the geography of health. *Social Science & Medicine, 50*(7–8), 1001–1014. doi:10.1016/S0277-9536(99)00350-0

Doherty, A., Misener, K., & Cuskelly, G. (2014). Toward a multidimensional framework of capacity in community sport clubs. *Nonprofit and Voluntary Sector Quarterly, 43*(2S), 124S–142S. doi:10.1177/0899764013509892

Frawley, S., & Cush, A. (2011). Major sport events and participation legacy: The case of the 2003 Rugby World Cup. *Managing Leisure, 16*, 65–76. https://doi.org/10.1080/13606719.2011.532605

Girginov, V., & Hills, L. (2008). A sustainable sports legacy: Creating a link between the London Olympics and sports participation. *The International Journal of the History of Sport, 25*, 2091–2116. doi:10.1080/09523360802439015

Glasgow City Council. (2010). *Glasgow 2014 Commonwealth Games Sustainability Plan.* Retrieved from http://www.glasgow.gov.uk/CHttpHandler.ashx?id=8465

Glasgow Sport. (2013). *2014 and Beyond, get ready with Glasgow Sport: A guide for sports clubs in Glasgow.* Glasgow, UK: Glasgow Life. Retrieved from http://publications.glasgowlife.org.uk/sport/2014-and-Beyond-Clubs/files/assets/basic-html/index.html#1

Graham, H. (Ed.). (2009). *Understanding health inequalities.* Maidenhead, UK: Open University Press.

Grix, J., & Carmichael, F. (2012). Why do governments invest in elite sport? A polemic. *International Journal of Sport Policy and Politics, 4*, 73–90. doi:10.1080/19406940.2011.627358

Hindson, A., Gidlow, B., & Peebles, C. (1994). The 'trickle-down' effect of top level sport: Myth or reality? A case study of the Olympics. *Australian Leisure and Recreation, 4*, 16–24.

Hogan, K., & Norton, K. (2000). The 'Price' of Olympic Gold. *Journal of Science and Medicine in Sport, 3*, 203–218. doi:10.1016/S1440-2440(00)80082-1

Hylton, K., & Totten, M. (2008). Community Sports Development. In K. Hylton & P. Bramham (Eds.), *Sports development: Policy, process and practice* (pp. 77–117). London, UK: Routledge.

Jarvie, G. (2003). Communitarianism, sport and social capital: 'Neighbourly insights into Scottish sport.' *International Review for the Sociology of Sport, 38*(2), 139–153. doi:10.1177/1012690203038002001

Krieger, J. (2000). *British politics in the Global Age: Can social democracy survive?* Cambridge, UK: Polity Press.

Mackintosh, C., Darko, N., & May-Wilkins, H. (2016). Unintended outcomes of the London 2012 Olympic Games: Local voices of resistance and the challenge for sport participation leverage in England. *Leisure Studies, 35*, 454–469.

Matthews, B., & Ross, L. (2010). *Research methods: A practical guide for the social sciences.* Harlow, UK: Pearson Education.

May, T., Harris, S., & Collins, M. (2013). Implementing community sport policy: Understanding the variety of voluntary club types and their attitudes to policy. *International Journal of Sport Policy and Politics, 5*(3), 397–419. doi:10.1080/19406940.2012.735688

McCartney, G., Hanlon, P., & Bond, L. (2013). How will the 2014 Commonwealth Games impact on Glasgow's health, and how will we know? *Evaluation, 19*(1), 24–39. doi:10.1177/1356389012471885

McCartney, G., Palmer, S., Winterbottom, J., Jones, R., Kendall, R., & Booker, D. (2010). A health impact assessment of the 2014 Commonwealth Games in Glasgow. *Public Health, 124*, 444–451. doi:10.1016/j.puhe.2010.04.004

McCartney, G., Thomas, S., Thomson, H., Scott, J., Hamilton, V., Hanlon, P., . . . Bond, L. (2010). The health and socio-economic impacts of major multi-sport events: Systematic review (1978-2008). *British Medical Journal, 2369.*

Millar, P., & Doherty, A. (2016). Capacity building in non-profit sport organizations: Development of a process model. *Sport Management Review, 19*, 365–377. doi:10.1016/j.smr.2016.01.002

Murphy, N.M., & Bauman, A. (2007). Mass sporting and physical activity events: Are they bread and circuses or public health interventions to increase population levels of physical activity? *Journal of Physical Activity and Health, 4*, 193–202. doi:17570888

Nichols, G., Padmore, J., Taylor, P., & Barrett, D. (2012). The relationship between types of sports club and English government policy to grow participation. *International Journal of Sport Policy and Politics, 4*(2), 187–200. doi:10.1080/19406940.2012.662693

Office for National Statistics. (2010). *Life expectancy at birth and at age 65 by local areas in the United Kingdom, 2007–09.* Retrieved from file:///C:/Users/e516250/Downloads/liex101_tcm77-198970.pdf

Pappous, A.S. (2011). Do the Olympic Games lead to a sustainable increase in grassroots sport participation? In J. Savery & K. Gilbert (Eds.), *Sustainability and sport* (pp. 81–87). Champaign, IL: Common Ground.

Pappous, A., & Hayday, E.J. (2016). A case study investigating the impact of the London 2012 Olympic and Paralympic Games on participation in two non-traditional English sports, Judo and Fencing. *Leisure Studies, 35*, 668–684.

Reid, F. (2012). Increasing sports participation in Scotland: Are voluntary sports clubs the answer? *International Journal of Sport Policy and Politics, 4*(2), 221–241. doi:10.1080/19406940.2012.662691

Scottish Government. (2014). *An evaluation of legacy from the Glasgow 2014 Commonwealth Games: Pre-Games report.* Retrieved from http://www.gov.scot/Resource/0044/00449031.pdf

Shaw, M., Smith, G.D., & Dorling, D. (2005). Health inequalities and New Labour: How the promises compare with real progress. *British Medical Journal, 330*(7498), 1016–1021. doi:10.1136/bmj.330.7498.1016

Skinner, J., Zakus, D.H., & Cowell, J. (2008). Development through sport: Building social capital in disadvantaged communities. *Sport Management Review, 11,* 253–275. doi:10.1016/S1441-3523(08)70112-8

Sport and Recreation Alliance. (2012). Olympic legacy: Three quarters of grassroots clubs say government hasn't done enough. *Sport and Recreation Alliance.* Retrieved from http://www.sportandrecreation.org.uk/news/olympicpoll

SportScotland. (2015). Scottish sport benefits from Glasgow Games legacy boost. Retrieved from http://www.sportscotland.org.uk/news/sportscotland/2015/scottish-sport-benefits-from-glasgow-games-legacy-boost/

Taks, M., Green, B.C., Misener, L., & Chalip, L. (2014). Evaluating sport development outcomes: The case of a medium-sized international sport event. *European Sport Management Quarterly, 14,* 213–237. doi:10.1080/16184742.2014.882370

Taylor, P., Barrett, D., & Nichols, G. (2009). *Survey of Sports Clubs 2009.* London, UK: CCPR.

Vail, S. (2007). Community development and sport participation. *Journal of Sport Management, 21,* 571–596. doi:10.1123/jsm.21.4.571

Veal, A.J., Toohey, K., & Frawley, S. (2012). The sport participation legacy of the Sydney 2000 Olympic Games and other international sporting events hosted in Australia. *Journal of Policy Research in Tourism, Leisure and Events, 4*(2), 155–184. doi:10.1080/19407963.2012.662619

Weed, M., Coren, E., Fiore, J., Mansfield, L., Wellard, I., Chatziefstathiou, D., & Dowse, S. (2009). *A systematic review of the evidence base for developing a physical activity and health legacy from the London 2012 Olympic and Paralympic Games.* London, UK: Centre for Sport, Physical Education and Activity Research, Department of Health.

Journal of Sport Management, 2017, 31, 27-43
https://doi.org/10.1123/jsm.2016-0077

Weather Conditions, Travel Distance, Rest, and Running Performance: The 2014 FIFA World Cup and Implications for the Future

Nicholas Watanabe

University of Mississippi

Pamela Wicker

German Sport University Cologne

Grace Yan

University of Mississippi

The awarding of the hosting of the Football World Cup to Russia and Qatar initiated discussions about temperature and travel distances related to the game. This study examines the effect of weather conditions, travel distances, and rest days—three factors potentially causing fatigue—on running performance using player-level and team-level data from the 2014 World Cup. The results show that the heat index (combining temperature and humidity) significantly decreased running performance (number of sprints, high-intensity running), while a clear sky was positively associated with distance covered at high intensity. Travel distance and rest were insignificant. When these models are used to predict running performance at the 2022 Qatar World Cup, the projections show that the combination of heat and wind could hinder the performance of both players and teams and create potentially dangerous conditions. The present study has implications for policy makers regarding the choice of future host countries.

Keywords: team performance, fatigue, running distance, World Cup, sports economics

The Fédération Internationale de Football Association (FIFA) World Cup, which is hosted once every 4 years, is considered the premier international football (soccer) tournament. For example, FIFA claimed a television audience of 3.2 billion for the 2014 tournament (Teixeira, 2014), indicating that the Football World Cup is one of the most watched, televised events in the world. Given the global attention, the ability to potentially attract large numbers of visitors and tourists (Solberg & Preuss, 2007)—although the economic effects were found to be often overstated (Allmers & Maennig, 2009)—as well as the connections with large and powerful corporations, the rights to host the FIFA World Cup are highly sought after and countries spend a large amount of money in bidding for and hosting the FIFA World Cup (de Nooij, van den Berg, & Koopmans, 2011; Heere et al., 2012).

This high level of notoriety associated with hosting a tournament has placed host countries and FIFA under intense scrutiny of the media and general public. Specifically, the awarding of the 2018 World Cup to Russia and the 2022 tournament to Qatar were critically discussed in regard to weather conditions in both future host countries, as well as the accusations of bribery in their selection (Pielke, 2013). Not deliberating over a full range of weather impacts and other conditions can thus be problematic. Given the size of Russia, there will be large travel distances and the possibility for great differences in temperature between host cities. Furthermore, extraordinarily high temperatures in general are predicted for Qatar. Thus, the question is whether and how these circumstances affect the *game*.

The game of football's core components are technical and tactical skills as well as physical performance (Rösch et al., 2010). The focus of this study is on the latter and specifically on running performance. There are indications that physical performance and the attractiveness of the game are related. Under the slogan "For the Good of the Game," FIFA took measures to make the game more dynamic and attractive at the end of the 1980s (Heineke, 2014). Within this initiative, several rules were changed

Nicholas Watanabe and Grace Yan are with the Department of Health, Exercise Science, and Recreation Management, University of Mississippi, Oxford, MS. Pamela Wicker is with the Department of Sport Economics and Sport Management, German Sport University Cologne, Cologne, Germany. Address author correspondence to Nicholas Watanabe at nmwatana@olemiss.edu.

with the aim of supporting a more offensive style of play: For example, goalkeepers were forbidden from picking up back passes, sanctions for (intentionally) delaying the game increased, and the offside rule changed with the aim of reducing the number of breaks in the game (Heineke, 2014). Thus, the rules of the game were changed to make the sport more attractive to the media and the spectators (Heineke, 2014; Meyen, 2014); put differently, if spectators did not value the speed and dynamics of the game, FIFA would have not changed the rules. Consequently, research documents that in recent years the speed and dynamics of the game have increased during Football World Cups (Meyen, 2014; Wallace & Norton, 2014). Since a dynamic and attacking game involves running, it is worth examining—with the World Cups in Russia and Qatar looming—whether and how weather conditions and travel affect the game and the players' running performance, respectively.

The purpose of this study is to examine the effect of weather conditions, traveling, and rest on running performance in football. The mechanism through which these three factors affect running performance is fatigue. As our research context, we select the 2014 World Cup in Brazil since it provides a unique environment for this examination given the wide range in climates, temperatures, and distances between match locations, as well as a more sophisticated use of technology to collect players' running data during matches. Our findings show that the heat index and a clear sky significantly affect running performance while controlling for player/ team-specific and match-specific variables. Based on these results, we were able to predict how the weather conditions in Russia and Qatar may affect the running performance of football players when the World Cup is hosted in these countries. Our findings have implications for sport managers and policy makers regarding the governance and identification of hosting criteria for future World Cups.

Conceptual Framework and Literature Review

The Concept of Fatigue

The concept of fatigue has been primarily approached as *metabolic fatigue*, which is associated with less energy and a feeling of tiredness (Bangsbo, Iaia, & Krustrup, 2007). From a physiological perspective, two types of fatigue can be distinguished: While *central fatigue* relates to changes in the central nervous system, *peripheral fatigue* is provoked by impairments of cardiovascular function caused by reduced oxygen delivery to the exercising muscles (Grantham et al., 2010). Fatigue typically leads to reduced running performance in the second half (Rampinini, Impellizzeri, Castagna, Coutts, & Wisloff, 2009) or toward the end of a football match (Bangsbo et al., 2007), while it can also occur temporarily during games and is subject to seasonal changes

(Mohr, Krustrup, & Bangsbo, 2003). Declines in running performance were found to be larger for less competitive teams (Rampinini et al., 2009) and mediocre players (Mohr et al., 2003). In addition to game-induced fatigue, which is caused by the physical demands of the game, further factors can add to fatigue such as weather conditions (particularly heat; Grantham et al., 2010), traveling (Ashman, Bowman, & Lambrinos, 2010), and rest (Scoppa, 2015), which can affect running performance in a game.

Factors Adding to Fatigue and Affecting Running Performance

Weather conditions. Playing football in extreme weather conditions such as a hot and humid environment poses challenges to the body (Grantham et al., 2010). The first challenge is dehydration and hyperthermia, which can also impair exercise performance (Maughan et al., 2010; Mohr, Krustrup, & Bangsbo, 2005). The second challenge relates to releasing heat because the normal mechanism of releasing heat from the skin to the surroundings is not possible in a hot environment with the problem being even greater in humid conditions. Since muscle temperatures are extremely high in football (i.e., >40 °C; Mohr et al., 2010), the body has to deal with an increase in internal body temperature that can lead to heat illness and heatstroke (Grantham et al., 2010).

The above issues lead to fatigue and are responsible for declines in running performance when football is played in a hot and humid environment (Mohr et al., 2005). For instance, the total distance run in a game declines significantly by 7% in extremely hot conditions ~43 °C) compared with temperate conditions (~21 °C; Mohr, Nybo, Grantham, & Racinais, 2012). Similarly, total distance covered by football players was significantly lower in hot and humid environments measured with the heat index (Özgünen et al., 2010). Furthermore, football players were found to demonstrate lower performances across several running parameters including sprints and high-intensity running in hot (31 °C) conditions (Mohr et al., 2010). Moreover, performance of tasks requiring cognition and skill—which are also required in football—is also reduced in a hot environment (Maughan et al., 2010).

When a tournament is hosted in hot and humid conditions, football teams usually spend some time in similar weather conditions so that players can acclimatize. Previous research argues that such acclimatization periods can be effective in the sense that football-specific physical performance significantly increases after a training camp in the heat (Buchheit, Voss, Nybo, Mohr, & Racinais, 2011). However, studies also indicate that the responses to acclimatization are highly individualized; only some players are able to maintain their activity level in the heat after an acclimatization camp (Racinais et al., 2012). Furthermore, acclimatization periods can only reduce the effect of hot environments; their effectiveness is limited in environments with high humidity (Maughan et al., 2010). Thus, training camps can be effective for some players and certain environmental circumstances but cannot fully mitigate the effect of heat and humidity.

While most studies have concentrated on the effect of heat and humidity on running performance in football, other weather conditions may be relevant too. Thornes (1977) already stated that "not only are temperature and humidity important in comprehending the impact of weather on sport, but also wind velocity, visibility, precipitation, sunshine and the state of the ground" (p. 261). These conditions may also lead to fatigue; for example, running on a muddy ground is more exhausting. Moreover, adverse conditions such as wind and rain may affect playing skills because of greasy balls, muddy pitches, and wind-affected kicks (Carmichael, Millington, & Simmons, 1999), thus affecting the style of play and the quality of the game directly. These aspects have been neglected in previous research.

Traveling. Teams may also experience fatigue as a result of the distances they have traveled (Pollard, Silva, & Medeiros, 2008). Previous research has focused on the effect of travel on team performance (i.e., winning probability) rather than running performance. Mixed findings were documented for the former (for an overview, see Carron, Loughhead, & Bray, 2005): On the one hand no significant effect of travel distance on team performance was reported (Armatas & Pollard, 2014), while on the other hand a significant negative effect was documented (Goumas, 2014; Pollard et al., 2008). Specifically, travel distance was found to increase an away team's probability of conceding goals while scoring fewer goals themselves (Brown, Van Raalte, Brewer, Winter, & Cornelius, 2002). Furthermore, there is evidence suggesting that the direction of travel is important; previous research also showed that teams traveling eastward performed worse because of jetlag (Ashman et al., 2010). Thus, the number of time zones may play a role as well; Qatar has 1; Brazil, 3; and Russia, 11. Given the above findings, it was acknowledged that a key component of the often documented home advantage is less traveling and more rest (Ashman et al., 2010). For the Football World Cup, a continental effect was detected, that is, teams from the host continent had a higher probability of reaching the final eight (Monks & Husch, 2009). Thus, there is evidence that traveling negatively affects overall team performance, but the effect on running performance has not yet been examined.

Rest. Insufficient time to rest can lead to fatigue (Entine & Small, 2008), and teams that do not have enough time to rest and recover between competitions will suffer a decline in their abilities as they advance through tournaments (Mohr et al., 2003; Rampinini et al., 2009). The relationship between rest days and team performance has been examined in previous studies, with the intuitive assumption that rest adds to performance being documented by Entine and Small (2008). Yet, other studies showed that the difference in rest days between a team and its opponent had no significant effect on match outcome (von Hanau, Wicker, & Soebbing, 2015). A study of FIFA World Cups and European Championships found that the previously documented positive relation between rest days and winning outcome fades in the 1990s, presumably as a result of improvements in training and player preparation as well as advances in sport medicine (Scoppa, 2015). Thus, a reduced amount of rest may still lead to fatigue, but the role of rest may be less pronounced in contemporary elite football tournaments.

Shortcomings of Previous Research and This Study's Contribution

To conclude, previous research has examined various fatigue-related factors and how they relate to running performance. Nevertheless, some shortcomings can be observed: First, previous studies focused on the effect of temperature and humidity on running performance; the effect of the full range of weather conditions (wind, rain, etc.) has been largely neglected. Second, the effect of travel distance and rest days on running performance has not yet been examined (studies only looked at team performance measures such as winning a game). Third, many studies were conducted through a sport science and physiology lens without considering the management implications of the findings. The present study aims to address these shortcomings and relates the findings to the selection of future hosts for sport mega-events.

Methods

Data Collection

This study uses both player-level and team-level data. The initial individual player data set includes all players who appeared in at least one game of the 2014 World Cup ($n = 1,777$ player-match observations). Goalkeepers were removed because their running performance cannot be compared with field players (Wicker, Prinz, Weimar, Deutscher, & Upmann, 2013). Another 3 players were excluded because of missing market value data. Thus, the final player-level data set consists of 1,644 player-match observations. The team-level data were aggregated from the player level and comprise $n = 128$ observations on a team-match basis (thus including both teams involved in a match).

Data were collected from various sources: Information on running performance, team/player characteristics, tactical formations, and weather were gathered from the official FIFA 2014 World Cup website (www.fifa.com). FIFA has employed a tracking system named Matrics to provide extensive data in real time that includes heat maps, attacking zones, running performance, and many other statistics. The player-level data on running performance (distance covered, sprints, etc.), attacking, and exact playing time were provided through individual published reports for each match. Because there is no available systematic information on running performance for prior World Cup tournaments, no historical data can be included. Travel distances were collected from maps.google.com. Information on market values was retrieved from a German football data website (www.transfermarkt.de).

Measures and Variables

An overview of the variables and their measurement is provided in Table 1. The summary statistics can be found in Table 2.

Running performance. In line with previous research (Weimar & Wicker, in press), running performance was captured with multiple measures, that is, the total distance covered per minute (*DistMin*) and the number of sprints per minute (*SprintMin*). In addition, a third measure of running performance was available at the 2014 World Cup: high-intensity running per minute (*HighDistMin*). While high-intensity running was defined as running at a speed between 19.8 kph and 25 kph, sprints were defined as running at a speed of over 25 kph at a distance up to 20 m (Di Salvo, Gregson,

Atkinson, Tordoff, & Drust, 2009). Considering that running performance is often a result of interactions between the two opposing teams in a match (Leard & Doyle, 2011), total distance covered (*OppDistMin*), number of sprints (*OppSprintsMin*), and distance covered at high intensity (*OppHighDistMin*) by opponents were also calculated. On average, teams in the 2014 World Cup ran about 109,967 m per match, which is about 1,113 m per minute for a squad. Field players ran about 9.8 km in a standard 90-min match (Table 2).

Fatigue-related variables. The first set of fatigue-related variables focuses on the weather conditions at each match. Specifically, the following variables were included: heat index (*HeatIndex*), average wind speed (*Wind*), precipitation (*Rain*), and clarity (*Clear*). The heat index is a combined measure of temperature and humidity and has already been used in previous research (Özgünen et al., 2010). Moreover, heat breaks (*HeatBreak*) was considered, which reflects when the play is stopped by referees to have players cool down and drink fluids. This was a special condition at the 2014 World Cup, where the regulation of allowing players to stop the match and recover from heat exhaustion was put into place (Blount, 2014). The variable *Altitude* captures the varying altitudes (in meters) of locations where matches were played during the 2014 World Cup.

Second, travel (*TravelDistance*) was measured using the straight-line distance from one game venue to the

Table 1   Variable List and Descriptions

Variable	Description
Running performance	
DistMin	Total distance run by a team/player in a match (in m/min)
OppDistMin	Total distance run by opponent in a match (in m/min)
SprintsMin	Total number of sprints per minute by a team/player in a match
OppSprintsMin	Total number of sprints by opponent per minute in a match
HighDistMin	Total distance run at high intensity by a team/player in a match (in m/min)
OppHighDistMin	Total distance run by an opponent at high intensity in a match (in m/min)
Fatigue-related variables	
Heat Index	Combined measure of temperature and humidity at the start of a match (in degrees Celsius)
Wind	Wind speed at the start of a match (in km/h)
Rain	Precipitation during a match (in cm)
Clear	Whether the sky was clear during a match (1 = yes)
HeatBreak	Presence of a heat break during a match (1 = yes)
Altitude	Altitude of stadium above sea level (in m)
TravelDistance	Distance traveled by a team before a match (in km)
RestDays	Number of days of rest from the previous match for the team

Table 1 *(continued)*

Variable	Description
Player- and team-specific variables (controls)	
Age	Age of player
AgeSq	Squared age of player
AverageAge	Average age of players on the team
SDAge	Standard deviation of the age of players on a team
Appear	Total number of appearances on the national team
TeamAppear	Total number of appearances on the national team by the current members of the squad
SDAppear	Standard deviation of appearances on the national team
Value	Market value of an individual player (in €)
TeamValue	Market value of all the players on a team (in €)
SDValue	Standard deviation of team market value (in €)
WinProb	Implied win probability calculated using betting odds
SouthAmerica	Player plays for a South American club (1 = yes)
PctSouthAm	Percentage of players who play for a South American club
Defense	Player is a defender (1 = yes)
Midfield	Player is a midfielder (1 = yes)
Forward	Player is a forward (1 = yes)
Match-specific variables (controls)	
PlayingTime	Total number of seconds a player was on the field of play
Started	Individual started a match (1 = yes)
TeamStartTime	Total number of seconds played by starters on a team in a match
TeamSubTime	Total number of seconds played by substitutes on a team in a match
YellowCard	The number of yellow cards collected by a player/team in a match
RedTimeLost	Total number of seconds lost by a team for having a player red carded
TotalPasses	Total number of passes by a team in a match
Possession	Percentage of ball possession by a team in a match
MatchNum	Match number for the team in the tournament
Eliminated	Team eliminated from the tournament before the match (1 = yes)
Advanced	Team secured moving on to the knockout stage before the match (1 = yes)
ThreeFourThree	Three-four-three formation (1 = yes)
FourThreeThree	Four-three-three formation (1 = yes)
FourFiveOne	Four-five-one formation (1 = yes)
FiveFourOne	Five-four-one formation (1 = yes)
FiveThreeTwo	Five-three-two formation (1 = yes)
ThreeFiveTwo	Three-tive-two formation (1 = yes)
FourFourTwo	Four-four-two formation (1 = yes)
Attack	Total number of runs and deliveries by a player into the attacking third

Table 2 Summary Statistics

Variable	Player models (n = 1,644)			Team models (n = 128)		
	M	Min	Max	M	Min	Max
DistMin	109	67.32	152	1,113	970	1,316
OppDistMin	101	88.21	120	1,113	970	1,316
SprintsMin	0.3997	0.0000	1.83	3.744	2.786	5.302
OppSprintsMin	0.3404	0.2533	0.4820	3.744	2.786	5.302
HighDistMin	29.71	11.24	80.49	284	215	397
OppHighDistMin	25.85	19.53	36.14	284	215	397
HeatIndex	26.05	11	40	25.97	11	40
Wind	12.82	3	27	12.75	3	27
Rain	0.1767	0	7.89	0.1811	0	7.89
Clear	0.2944	0	1	0.2969	0	1
HeatBreak	0.0316	0	1	0.0313	0	1
Altitude	357	8	1,172	356	8	1,172
TravelDistance	1,573	0	7,296	1,571	0	7,296
RestDays	4.82	2	12	4.83	2	12
Age	26.69	18	37	—	—	—
AgeSq	725	324	1369	—	—	—
AverageAge	—	—	—	26.90	24.9	28.5
SDAge	—	—	—	3.50	1.66	5.70
Appear	42.64	0	145	—	—	—
TeamAppear	—	—	—	758	364	1,375
SDAppear	—	—	—	28.81	10.10	47.87
Value (in TSD €)	12,000	250	120,000	—	—	—
TeamValue (in TSD €)	—	—	—	162,000	13,700	427,000
SDValue (in TSD €)	—	—	—	9,740	694	31,300
WinProb	0.3950	0.0444	0.9190	0.3942	0.0444	0.9190
SouthAmerica	0.0328	0	1	—	—	—
PctSouthAm	—	—	—	3.29	0	38.46
Defense	0.3425	0	1	—	—	—
Midfield	0.3826	0	1	—	—	—
Forward	0.2749	0	1	—	—	—
PlayingTime	4,643	82	7,820	—	—	—
Started	0.7774	0	1	—	—	—
TeamStartTime	—	—	—	60,619	50,165	81,025
TeamSubTime	—	—	—	5,144	1,057	10,815
YellowCard	0.1095	0	2	1.46	0	6
RedTimeLost	—	—	—	123	0	3,544
TotalPasses	517	242	940	519	242	940
Possession	49.97	32	70	49.92	28	70
MatchNum	32.47	1	64	32.50	1	64
Eliminated	0.0383	0	1	0.0391	0	1
Advanced	0.0316	0	1	0.0313	0	1
ThreeFourThree	0.0225	0	1	0.0234	0	1
FourThreeThree	0.2743	0	1	0.2734	0	1

Table 2 *(continued)*

Variable	Player models (*n* = 1,644)			Team models (*n* = 128)		
	M	Min	Max	*M*	Min	Max
FourFiveOne	0.3759	0	1	0.3750	0	1
FiveFourOne	0.0554	0	1	0.0547	0	1
FiveThreeTwo	0.0547	0	1	0.0547	0	1
ThreeFiveTwo	0.0395	0	1	0.0391	0	1
Attack	4.43	0	32	—	—	—

Note. Marginal differences between player-level and team-level data were caused by missing values for some players, as well as some teams' using different numbers of players in matches.

next. While travel distance could also be captured with the distance between the accommodation of teams and the venue of the game, this option was not preferred because the accommodation choices are subjective and determined by the individual teams. Since tournament organizers and federations cannot be held responsible for these distances, this study employed the objective travel distance from one venue to the next. On average, teams traveled 1,571 km between matches.

Third, the number of rest days between two matches (*RestDays*) was included. For opening matches, the number of days teams rested between their previous international friendly and the opening of the World Cup was used. While some teams played their last warm-up friendly 12 days before their first World Cup match, most teams played friendlies close to the start of the tournament. On average, teams had approximately 5 rest days between matches.

Player- and team-specific variables (controls). Several player- and team-specific variables were included because they can also affect running performance. The following variables were used at the player level: age (*Age*) and its squared term (*AgeSq*) because younger players may reveal stronger abilities in running, the number of appearances on the national team (*Appear*), market value (*Value*), and whether the player played club football in South America during the previous season (*SouthAmerica*) to capture familiarity with the climate. The variables *Defense*, *Midfield*, and *Forward* measure the position the player was listed at by his team.

Similar variables were used at the team level: average age (*AverageAge*) and its standard deviation (*SDAge*), total appearances for the national team (*Appear*) and its standard deviation (*SDAppear*), total market value of the team (*TeamValue*) to capture the quality and potential of each squad and its standard deviation (*SDValue*), and the percentage of the squad that played professionally in South America before the start of the tournament (*PctSouthAm*). The standard deviation variables were included to capture the degree of heterogeneity within teams. Finally, the implied win probability (*WinProb*) was calculated for each team in every match by using betting odds data to capture the market predictions of team ability in each match.

Match-specific variables (controls). This study employs a group of match-specific variables that were also found to affect running performance (Bradley & Noakes, 2013; Lago, Casais, Dominguez, & Sampaio, 2010). On the player level, these were the exact number of seconds played by individual players (*PlayingTime*) and whether these individuals started a match (*Started*). On the team level, we used the time played by all starters (*TeamStartTime*) and substitutes (*TeamSubTime*). The use of the exact number of seconds of playing time helps to account for the varying match lengths in detail (including extra time). Since each substitute potentially enhances the overall running capability of a team, the time played by starters and substitutes provides a better control than simply counting the number of times a team changed players during a match.

In addition, the number of yellow cards (*YellowCard*) was collected for every player and team in each match. Players with yellow cards are cautioned and placed in a situation where another card will lead to their removal from the match. Thus, they may not play as aggressively and may decrease their running performance. For red cards, the amount of time teams lost due to having a player ejected for receiving a red card (*RedTimeLost*) was included because this variable also reflects when the player received the red card. To control for how often teams held the ball and passed during a match, variables for the total number of passes (*TotalPasses*) and the percentage of ball possession (*Possession*) were included.

The stage of the tournament and the relevance of a match may also influence running performance. *MatchNum* measures the number of the match in the tournament. This variable helps to control for how far a team has progressed in the tournament; teams may demonstrate higher running performance in matches with high stakes (such as the Final). In addition, while all teams play three matches in the group stage, in some cases teams have already been eliminated (*Eliminated*) or secured advancement (*Advanced*) to the next round before playing their third group stage match. Since these teams do not have as much at stake in the third game as those still competing to advance, they may run less in these matches.

Running performance may also be affected by the tactics developed by the head coach before the match—which are difficult to observe and to measure. Previous research examining running performance in the Bundesliga used coach dummies because each coach tends to pursue a certain tactic (Weimar & Wicker, in press), yet this option is not feasible in this study because coaches did not change during the World Cup. To capture the tactical formation, we included the starting formations for each team as listed in the tactical lineup files released along with each match on the FIFA World Cup website. Altogether, teams used seven different types of formations, which were categorized in the traditional format listing the number of defenders, midfielders, and then forwards in order (*ThreeFourThree, FourThreeThree, FourFiveOne, FiveFourOne, FiveThreeTwo, ThreeFiveTwo*, and *FourFourTwo*). For example, a team playing the most common format known as a *Four-Four-Two* would have four defenders, four midfielders, and two forwards. These variables do not, however, capture whether a team has shifted its tactical formation during a match.

Empirical Evidence on the Relevance of Running Performance

An important question that arises is whether running performance is relevant to the attractiveness of the game and whether fans care about this, as well as whether spectators get to see the same number of goals and opportunities when players run less. With our data we are able to empirically support the initial statement from FIFA that physical running performance and game attractiveness are related. We do this in two steps. First, we report average running performance of all teams at the 2014 World Cup in Table 3. This table gives some indications that teams that were less successful at the World Cup and have performed below expectations demonstrated low levels of running performance. Following Rampinini et al. (2009), reduced levels of running performance are typical for less competitive teams.

Second, recall that several rules were changed to support a more offensive style of play that can be reflected by the number of attacks in a match. The variable *Attack* is thus constructed at the player level by aggregating the total number of runs and deliveries (passes) that each player made into the attacking third of the field. Three regression models were estimated to examine how running performance affects *Attack* while controlling for weather, travel, and rest, as well as player-specific and match-specific variables (Table 4). The results show that all three measures of running performance have a statistically significant and positive effect on *Attack*. Thus, running performance is positively related to a more attacking style of play and, consequently, is relevant to the attractiveness of a match.

Model Specification

Altogether, six regression models were estimated to examine the effect of fatigue-related variables (weather, travel, rest) on running performance while controlling for team/player- and match-specific factors. The first set of models (Models 4–6) was based on player-level data, the second set (Models 7–9) on team-level data. The three measures of running performance (*DistMin, SprintsMin, HighDistMin*) serve as the dependent variables in both sets of models. Models 4–6 were estimated with fixed effects because resistance to heat or humidity is time invariant, yet the fixed effects caused some variables to be omitted because they were time invariant during the World Cup (i.e., *Age, Value, SouthAmerica*). In addition, because some players played different positions during the tournament, the position dummies were not time invariant. Since the running performance of a player or team is also affected by the running performance of the opponent, the respective running measure for the opponent is included in all models. Breusch–Pagan tests have found no presence of heteroscedasticity. Standard errors were clustered by teams because observations among teams may be related to one another. The following general regression function is estimated using ordinary least squares:

$$\text{Running Performance} = \beta_0 + \beta_1 \text{ Rest} + \beta_2 \text{ Travel} + \beta_3 \text{ Weather} + \beta_4 \text{ Team/Player Specific Variables} + \beta_5 \text{ Match Specific Variables} + \varepsilon \qquad (1)$$

Results and Discussion

Table 5 shows the player-level models examining distance run per minute (Model 4), sprints per minute (Model 5), and high-intensity running per minute (Model 6), while Table 6 displays the results of the corresponding team-level models. The distance that opponents ran was positive and statistically significant in all models, indicating that when the opponents in a match ran further or sprinted more, both players and teams increased their running performances. The models explain between 23% and 37% of the variation in running performance at the player level and between 59% and 63% at the team level, respectively.

Fatigue-Related Variables (Weather, Travel, Rest) and Running Performance

Starting with weather conditions, heat is the factor that is highly suspected for potentially exacerbating player fatigue and leading to reduced running performance. The player-level results (Table 5) show that the heat index, a combined measure of both air temperature and humidity, had a significant negative effect on total distance covered and high-intensity running per minute. This finding implies that the higher the heat index, the lower the running performance in terms of the distance run per minute and the total distance run at high intensity per minute. The team-level models (Table 6) also document a negative effect of heat index on high-intensity running. Thus, it seems that heat and humidity particularly affect the amount of running that requires higher levels of

Table 3   Running Performance of Teams at the 2014 World Cup (Sorted in Descending Order by Distance per Minute)

Team	Round advanced to	No. of matches	Distance per minute (mean in m)	Total distance (mean in m)
Russia	Group Stage	3	1,243	115,812
Australia	Group Stage	3	1,241	118,104
Bosnia	Group Stage	3	1,187	112,591
United States	Round of 16	4	1,176	124,190
Korea	Group Stage	3	1,173	111,001
Germany	Final	7	1,168	120,891
Chile	Round of 16	4	1,155	120,300
Belgium	Quarter-finals	5	1,148	115,370
Portugal	Group Stage	3	1,144	107,681
Switzerland	Round of 16	4	1,139	118,227
Ghana	Group Stage	3	1,137	110,935
Spain	Group Stage	3	1,131	108,486
Algeria	Round of 16	4	1,128	115,500
Iran	Group Stage	3	1,127	107,825
The Netherlands	Third Place	7	1,122	118,030
Italy	Group Stage	3	1,117	107,105
England	Group Stage	3	1,113	106,315
Costa Rica	Quarter-finals	5	1,103	119,317
Japan	Group Stage	3	1,103	105,829
France	Quarter-finals	5	1,098	105,676
Mexico	Round of 16	4	1,096	106,319
Croatia	Group Stage	3	1,092	104,784
Uruguay	Round of 16	4	1,089	104,859
Colombia	Quarter-finals	5	1,087	103,299
Argentina	Final	7	1,067	117,409
Brazil	Third Place	7	1,066	106,792
Greece	Round of 16	4	1,058	109,162
Nigeria	Round of 16	4	1,053	100,531
Cameroon	Group Stage	3	1,044	97,314
Ecuador	Group Stage	3	1,041	98,751
Honduras	Group Stage	3	1,015	96,110
Côte D'Ivoire	Group Stage	3	989	95,784

Table 4   Player-Level Regression Results for Attack

	Model 1		Model 2		Model 3	
	Coeff.	p > |t|	Coeff.	p > |t|	Coeff.	p > |t|
DistMin	0.0231	0.055*	—	—	—	—
SprintsMin	—	—	1.787	0.041**	—	—
HighDistMin	—	—	—	—	0.0459	0.011**
OppDistMin	0.0124	0.337	0.2821	0.908	0.0009	0.977
HeatIndex	0.0139	0.412	0.0171	0.314	0.0208	0.225
Wind	−0.0205	0.109	−0.0249	0.061*	−0.0256	0.058*
Rain	0.0862	0.195	0.0776	0.280	0.0854	0.211
Clear	0.1277	0.590	0.1533	0.516	0.1274	0.583
HeatBreak	0.3918	0.306	0.4445	0.218	0.3959	0.300
Altitude	<0.0001	0.814	<0.0001	0.901	<0.0001	0.809
TravelDistance	−0.0001	0.171	−0.0001	0.278	−0.0001	0.254
RestDays	−0.0231	0.792	−0.0091	0.918	−0.0206	0.813
Age	−0.4193	0.255	−0.4599	0.229	−0.4531	0.227
AgeSq	0.0047	0.465	0.0056	0.407	0.0054	0.410
Appear	0.0244	0.001***	0.0247	0.001***	0.0249	0.001***
Value	<0.0001	0.012**	<0.0001	0.016**	<0.0001	0.015**
SouthAmerica	−0.1326	0.871	−0.1426	0.865	−0.1451	0.860
Midfield	1.903	<0.001***	2.027	<0.001***	1.814	<0.001***
Forward	0.1201	0.608	0.0356	0.880	0.0386	0.868
PlayingTime	0.0012	<0.001***	0.0012	<0.001***	0.0012	<0.001***
Started	−1.123	<0.001***	−0.9949	0.001***	−0.9771	0.002***
YellowCard	−0.4888	0.042**	−0.4469	0.066*	−0.4533	0.061*
TotalPasses	0.0020	0.132	0.0024	0.04**	0.0021	0.069*
Possession	0.0883	<0.001***	0.0837	<0.001***	0.0871	<0.001***
MatchNum	−0.0108	0.281	−0.0117	0.236	−0.0116	0.250
Eliminated	−0.7525	0.026**	−0.7373	0.019**	−0.7361	0.026**
Advanced	−0.9560	0.121	−0.7814	0.199	−0.8048	0.187
ThreeFourThree	0.0148	0.965	−0.0942	0.775	−0.0982	0.763
FourThreeThree	0.3737	0.066*	0.4028	0.045**	0.3355	0.105
FourFiveOne	0.5144	0.086*	0.5631	0.048**	0.4902	0.081*
FiveFourOne	−0.2356	0.589	−0.1616	0.717	−0.3022	0.477
FiveThreeTwo	−0.0236	0.946	0.0524	0.888	−0.0535	0.881
ThreeFiveTwo	−0.8271	0.020**	−0.7135	0.034**	−0.8526	0.013**
constant	−3.430	0.495	−0.1620	0.975	−0.8825	0.861
R^2	.3663		.3663		.3679	

Note. Reference categories are *Defense* and *FourFourTwo*. Coeff. = coefficient.

*$p < .1$. **$p < .05$. ***$p < .01$.

Table 5 **Player-Level Regression Results for Running Performance (Including Fixed Effects)**

Variable	Model 4: DistMin		Model 5: SprintsMin		Model 6: HighDistMin	
	Coeff.	$p > \lvert t \rvert$	Coeff.	$p > \lvert t \rvert$	Coeff.	$p > \lvert t \rvert$
OppDistMin	0.5927	<0.001***	—	—	—	—
OppSprintsMin	—	—	0.5704	<0.001***	—	—
OppHighDistMin	—	—	—	—	0.5028	<0.001***
HeatIndex	−0.1613	0.040**	−0.0011	0.214	−0.1601	0.004***
Wind	−0.0285	0.527	−0.0001	0.868	−0.0009	0.976
Rain	0.0869	0.607	0.0023	0.215	−0.0124	0.863
Clear	0.9362	0.171	−0.0005	0.939	0.7238	0.041**
HeatBreak	−0.4988	0.758	−0.0173	0.353	−0.5603	0.418
Altitude	0.0010	0.329	0.0000	0.029**	0.0001	0.768
TravelDistance	0.0004	0.231	0.0000	0.558	0.0002	0.306
RestDays	0.1948	0.543	−0.0019	0.625	0.0891	0.672
Age	—	—	—	—	—	—
AgeSq	—	—	—	—	—	—
Appear	—	—	—	—	—	—
Value	—	—	—	—	—	—
WinProb	4.27	0.028**	−0.0254	0.275	0.3228	0.760
SouthAmerica	—	—	—	—	—	—
Midfield	−2.00	0.303	0.0182	0.763	−1.34	0.282
Forward	−5.05	0.006***	0.0162	0.856	−3.21	0.130
PlayingTime	−0.0017	<0.001***	<0.0001	<0.001***	−0.0011	<0.001***
Started	0.7530	0.517	−0.0637	<0.001***	−1.79	0.015**
YellowCard	0.0784	0.917	−0.0101	0.204	−0.3487	0.422
TotalPasses	−0.0078	0.050**	0.0000	0.449	−0.0019	0.419
Possession	−0.1192	0.131	−0.0003	0.691	−0.0348	0.427
MatchNum	0.0275	0.157	0.0003	0.315	0.0074	0.637
Eliminated	−2.39	0.289	−0.0582	<0.001***	−1.81	0.147
Advanced	−1.87	0.331	0.0043	0.845	0.0065	0.994
ThreeFourThree	1.52	0.267	0.0322	0.114	1.82	0.049**
FourThreeThree	−0.0234	0.977	−0.0035	0.813	0.3671	0.479
FourFiveOne	0.7188	0.306	−0.0031	0.823	0.8969	0.078*
FiveFourOne	2.62	0.106	0.0404	0.145	2.22	0.039**
FiveThreeTwo	1.39	0.139	0.0144	0.475	2.00	0.006***
ThreeFiveTwo	0.3674	0.715	0.0224	0.350	1.20	0.180
constant	67.45	<0.001***	0.3927	<0.001***	29.67	<0.001***
R^2	.3723		.2275		.3140	

Note. Reference categories are *Defense* and *FourFourTwo*. Coeff. = coefficient.

*$p < .1$. **$p < .05$. ***$p < .01$.

Table 6 Team-Level Regression Results for Running Performance

	Model 7: DistMin		Model 8: SprintMin		Model 9: HighDistMin	
	Coeff.	*p > |t|*	Coeff.	*p > |t|*	Coeff.	*p > |t|*
OppDistMin	0.4133	<0.001***	—	—	—	—
OppSprintMin	—	—	0.5081	<0.001***	—	—
OppHighDistMin	—	—	—	—	0.3720	<0.001***
HeatIndex	–0.2297	0.825	–0.0059	0.466	–0.9822	0.066*
Wind	–0.6929	0.392	0.0010	0.872	0.0838	0.832
Rain	–3.16	0.493	–0.0184	0.605	–2.49	0.277
Clear	12.37	0.261	0.0906	0.288	7.90	0.150
HeatBreak	–18.114	0.528	–0.1532	0.490	–8.07	0.571
Altitude	0.0011	0.930	<0.0001	0.679	–0.0004	0.945
TravelDistance	0.0037	0.473	<0.0001	0.241	0.0023	0.372
RestDays	4.06	0.397	–0.0196	0.593	1.56	0.510
AverageAge	–6.71	0.294	0.0093	0.851	–2.02	0.529
SDAge	–9.81	0.191	–0.1073	0.064*	–3.97	0.286
TeamAppear	–0.0389	0.233	–0.0004	0.130	–0.0292	0.073*
SDAppear	0.8002	0.374	–0.0006	0.925	0.3072	0.490
TeamValue	0.0000	0.795	<0.0001	0.224	<0.0001	0.891
SDValue	0.0000	0.973	<0.0001	0.857	<0.0001	0.957
WinProb	–8.72	0.774	–0.4824	0.041**	–25.00	0.100*
PctSouthAm	8.43	0.920	1.39	0.034**	58.45	0.164
TeamStartTime	–0.0044	<0.001***	<0.0001	0.077*	–0.0021	0.001***
TeamSubTime	–0.0012	0.640	<0.0001	0.360	–0.0008	0.537
YellowCard	–2.30	0.642	–0.0591	0.122	–1.28	0.601
RedTimeLost	–0.0118	0.162	<0.0001	0.495	–0.0062	0.139
TotalPasses	0.3120	<0.001***	0.0015	0.018**	0.1303	0.001***
Possession	–4.98	<0.001***	–0.0133	0.091*	–1.72	0.001***
MatchNum	0.6538	0.120	0.0055	0.089*	0.4297	0.041**
Eliminated	1.15	0.963	–0.1630	0.397	–8.36	0.497
Advanced	–7.85	0.776	0.0016	0.994	–3.90	0.772
ThreeFourThree	27.42	0.400	0.3311	0.187	19.15	0.237
FourThreeThree	16.41	0.305	0.2092	0.091*	13.65	0.087*
FourFiveOne	31.56	0.038**	0.3799	0.001***	19.93	0.009***
FiveFourOne	50.94	0.044**	0.3006	0.123	35.54	0.005***
FiveThreeTwo	51.24	0.026**	0.2360	0.180	25.49	0.026**
ThreeFiveTwo	72.50	0.005***	0.3998	0.044**	40.45	0.002***
Constant	1,184	<0.001***	3.27	0.038**	398	<0.001***
R^2	.6307		.6015		.5860	

Note. Reference categories are *Defense* and *FourFourTwo*. Coeff. = coefficient.

*$p < .1$. **$p < .05$. ***$p < .01$.

exertion. These findings are in line with previous research documenting that especially high-intensity running deteriorates as temperature increases (Mohr et al., 2010).

While wind speed is insignificant in the models examining running performance at the player and team level, it has a significant negative effect on attacking (Table 4): The higher the wind speed, the lower the number of runs and deliveries of a player into the attacking third in a match. According to these results, attacking is hampered by increased winds, which could come about because of the erratic nature of the wind carrying the ball during play. Thus, wind speed directly affects the attractiveness of the game. When the sky was clear, players ran further distances at high intensity. The coefficients indicate that when the sky was clear, players ran about 0.72 m more per minute at high intensity (Table 5). Thus, good weather in terms of a clear sky affects running performance and, consequently, also the attractiveness of the game.

Rain was found to be insignificant in all models, suggesting that precipitation did not have any relationship with total distance run, sprinting, or high-intensity running at the World Cup. Similarly, heat breaks were found to have no statistically significant relationship with running performance. This finding indicates that the implementation of including heat breaks for players during matches seems an effective policy for international football tournaments played in hot and humid conditions, as it allows players to rest without causing significant fluctuations in their running performance.

Altitude had no significant effect in all models except the player-level model analyzing number of sprints where altitude showed a positive effect. Furthermore, familiarity with the climate (*SouthAmerica*) at the 2014 World Cup had a significant positive effect in the team-level model examining number of sprints per minute (Table 6). Thus, the higher the share of players playing for a South American club, the higher the number of sprints per minute performed during a match. However, the insignificance of this variable in the other team-level models indicates that familiarity with the climate is not related to covering more distance at regular or high intensity during a match. Thus, there does not seem to be an acclimatization advantage of players who play regularly on the continent. In addition, the pre–World Cup training camps may have indeed been successful in adapting players to the climate, as shown in prior research (Buchheit et al., 2011).

Much has been discussed about the existence of a wide range of travel times and distances at the 2014 Brazil World Cup—some teams had to fly 5 hr from one host site to the next, while other teams had schedules requiring shorter travel distances. The results of this study reveal that travel distance has no statistically significant effect on running performance—similar to some previous studies examining the effect of travel on team performance (e.g., Armatas & Pollard, 2014). It is possible that with the use of chartered planes and buses, travel for players during the tournament is likely not as physically and mentally taxing, and thus even for a competition within a country as large as Brazil, there seems to be no noticeable effect of travel distance on running performance.

The number of rest days between matches was insignificant in all models run with either player-level or team-level data. These results are in line with Scoppa (2015), who noted that teams that have at least 3 rest days do not witness any great decline in performance and match outcomes, suggesting that rest may not be important in contemporary elite football tournaments. This result can also be attributed to tournament schedules dictated by television viewing patterns and the demands of broadcasting creating adequate rest periods for players.

Player/Team- and Match-Specific Variables and Running Performance

Starting with player- and team-specific variables, age was insignificant in all models, while its standard deviation was significant in Model 8. Hence, heterogeneous teams in terms of age performed significantly fewer sprints per minute. From this, it may be possible that teams that have a relatively similar age among the squad sprint more, but that the overall age of the team did not matter. Thus, the intuitive assumption that younger players prefer a more physical style of play or that they have to run more to compensate for a lack of tactical skills could not be supported by these results. In fact, the results show that high-quality players, that is, those with a high level of tactical and technical skills that should be reflected in the win probability set by the betting market, cover greater distances during a match (Model 4). Thus, the results support the notion that player quality and running distance are complements rather than substitutes. However, the higher a team's probability of winning a game, the fewer sprints per minute were performed (Model 8) and the less distance was run at high intensity (Model 9). This finding is similar to previous research suggesting that good teams cover greater distances because they seek good positioning on the field, while sprinting or running at high intensity is rather needed to chase the ball and/or opponent (Weimar & Wicker, in press).

Turning to match-specific variables, the amount of time a player was on the field (*PlayingTime*) has a significant negative effect on total distance covered and distance run at high intensity. Thus, running performance declines the longer a match lasts (Bangsbo et al., 2007). Interestingly, the number of sprints rises with increasing playing time, indicating that players run fast to try to score goals toward the end of a match—an assumption that is supported by the positive effect of playing time in the *Attack* models. The same pattern of effects can be found in the team-level models for *TeamStartTime*, as the longer the starters on a team played, the lower their collective running performance for total distance and distance run at high intensity.

Having received a yellow card significantly reduced the number of attacks attempted by players but did not significantly affect running performance. At the team level, the amount of time lost for a team due to red cards

(*RedTimeLost*) had no significant effect on total distance covered, sprinting, and distance run at high intensity. Thus, teams that had players missing for longer periods of time because of being sent off by the referee did not change their running performance.

The total number of passes is positively related to running performance at the team level and with attacking at the player level. Ball possession has a significant positive effect on attacking, but it is associated with significantly lower levels of running performance at the team level. Thus, teams that control the ball (have to) run less and vice versa. Examining the coefficients, the effects of passing did not greatly affect the amount of running, with each pass getting a team to run about 0.31 m more per minute. On the other hand, a loss of 1% in ball possession meant that a team had to run about 5 m more per minute in total and 1.7 m more per minute at high intensity, respectively. While passing was associated with slightly more running, not having possession of the ball and having to constantly chase it had a greater effect on the distance a team had to run.

The more relevant the match is (*MatchNum*), the greater the running performance of teams in terms of number of sprints and high-intensity running. Thus, there seems to be a ramping up effect; teams significantly increase their running performance as a group as they progress to the later stages of the tournament. While match number does not affect attacking, teams that have already been eliminated before a match attack significantly less and their players perform significantly fewer sprints. Having already advanced to the next round before a match affects neither running performance nor attacking.

The tactical starting formation of a team was significantly related to running performance and attacking (recall that the figures indicate the number of defenders, midfielders, and attackers). For example, players whose teams started matches using either a 3-4-3, 4-5-1, 5-4-1, 5-3-2, or 3-5-2 formation demonstrated significantly higher running performance in terms of high-intensity running than teams starting with a 4-4-2 formation (reference category). Moreover, the formations 4-3-3 and 4-5-1 led to significantly more and the 3-5-2 formation led to significantly fewer attacks than the 4-4-2 formation. Thus, the tactical formations selected by the head coach and how players interpreted their roles also explain running performance and attacking, respectively.

Conclusion

Summary and Limitations

This study examined the effect of various weather conditions, travel, and rest—all factors potentially causing fatigue—on running performance at the 2014 Football World Cup. Before the actual analysis was conducted, this study had provided empirical evidence for the assumptions by FIFA that running performance is associated with a more attacking style of play and, consequently,

increases the attractiveness of the game. The results of the main regression analyses show that heat index (a combined measure of temperature and humidity) significantly decreased running performance in terms of distance covered, sprinting, and high-intensity running, while a clear sky was associated with greater distance covered at high intensity. Travel distance and rest days had no significant relationship with running performance, suggesting that these aspects play a minor role in contemporary elite football tournaments, probably because TV broadcast cycles have put a limit on how many matches can be broadcast within a relatively short amount of time (Scoppa, 2015).

Meanwhile, the limitations of this study must also be recognized. First, while this study is based upon a complete sample of 2014 World Cup matches and used both player-level and team-level data, a larger data set covering several World Cup tournaments would be preferred to check the robustness of this study's findings. However, the technology that FIFA partners with to track and publish data during the tournament is a relatively new system, which does not provide data for previous competitions. Second, the weather variables are basic measures of weather at the time the match began. While the modeling helps to control for a large number of factors, meteorological and physiological measures based upon more advanced tracking would further enhance our understanding of the role of weather. However, these measurements are not fully available at the 2014 World Cup. Moreover, future studies should consider the fact that weather conditions may change during matches. Third, while this research examines the ability of players to demonstrate running performance in various weather conditions, it is not a full prediction as to how weather factors can impact player health. As players continue to show high levels of running performance in World Cup games, the health condition of players in extreme weather may be exacerbated. Future studies should examine how weather conditions and running performance affect player health (e.g., dehydration, hyperthermia, injury prevalence).

Managerial Implications

The awarding of the hosting of the 2018 World Cup to Russia and the 2022 tournament to Qatar has attracted voluminous discussions. Particularly, predicted year-round high temperatures in Qatar were seen as problematic. With this in mind, the specific findings of this study contribute to illuminating potential scenarios where running performances and also the attractiveness of the game can be affected by compounding factors of weather and tournament arrangements. For a comparative analysis, Table 7 provides an overview of the weather conditions (average temperature, wind speed, humidity, and rain) in Brazil during the World Cup and the expected conditions in Russia and Qatar. In this table, the sites that are chosen for Brazil and Russia manifest the greatest variations in weather conditions. Meanwhile, considering the

Table 7   Weather Conditions in Different Host Locations of the World Cups in 2014, 2018, and 2022

Host location	Manaus (2014)	Rio de Janeiro (2014)	Moscow (2018)	Sochi (2018)	Doha (2022)
Month	June	June	June	June	November
Average low temperature (°C)	24	19	13	15	20
Average high temperature (°C)	31	23	22	24	30
Record high temperature (°C)	35	33	34	35	39
Average wind speed (km/h)	6	9	4	10	13
Record wind speed (km/h)	83	93	22	54	61
Humidity (%)	78	78	73	7	63
Average precipitation (mm/month)	30	42	93	57	0

relatively small size of Qatar, only Doha is included, as the venues are all within a short driving distance from the main host city.

Although FIFA has moved the tournament in Qatar to November to avoid extreme temperature, the highest temperature may still get close to 40 °C. In light of the results of this study, it is possible that players still demonstrate considerable running performance even in high temperatures during the World Cup. However, the present results found that total distance run and distance run at high intensity were significantly reduced in hot and humid conditions. Specifically, players ran about 0.16 m less per minute at both normal distances and high intensity for each degree increase in the heat index, or about 14 m less in a 90-min match. For the case of Doha, where the average heat index is 33.4 °C (or 7.4 °C hotter than the average for Brazil), this would translate to players running approximately 103.6 m less at high intensity per match during the 2022 tournament. As this research has shown links between high-intensity running and attacking opportunities, it is possible that the effects of heat in Doha could negatively affect game attractiveness.

Given these weather conditions, it is necessary for tournament organizers to take precautionary measures to ensure player safety during competitions. While the implementation of heat breaks was a step forward at the 2014 World Cup, not all jurisdictions have policies or regulations with specific and systematic attention to the crucial impact of weather conditions. Additional policies reflecting concerns about the weather, rather than about maximizing broadcast viewership, when designing match schedules, should be implemented. For example, considering that the findings of this study and prior research (Mohr et al., 2010) revealed a significant negative relationship between heat and running performance in extreme conditions, the implementation of a temperature threshold may be considered. This may be particularly relevant in Qatar, where players may be exposed to temperatures close to 40 °C for an enduring amount of time. Although adjustments ex post can be made, the temperature at potential host destinations should be taken into account when selecting host locations for sport mega-events in the future.

In addition, the wind speed in Doha is worth noting. As can be seen from Table 7, the average Doha wind speed during November is 13 kph—twice as strong compared with Manaus—with maximum wind speeds reaching 61 kph. According to the coefficients, it means that teams on average would attack significantly less per match when all other variables are held constant. Thus, wind speed compounded by heat may present a daunting challenge for players to deliver quality performances, as well as for FIFA and tournament organizers to manage related consequences. For Qatar, the envisaged roof constructions for stadia should not only allow cooling down the facility but also mitigating the impact of strong wind. For the case of Russia, it would seem that some locations like Sochi, where the wind is stronger, could potentially see reductions in attacking opportunities during matches.

However, moving sporting tournaments to another time in the year because of weather conditions, as in the case of the 2022 Qatar World Cup, also has repercussions for football competitions and seasons in countries worldwide. League competitions (including cups) within countries and also international competitions like the UEFA Champions and Europa League are characterized by dense schedules that would need revision. Typically, major tournaments like the World Cup are held in the postseason period. Thus, moving a tournament to another time of the year requires a long break during the regular season, which may affect the competition.

Finally, one purpose of this paper was to build cognizance of factors related to fatigue, how they affect running performance, and how all that may be taken into account in the complex interplays between tournament arrangements, environmental conditions, and the performance of players and teams. A further step toward improved practices requires collaborated efforts, as noted by Müller (2015): "Two main actors are responsible for implementing these changes—hosts and event-governing bodies—and in many cases both need to work together for a change to be most effective" (p. 13). Surely, if powerful federations and host governments are willing to work together to initiate changes, it would enhance the governing of sport by bringing together player welfare, consumer interests, and organizational behaviors in the long run. Such collaboration is most likely needed to ensure that future mega-events such as the World Cup will continue to provide entertaining matches for fans while also protecting the health and safety of players.

References

Allmers, S., & Maennig, W. (2009). Economic impacts of the FIFA Soccer World Cups in France 1998, Germany 2006, and outlook for South Africa 2010. *Eastern Economic Journal, 35,* 500–519. doi:10.1057/eej.2009.30

Armatas, V., & Pollard, R. (2014). Home advantage in Greek football. *European Journal of Sport Science, 14*(2), 116–122. doi:10.1080/17461391.2012.736537

Ashman, T., Bowman, R.A., & Lambrinos, J. (2010). The role of fatigue in NBA wagering markets: The surprising "home disadvantage situation." *Journal of Sports Economics, 11*(6), 602–613. doi:10.1177/1527002509357545

Bangsbo, J., Iaia, F.M., & Krustrup, P. (2007). Metabolic response and fatigue in soccer. *International Journal of Sports Physiology and Performance, 2*(2), 111–127. doi:10.1123/ijspp.2.2.111

Blount, J. (2014). Judge orders World Cup water breaks if heat reaches 32 degrees C. *Reuters.* Retrieved July, 28, 2015, from http://uk.reuters.com/article/2014/06/20/us-soccer-world-water-injunction-idUKKBN0EV29F20140620

Bradley, P.S., & Noakes, T.D. (2013). Match running performance fluctuations in elite soccer: Indicative of fatigue, pacing or situational influences? *Journal of Sports Sciences, 31*(15), 1627–1638. doi:10.1080/02640414.2013.796062

Brown, T.D., Jr., Van Raalte, J.L., Brewer, B.W., Winter, C.R., & Cornelius, A.E. (2002). World Cup soccer home advantage. *Journal of Sport Behavior, 25,* 134–144.

Buchheit, M., Voss, S.C., Nybo, L., Mohr, M., & Racinais, S. (2011). Physiological and performance adaptations to an in-season soccer camp in the heat: Associations with heart rate and heart rate variability. *Scandinavian Journal of Medicine & Science in Sports, 21,* e477–e485. doi:10.1111/j.1600-0838.2011.01378.x

Carmichael, F., Millington, J., & Simmons, R. (1999). Elasticity of demand for Rugby League attendance and the impact of BskyB. *Applied Economics Letters, 6*(12), 797–800. doi:10.1080/135048599352196

Carron, A.V., Loughhead, T.M., & Bray, S.R. (2005). The home advantage in sport competitions: Courneya and Carron's (1992) conceptual framework a decade later. *Journal of Sports Sciences, 23*(4), 395–407. doi:10.1080/02640410400021542

de Nooij, M., van den Berg, M., & Koopmans, C. (2011). Bread or games? A social cost-benefit analysis of the World Cup bid of the Netherlands and the winning Russian bid. *Journal of Sports Economics, 14*(5), 521–545. doi:10.1177/1527002511429825

Di Salvo, V., Gregson, W., Atkinson, G., Tordoff, P., & Drust, B. (2009). Analysis of high intensity activity in Premier League soccer. *International Journal of Sports Medicine, 30*(3), 205–212. doi:10.1055/s-0028-1105950

Entine, O., & Small, D.S. (2008). The role of rest in the NBA home-court advantage. *Journal of Quantitative Analysis in Sports, 4*(2), 1–9. doi:10.2202/1559-0410.1106

FIFA. (2014). *2014 FIFA World Cup in Numbers.* Retrieved July 15, 2015, from http://www.fifa.com/worldcup/news/y=2014/m=9/news=2014-fifa-world-cup-braziltm-in-numbers-2443025.html

Goumas, C. (2014). Home advantage and referee bias in European football. *European Journal of Sport Science, 14*(Suppl. 1), S243–S249. doi:10.1080/17461391.2012.686062

Grantham, J., Cheung, S.S., Connes, P., Febbraio, M.A., Gaoua, N., González-Alonso, J., . . . Dvorak, J. (2010). Current knowledge on playing football in hot environments. *Scandinavian Journal of Medicine & Science in Sports, 20*(Suppl. 3), 161–167. doi:10.1111/j.1600-0838.2010.01216.x

Heere, B., Kim, C., Yoshida, M., Nakamura, H., Ogura, T., Chung, K.S., & Lim, S.Y. (2012). The impact of World Cup 2002 on the bilateral relationship between South Korea and Japan. *Journal of Sport Management, 26*(2), 127–142. doi:10.1123/jsm.26.2.127

Heineke, S. (2014). *Fit fürs Fernsehen?* Cologne, Germany: Herbert von Halem.

Lago, C., Casais, L., Dominguez, E., & Sampaio, J. (2010). The effects of situational variables on distance covered at various speeds in elite soccer. *European Journal of Sport Science, 10*(2), 103–109. doi:10.1080/17461390903273994

Leard, B., & Doyle, J.M. (2011). The effect of home advantage, momentum, and fighting on winning the National Hockey League. *Journal of Sports Economics, 12*(5), 538–560. doi:10.1177/1527002510389869

Maughan, R.J., Shirreffs, S.M., Özgünen, K.T., Kurdak, S.S., Ersoz, G., Binnet, M.S., & Dvorak, J. (2010). Living, training and playing in the heat: Challenges to the football player and strategies for coping with environmental extremes. *Scandinavian Journal of Medicine & Science in Sports, 20*(Suppl. 3), 117–124. doi:10.1111/j.1600-0838.2010.01221.x

Meyen, M. (2014). Medialisierung des deutschen Spitzenfußballs. *Medien und Kommunikation, 62*(3), 377–394. doi:10.5771/1615-634x-2014-3-377

Mohr, M., Krustrup, P., & Bangsbo, J. (2003). Match performance of high-standard soccer players with special reference to development of fatigue. *Journal of Sports Sciences, 21,* 519–528. doi:10.1080/0264041031000071182

Mohr, M., Krustrup, P., & Bangsbo, J. (2005). Fatigue in soccer: A brief review. *Journal of Sports Sciences, 23*(6), 593–599. doi:10.1080/02640410400021286

Mohr, M., Muijka, I., Santisteban, J., Randers, M.B., Bischoff, R., Solano, R., . . ., Krustrup P. (2010). Examination of fatigue development in elite soccer in a hot environment: A multi-experimental approach. *Scandinavian Journal of Medicine & Science in Sports, 20,* 125–132. doi:10.1111/j.1600-0838.2010.01217.x

Mohr, M., Nybo, L., Grantham, J., & Racinais, S. (2012). Physiological responses and physical performance during football in the heat. *PLoS One, 7*(6), e39202. doi:10.1371/journal.pone.0039202

Monks, J., & Husch, J. (2009). The impact of seeding, home continent, and hosting on FIFA World Cup results. *Journal of Sports Economics, 10*(4), 391–408. doi:10.1177/1527002508328757

Müller, M. (2015). The mega-event syndrome: Why so much goes wrong in mega-event planning and what to do about it. *Journal of the American Planning Association, 81*(1), 6–17.

Özgünen, K.T., Kurdak, S.S., Maughan, R.J., Zeren, C., Korkmaz, S., ... Dvorak, J. (2010). Effect of hot environmental conditions on physical activity patterns and temperature response of football players. *Scandinavian Journal of Medicine & Science in Sports, 20*(Suppl. 3), 140–147. doi:10.1111/j.1600-0838.2010.01219.x

Pielke, R. (2013). How can FIFA be held accountable? *Sport Management Review, 16*(3), 255–267. doi:10.1016/j.smr.2012.12.007

Pollard, R., Silva, C.D., & Medeiros, N.C. (2008). Home advantage in football in Brazil: Differences between teams and the effects of distance traveled. *Revista Brasileira de Futebol, 1*(1), 3–10.

Racinais, S., Mohr, M., Buchheit, M., Voss, S.C., Gaoua, N., Grantham, J., & Nybo, L. (2012). Individual responses to short-term heat acclimatisation as predictors of football performance in a hot, dry environment. *British Journal of Sports Medicine, 46,* 810–815. doi:10.1136/bjsports-2012-091227

Rampinini, E., Impellizzeri, F.M., Castagna, C., Coutts, A.J., & Wisloff, U. (2009). Technical performance during soccer matches of the Italian Serie A league: Effect of fatigue and competitive level. *Journal of Science and Medicine in Sport, 12,* 227–233. doi:10.1016/j.jsams.2007.10.002

Rösch, D., Hodgson, R., Peterson, L., Graf-Baumans, T., Junge, A., Chomiak, J., & Dvorak, J. (2010). Assessment and evaluation of football performance. *American Journal of Sports Medicine, 28*(5), S29–S39.

Scoppa, V. (2015). Fatigue and team performance in soccer: Evidence from the FIFA World Cup and the UEFA European Championship. *Journal of Sports Economics, 16*(5), 482–507. doi:10.1177/1527002513502794

Solberg, H.A., & Preuss, H. (2007). Major sport events and long-term tourism impacts. *Journal of Sport Management, 21*(2), 213–234. doi:10.1123/jsm.21.2.213

Teixeira, T. (2014). *World Cup Soccer: 770 billion minutes of attention.* Retrieved March 03, 2016, from http://www.forbes.com/sites/hbsworkingknowledge/2014/06/13/world-cup-soccer-770-billion-minutes-of-attention/

Thornes, J.E. (1977). The effect of weather on sport. *Weather, 32*(7), 258–268. doi:10.1002/j.1477-8696.1977.tb04568.x

von Hanau, T., Wicker, P., & Soebbing, B.P. (2015). Determinants of expected vs. actual match outcome: An examination of the German Bundesliga. *Soccer and Society, 16*(1), 63–75. doi:10.1080/14660970.2014.882823

Wallace, J.L., & Norton, K.I. (2014). Evolution of World Cup soccer final games 1966–2010: Game structure, speed and play patterns. *Journal of Science and Medicine in Sport, 17,* 223–228. doi:10.1016/j.jsams.2013.03.016

Weimar, D., & Wicker, P. (in press). Moneyball revisited: Effort and team performance in professional soccer. *Journal of Sports Economics.*

Wicker, P., Prinz, J., Weimar, D., Deutscher, C., & Upmann, T. (2013). No pain, no gain? Effort and productivity in professional soccer. *International Journal of Sport Finance, 8*(2), 124–139.

Journal of Sport Management, 2017, 31, 44-60
https://doi.org/10.1123/jsm.2015-0314
© 2017 Human Kinetics, Inc.

Human Kinetics
ARTICLE

To Extend or Not Extend a Human Brand: An Analysis of Perceived Fit and Attitudes Toward Athlete Brand Extensions

Patrick Walsh

Syracuse University

Antonio Williams

Indiana University

While athletes have been building and leveraging their brands for many years by introducing brand extensions, research on sport brand extensions has primarily focused on factors that influence the success of team-related extensions. However, as there is potential risk involved when introducing brand extensions, it is important for athletes to understand how consumers respond to extensions they may introduce. Through the use of self-administered web-based surveys this study provides the initial examination of this topic by exposing participants (n = 292) to hypothetical brand extensions and investigating factors that may influence perceived fit and attitudes toward athlete brand extensions. Partial least squares path modeling suggests that athlete prestige had the most significant effect on fit and attitudes for a brand extension that is considered to be a fit with an athlete's image, while athlete attachment had the most influence on fit and attitudes for a brand extension with low perceived fit.

Keywords: celebrity brand, brand equity, branding, brand management, brand evaluation

When an organization uses their preexisting brand name to introduce a new product, this is typically referred to as a brand extension (Aaker, 1991). This is a common practice in sport, and recent research has attempted to understand how consumers react to team-related extensions and what factors might impact the success of a team's brand extension (e.g., Walsh & Lee, 2012; Walsh & Ross, 2010). While there has been a recent focus on the study of brand extensions in sport, this research has primarily focused on sport teams. However, athletes are also capitalizing on their own personal brand via brand extensions. For example, former National Football League (NFL) star John Elway has used his brand name to introduce four steakhouses called Elway's, tennis pro Venus Williams has extended her brand into clothing with a line of sportswear called EleVen by Venus Williams, and golfer John Daly has his own alcoholic beverage brand called The Original John Daly Cocktail.

When successful, brand extensions such as these can be financially lucrative for athletes and provide long term-term brand viability (Kowalczyk & Royne, 2013). This success often occurs when the consumer is familiar with the parent brand (i.e., the brand that introduces the extension) and due to the belief that the "consumers trust that a new brand extension will fulfill the brand's promise and they expect a brand extension to be consistent with the parent brand's core associations" (Loken, Joiner, & Houston, 2010, p. 13). This consistency between the parent brand and the brand extension is commonly referred to as perceived fit. Perceived fit is important to consider as research would indicate that when the image of the brand extension is consistent with the image of the parent brand, the positive associations and attitudes a consumer has for the parent brand will be passed on to the new brand extension (e.g., Bhat & Reddy, 2001; Loken et al., 2010; Park, Milberg, & Lawson, 1991). This fit can be established in a variety of ways, most prominently being a fit between the product category of the parent brand and the brand extension product category and a fit between the image of the parent brand and the image of the new brand extension.

All of these factors provide well-known athletes with the opportunity to extend their brand into targeted new business ventures that capitalize on the athlete's brand.

Patrick Walsh is with the David B. Falk College of Sport and Human Dynamics, Syracuse University, Syracuse, NY. Antonio Williams is with the School of Public Health, Indiana University, Bloomington, IN. Address author correspondence to Patrick Walsh at ptwalsh@syr.edu.

However, there is also risk involved when introducing brand extensions (Walsh & Ross, 2010). For instance, if a brand extension were to fail, or if the brand extension is perceived to not match the image of the parent brand, research has suggested that the image of the parent brand could be negatively altered (John, Loken, & Joiner, 1998; Loken & John, 1993; Walsh & Lee, 2012). This dilution of the parent brand image will generally occur as the negative image that the consumer holds for the brand extension may now be passed on to the parent brand (John, et al., 1998; Loken, Barsalou, & Joiner, 2007; Loken & John, 1993; Walsh & Lee, 2012). For example, if an athlete were to open up a restaurant that bears his or her name, and the restaurant either is not a strong fit with the image of the athlete or were to cease operating because of lack of interest, poor food, and so forth, this could reflect negatively on the athlete and potentially change the preexisting attitudes that consumers have for that particular athlete. While this dilution may not occur for all consumers or fans of the athlete, any potential for dilution of the parent brand over time is important to understand as this may impact a brand's ability to influence marketplace outcomes in sport such as media exposure, loyalty, and the ability to generate sponsorship revenue and introduce additional brand extensions (Ross, 2006; Williams, Walsh, & Rhenwrick, 2015).

In addition, it is time-consuming and costly to introduce and market new brand extensions. Using the same example of an athlete brand extension of a restaurant, some of the costs incurred would include construction costs and/or rental of an existing facility, purchasing the equipment necessary to operate the restaurant, staffing costs, inventory, marketing the restaurant, and so on. Should the restaurant fail, these are then sunken costs that the athlete could not recover. Taking all of these risks into consideration, it is important to understand the types of potential extension products and/or services that best fit an athlete's brand image and how consumers respond to athlete brand extensions. This study will be the first to address this topic and will specifically examine the perceived fit between athletes and potential brand extension product categories and the attitudes consumers have toward athlete brand extensions.

Athletes as Brands

The appeal of sports has allowed its most prominent figures, the athletes, to become recognizable personalities outside of sports, and for many the combination of their athletic performances and public personas has led to brand status. As such, a human brand may be considered to be an individual, such as an athlete, who is used in marketing and communication efforts (Thomson, 2006). Similarly, a celebrity brand is a human brand possessing a unique set of associations and features that are professionally managed (Thomson, 2006), or alternatively is a "well-known or famous person who professionally labels and manages him or herself to consumers and other stakeholders for the purpose of commercially

leveraging this unique image" (Kowalczyk & Royne, 2013, p. 212).

Given that professional athletes are increasingly used as brand ambassadors, endorsers, and spokespersons for numerous products for an array of sport and nonsport entities (Baker & Boyd, 1997; Jones & Schumann, 2000; Stone, Joseph, & Jones, 2003), it is reasonable to consider athletes as brands in and of themselves. Recent research by Arai, Ko, and Ross (2014) described the athlete brand as any athlete who has established value in the marketplace through the use of his or her name, likeness, or other brand elements. By considering athletes as brands, the athlete and his or her stakeholders (e.g., sponsors, team, leagues) have the ability to shape consumer perceptions of the brand to build a connection between consumers and the athlete (Kristiansen & Williams, 2015). Companies spend millions of dollars each year creating, building, and managing the connection between their consumers and athletes (Thomson, 2006). The connection is based on the premise that the associations consumers hold for the athlete may transfer onto the organization and/or its products and services via marketing communication tactics and use of the marketing mix (Williams et al., 2015).

Moreover, Carlson and Donavan (2013) described the cognitive connection between consumers and athletes as a form of athlete identification (athlete ID). Their findings suggest that athlete ID has a pivotal role in fostering the emotional attachment consumers feel toward athletes. This emotional attachment that an individual has with an athlete was labeled as athlete attachment. More importantly, they suggest that the presence of this emotional attachment, or lack thereof, may predict consumers' consumption behaviors, emotional attachment toward the team/league, viewership, and retail spending (Carlson & Donavan, 2013). They also suggest athlete prestige and athlete distinctiveness are both key predictors of identification. That is, consumers are more likely to identify with athletes who have a strong reputation with the public, are well respected, and are a status symbol (i.e., athlete prestige), and who are also unique when compared with other athletes in and outside of their sport (i.e., athlete distinctiveness).

In line with recent athlete marketing literature (e.g., Arai et al., 2014; Carlson & Donavan, 2013; Kristiansen & Williams, 2015; Williams et al., 2015) we consider the athlete as a human brand. Based on this approach, we posit that athlete brands possess equity in the minds' of consumers that adds or subtracts from their perceived value in the marketplace (Keller, 1993; Williams et al., 2015). In the context of this, therefore, the athlete is considered a parent brand, and any product or service introduced in the marketplace bearing the athlete's name, likeness, or persona is deemed a brand extension.

While there are no known studies that have specifically examined athlete brand extensions, Kowalczyk and Royne (2013) introduced the concept of celebrity brand extensions and made an important contribution to distinguishing the difference between a celebrity brand extension and a celebrity endorsement. They posit that a celebrity brand, and as such a celebrity brand extension, is different from a celebrity endorser in that the endorser is paid to use their recognition to promote a particular product, whereas a celebrity brand maintains control of the product it specifically introduces and markets as a brand extension.

In addition to operationalizing this difference, Kowalczyk and Royne (2013) also examined how perceived fit and an individual's level of celebrity worship impacted attitudes toward celebrity brand extensions. Their results suggest that perceived fit between the celebrity brand and celebrity brand extensions has a positive effect on attitudes toward the extension. In addition, they found that celebrity worship weakens the relationship that fit has on the attitudes toward celebrity brand extensions. In other words, those who felt more attached to the celebrity had less positive attitudes toward the brand extension, perhaps contributing to a feeling of the celebrity's "selling out" or becoming too commercial (Kowalczyk & Royne, 2013).

Theoretical Background

When an organization introduces a new product to the market, consumers are faced with the task of forming summary judgments about this new product. One theory that explains how consumers process and make judgments about new products and brand extensions is categorization theory. Categorization theory has its base in psychology and indicates that human beings take like objects they are exposed to and place them into categories in an effort to understand and process new information (Rosch, 1975). Thus, individuals do not need to formulate new information when they are exposed to a new stimulus; rather, previously stored categories of information are used to make summary judgments (Sujan & Tybout, 1988). This basic premise of categorization theory has been applied to consumer behavior and is based on the assumption that consumers classify like products or services, known as a consumer category, to be related in some way, and they develop mental representations of these categories, known as categorical representations, which are then used to make judgments about the new product (Loken, Barsalou, & Joiner, 2007). In other words, consumers are using their preexisting beliefs about the parent brand and its product category to form opinions and attitudes toward a potential new product or service (Loken, 2006). This process is referred to as categorization, and the judgments made about the new products are known as category inferences (Cohen & Basu, 1987; Loken et al., 2007). For example, if an athlete were to introduce a new brand extension, the consumers will rely on the beliefs they have formed about this particular athlete (i.e., the parent brand category) to make summary judgments about the athlete's brand extension. As consumers are exposed to a number of products and marketing messages on a daily basis, this categorization process aids in the processing of the new product information they are exposed to.

One model that may help explain this categorization process as it relates to athlete brand extensions is the celebrity meaning transfer model proposed by McCracken (1989). While this model used athlete endorsements, which as previous explained are different in form than athlete brand extensions, there are some basic principles of the model that could be applied to athlete brand extensions. This meaning transfer model suggests that athletes are comprised of different cultural "meanings," which are descriptors or properties that are representative of the athlete (McCracken, 1989). These meanings are established based on the roles the athlete may play (e.g., their performance, their behavior on and off the field) and how these roles then shape the athlete's image. When an athlete introduces a brand extension, this model would suggest that these meanings would then pass on to the brand extension through various marketing activities that may attempt to connect the athlete's attributes with the new extension. Ultimately, according to this model, the success of an athlete brand extension will rely on the meanings that the athlete brings to the product (McCracken, 1989). In other words, the extension will be a success when it takes on the specific qualities of the athlete, which would need to be highlighted in the marketing materials that promote the extension. As such, the meaning transfer acts as a form of categorization in that the athlete's meaning represents the product category and those meanings may transfer to the brand extension.

An important element of this categorization process is that the category representations made by the consumer must be stable and flexible at the same time (Loken, 2006; Loken et al., 2007). In other words, to engage in the categorization process, consumers must have stable, and readily accessible in memory, preexisting representations of the product category to be able to make some summary judgments when they are faced with a new product. In addition, these representations must be flexible enough to allow the consumer to respond to unexpected occurrences in the marketplace. As this relates to brand extensions, category inferences in which the attributes of the parent brand are passed along to the brand extension are more likely to be made when there is a similarity between the parent brand category and the category of the new brand extension (Loken et al., 2007). In this instance consumers will make judgments about the relationship between the brand extension and the parent brand by accessing their stable category representations and utilizing their preexisting attitudes and opinions of the parent brand. However, if the brand extension is viewed as not belonging to the parent brand's category, the potential for category inferences from the parent brand to the brand extension is lessened (Loken at al., 2007), and consumers may choose either to be flexible in their representation in determining whether the new brand extension belongs to the parent brand product category or not to be flexible in this regard. Similarly, McCracken (1989) would suggest that it would ultimately be the consumer who will decide if the athlete's meaning is transferred to the brand extension and if the categories are similar.

This concept of category similarity is commonly referred to in the brand extension literature as the perceived fit between the parent brand and the brand extension. Specifically, there is a long line of research suggesting that brand extensions for consumer-based products are more likely to be received favorably by consumers if the new extension shares some similar functions or features to the parent brand, if the product categories are similar, or if the brand extension is positioned in a similar fashion to the parent brand (e.g., Bhat & Reddy, 2001; Bottomley & Doyle, 1996; Bottomley & Holden, 2001; Park, Milberg, & Lawson, 1991). This process would take place during the encoding phase of categorization (i.e., when an individual is exposed to the extension). Specifically, if the extension is perceived to be similar to the parent brand's product category, it will "be assimilated to the category and take on its features and effect" (Loken, 2006, p. 456). While there is not one set measure of fit, scales have measured the similarity, consistency, typicality, and representativeness between the image of the parent brand and brand extension (Loken & John, 1993); if the product is a good, logical, and appropriate fit with the parent brand (Keller & Aaker, 1992); if the parent brand and brand extension are similar, go together well, or if the new product is a natural extension of the parent brand (Fedorikhin, Park, & Thomson, 2008); or have simply asked what product(s) are the best examples of the parent brand image (John et al., 1998). In sport-related literature, fit has been examined using similar one-item comparisons asking participants to respond to how similar they believe the image of a team and image of the brand extension product category is (Walsh & Ross, 2010), as well as examining fit using scales that measured functional, reputational, and affective image (Walsh, Chien, & Ross, 2012). The way a product is marketed could also to be used to establish fit. Specifically, Spiggle, Nguyen, and Caravella's (2012) concept of brand extension authenticity would suggest that if a brand extension is marketed in a similar fashion to the parent brand, this will have a positive effect on purchase intentions, attitudes toward the extension, and consumer willingness to recommend an extension. For sport-related brands and brand extensions, perceived fit has also been found to significantly influence evaluation of brand extensions introduced by professional sport teams (Papadimitriou, Apostolopoulou, & Loukas, 2004).

In addition to perceived fit between the parent brand and brand extension, consumers will use their preexisting attitudes toward the parent brand to make category inferences when evaluating brand extensions (Aaker & Keller, 1990; Broniarczyk & Alba, 1994; Loken, 2006). One aspect of attitudes that has been found to have a significant influence on brand extension evaluation both in and outside of sport is how attached a consumer feels to the parent brand. At the categorization stage consumers who are attached to the parent brand are more likely to pass their opinions of the parent brand on to the brand extension (Fedorikhin et al., 2008). This occurs as emotionally attached consumers are more likely to have built a strong and stable brand image of the parent brand, which is then easily accessible during categorization. This accessibility increases the likelihood of using the parent brand to make judgments regarding the brand extension and leads to higher levels of support and purchase intent for the brand extension (Fedorikhin et al., 2008). Similar to emotional attachment, team identification has been determined to be a significant influencer of evaluations of sport-related extensions, with previous research capturing both the cognitive and emotional aspects of identification (Apostolopoulou, 2002; Walsh & Lee, 2012; Walsh & Ross, 2010).

Hypothesis and Research Questions

As evidenced by the literature presented, there is a strong body of literature that has examined how consumers evaluate brand extensions of consumer-based goods and services outside of sport, and there is a growing line of literature examining brand extensions within sport. However, there is very limited literature that has explored brand extensions introduced by human brands (Kowalczyk & Royne, 2013), and there are no known studies to date that have examined brand extensions from the perspective of the professional athletes who utilizes their brand to introduce brand extensions.

While the celebrity brand extension study conducted by Kowalczyk and Royne (2013) may provide some potential insight into how individuals could respond to athlete brand extensions, previous brand extension literature in sport has uncovered that consumers often react differently to sport-related extensions when compared with extensions developed in other non-sport-related product categories (Walsh & Ross, 2010; Walsh et al., 2012). Therefore, while Kowalczyk and Royne (2013) examined the constructs of fit and attitudes as they relate to celebrity brand extensions, it is important to understand whether consumer views of fit and attitudes toward athlete brand extensions differ from those of other celebrity types, and of that of general consumer-based goods and/or services.

This is particularly important to understand as brand extension literature would suggest that any failed brand extension could negatively alter the image of the parent brand (e.g., Loken & John, 1993; Walsh & Lee, 2012), in this case a professional athlete's image. Therefore, it is important for athletes to first understand what types of products or services may be best to introduce as brand extension. Categorization theory would suggest that product categories that relate to sport would have the highest degrees of fit with the image of a professional athlete. Previous brand extension research in sport has also claimed that perceived fit for a brand extension introduced by a sport brand will be higher for brand extensions that relate to sport (Papadimitriou et al., 2004). This would occur as the consumer is using previous knowledge of the category (i.e., athletes) to make inferences regarding the connection between the parent brand and the new product or service (Loken 2006; Loken et al., 2007).

Based on this previous literature, the following hypothesis was developed:

H1: Products/services that relate to sport will be considered to have higher levels of perceived fit than products/services that do not relate to sport.

In addition, it is important to examine what factors may influence both perceived fit and the attitudes consumers have for athlete brand extensions. Previous literature has determined that parent brand image and emotional attachment to the parent brand are two factors that could influence consumer response toward brand extensions (e.g., Apostolopoulou, 2002; Fedorikhin et al., 2008; Walsh & Ross, 2010; Walsh & Lee, 2012). In the setting of our particular study, athlete brand image will be represented by the athlete's level of prestige and distinctiveness (Carlson & Donavan, 2013), while athlete attachment can be used as a measure to understand the level of emotional attachment an individual has with a particular athlete (Carlson & Donavan, 2013). Prestige and distinctiveness were chosen to represent athlete brand image in this study as they have been used in previous literature as a measure for athlete brands (Carlson & Donavan, 2013). In addition, prestige and distinctiveness are factors that may influence brand extension evaluation. For instance, from a brand extension perspective, brands high in levels of prestige are more likely to be extendable into a variety of product categories with varying degrees of fit (Park et al., 1991). Distinctiveness is also representative of some elements that have been examined in past brand extension research, most notably brand extension authenticity. A major component of a brand extension being seen as an authentic extension of the parent brand is its ability to capture the uniqueness of the parent brand's identity (Spiggle et al., 2012). Athlete distinctiveness measures how unique an athlete is compared with others in his or her sport, and as such relates directly to the athlete's brand identity as discussed by Spiggle et al. (2012). In addition, as previously mentioned, during the categorization process consumers who are attached to the parent brand are more likely to transfer affect from the parent brand to the new brand extension (Fedorikhin et al., 2008). As such, athlete attachment was chosen as a unit of measurement for this particular study.

Having been examined in the context of both athlete brands and brand extensions, athlete prestige, distinctiveness, and attachment were deemed appropriate measures to use in this study. While the studies mentioned above do provide some background information to form the base of this particular study, it is important to note that the majority of previous brand extension research took place outside of sport with general consumer-based goods, not sport or human brands. The unique nature of human brands necessitates that initial research be conducted to determine whether theories and principles from outside of sport, and that were applied with nonsport, nonhuman consumer goods in mind, are applicable in this setting. In addition, previous research on brand extensions in sport has found that some of the principles and models that have been used in brand extension literature of nonsport-related brand extensions are not applicable when applying them to brand extensions of sport teams (Walsh & Ross, 2010; Walsh et al., 2012). Given that there have been some contradictions when applying traditional brand extension models and theories to sport brand extensions, and that this is the first attempt to examine athlete brand extensions, research questions were deemed to be appropriate in this exploratory setting. As such, the following research questions were developed:

RQ1: Do athlete prestige, distinctiveness, and attachment influence perceived fit of brand extensions introduced by athletes?

RQ2: Do athlete prestige, distinctiveness, and attachment influence attitudes toward brand extensions introduced by athletes?

Methodology

To address the hypothesis and research questions, two self-administered web-based surveys were conducted. The purpose of the first pretest survey was twofold. First, the pretest was designed to measure the perceived fit between a variety of different products/services and an athlete's image, which would then be used to develop hypothetical brand extensions for the main test. The second purpose of the pretest survey was to measure the perceived levels of athlete prestige and distinctiveness for a variety of professional athletes. This was done in order to choose an athlete with a strong image to be used as a point of analysis in the main test. Each of these items were then used in the development of the survey for the main test, which exposed participants to hypothetical brand extensions with varying degrees of perceived fit for the participants' favorite athlete and one athlete chosen based on the pretest results. Partial least squares (PLS) path modeling was conducted to determine the influence athlete prestige, athlete distinctiveness, and athlete attachment had on the perceived fit and attitudes toward each of the extensions. What follows is an in-depth overview of the pretest methods and results, followed by a discussion of the methods and results for the main test.

Pretest Methods

The pretest survey ($N = 43$) was conducted utilizing two samples. The first was a convenience sample of students at a large midwestern university in the United States. In addition to the convenience sample, a link to the pretest survey was posted on the researchers' Facebook and Twitter accounts to obtain a broader sample than would be afforded by only using the student convenience sample, thus resulting in collecting a similar sample size to pretests from previous brand extension literature (e.g., Keller & Aaker, 1992; Punyatoya, 2013; Sood & Keller, 2012; Yeo & Park, 2006; Zhang & Sood, 2002).

In an effort to understand what types of products may be a good fit for an athlete brand extension, and address H1, the pretest respondents were asked to measure the perceived fit between 35 different product types and an athlete's image. Specifically, similar to brand extension research conducted by Walsh and Ross (2010), respondents were asked to respond to a 7-point Likert scale measuring how dissimilar or similar they felt the 35 products are with the image of their favorite athlete. The products were chosen to represent a wide variety of products athletes have associated themselves with and included items such as restaurants, clothing, personal fragrances, car dealerships, beverages, and food items to name a few.

Pretest participants then measured their perceived image of 10 professional athletes who appeared on SportsPro Media's list of the world's most marketed athletes in 2014 (Cushnan, 2014)—Tom Brady, Peyton Manning, Roger Federer, Serena Williams, Maria Sharapova, LeBron James, Kobe Bryant, Rory McIlroy, Tiger Woods, and Danica Patrick. Specifically, as brand extension success may rely on the preexisting attitudes and the image one holds for the parent brand, each of the 10 athletes' level of prestige and distinctiveness (Carlson & Donavan, 2013) was measured. As previously mentioned, athlete prestige and distinctiveness are being used as they have been shown to be a good measure of athlete brand image and are factors that could influence

brand extension evaluation (Carlson & Donavan, 2013; Park et al., 1991; Spiggle et al., 2012). To measure athlete prestige, participants were asked on a 7-point scale the extent to which they *strongly disagree* (1) or *strongly agree* (7) with the following three statements: <insert athlete> has a good reputation with the general public, <insert athlete> is a status symbol, and <insert athlete> is highly respected. Using the same 7-point scale anchored by *strongly disagree* (1) and *strongly agree* (7) to measure athlete distinctiveness, participants responded to the following: <insert athlete> is very unique when compared with other players in his/her sport, <insert athlete> is unlike any other athlete in his/her sport, and <insert athlete> is a rare athlete. A full listing of all the main items used in the pretest and main test can be found in Table 1.

Pretest Results

The average age of the pretest respondents ($N = 43$) was 32.66 years old, and the majority of the respondents were male (77%) and were White/Caucasian (64%). In addition, the sample was highly educated as 26% ($n = 10$) had earned a bachelor's degree and 49% ($n = 19$) had earned a master's degree.

As previously mentioned, the purpose of the pretest was to gather information that would be used to develop the survey for the main test. The first piece of information the pretest examined was the perceived image fit between

Table 1   Scale Items

Athlete Prestige (Carlson & Donavan, 2013)
<insert athlete> has a good reputation with the general public
<insert athlete> is highly respected
<insert athlete> is a status symbol
Athlete Distinctiveness (Carlson & Donavan, 2013)
<insert athlete> is very unique when compared with other players in his/her sport
<insert athlete> is unlike any other athlete in his/her sport
<insert athlete> is a rare athlete
Athlete Attachment (Carlson & Donavan, 2013)
I would experience an emotional loss if I had to stop being a <insert athlete> fan
When someone criticizes <insert athlete> it feels like a personal insult
If a story in the media criticized <insert athlete> it would affect me negatively
Perceived Fit (Keller & Aaker, 1992)
The product is a good fit with <insert athlete>
The product is a logical fit with <insert athlete>
The product is appropriate to be related to <insert athlete>
Attitudes Toward the Extension (Batra & Homer, 2004)
This product is good
I have a favorable attitude toward this product
I have positive feelings toward this product

Note. All items were measured on a 7-point scale anchored by *strongly disagree* (1) and *strongly agree* (7).

athletes and a number of potential products or services they may associate themselves with. The results of the pretest addressed H1 and allowed for the understanding as to which products or services would be considered appropriate choices for both the high-perceived-fit and low-perceived-fit brand extension (see Table 2). Supporting H1, the four items with the highest perceived image fit were athletic clothing/sportswear ($M = 6.09$), athletic shoes ($M = 6.04$), the sports camp/academy ($M = 6.04$), and sports training facility ($M = 5.93$). Conversely, the four that had the lowest perceived image fit were cosmetics ($M = 1.79$), salsa ($M = 1.86$), car wash ($M = 2.02$), and salad dressing ($M = 2.07$).

Based on these results, the high-perceived-fit brand extension that was chosen to use in the main test was athletic clothing/sportswear, while the low-perceived-fit brand extension chosen was salad dressing. While there were three products that had lower mean scores than salad dressing, cosmetics was not chosen as the athlete chosen in the main test was a male athlete and we felt it was best to present the most realistic option possible as male athletes typically do not have cosmetic brand extensions. In addition, as the athlete chosen was a football player, we decided against using salsa as the low-perceived-fit brand extension as salsa is commonly advertised during football television broadcasts and found during football tailgates, parties, and so forth. Therefore, salsa could be seen as being a better fit for football players than some athletes in other sports. In a similar vein, car wash was not

chosen as the athlete chosen for analysis in the main test (Peyton Manning) is commonly associated with a prominent car brand (i.e., Buick) and we wanted to eliminate any potential for associations with cars in this instance that could influence perceived fit. As such, salad dressing was chosen to best represent a realistic low-perceived-fit brand extension in this particular study setting.

The second purpose of the pretest was to choose an athlete for examination in the main test who had high mean scores on both athlete prestige and distinctiveness. The top three athletes from a prestige perspective were Peyton Manning ($M = 6.14$), Roger Federer ($M = 5.96$), and Rory McIlroy ($M = 5.52$), while the top rated athletes for distinctiveness were Serena Williams ($M = 5.97$), Tiger Woods ($M = 5.82$), and LeBron James ($M = 5.80$). The mean of the prestige and distinctiveness scores was then computed for each athlete, and taking both of these factors into consideration, Peyton Manning was chosen as the athlete who would be used in the main test. As noted in Table 3, Manning was rated the highest on athlete prestige and was the second highest rated athlete if you take the average of both prestige and distinctiveness into consideration. While Roger Federer was rated slightly above Peyton Manning if you combine both prestige and distinctiveness, Manning was chosen as this study used a sample based in the United States where American football is the most popular spectator sport. As such, due to his prevalence throughout the media and his association with the most popular spectator sport

Table 2   Image Fit of Products and Services From Pretest

Product/service		Product/service	
Athletic Clothing/Sportswear	6.09	Nonalcoholic beverage (iced tea, lemonade, etc.)	3.53
Athletic Shoes	6.05	Car Dealership	3.53
Sports Camp or Academy	6.05	Cologne or Perfume	3.37
Sports Training Facility	5.93	Beer	3.37
Sporting Goods Store	5.58	Wine	3.35
Sport Energy Drink	5.49	Financial/Business Planning	3.23
Health Club or Fitness Center	5.39	Jewelry	3.11
Sport Energy Bar	4.76	Soda	3.09
Sports Bar and Grill	4.65	Grocery Store	2.81
Luxury Car Dealership	4.64	Fast-Food Restaurant	2.44
Bottled/Flavored Water	4.56	Pasta Sauce	2.28
Casual Dining Restaurant	4.21	Furniture Store	2.21
Business Attire (suits, ties, etc.)	4.16	Candy	2.21
Upscale Restaurant	4.00	Salad Dressing	2.07
Night Club	3.74	Car Wash	2.02
Dress Shoes	3.74	Salsa	1.86
Designer Clothing	3.63	Cosmetics	1.79
Cereal	3.63		

Note. The table presents the mean results, on a scale of 1 (*dissimilar*) to 7 (*similar*), of the single-item question "Please rate how similar or dissimilar the following products/services are with the image of your favorite athlete."

Table 3   Athlete Prestige and Distinctiveness of Top Marketed Athletes From Pretest

Athlete	Prestige	Distinctiveness	Average of both
Roger Federer	5.96	5.61	5.79
Peyton Manning	6.14	5.32	5.73
Serena Williams	5.45	5.97	5.71
LeBron James	5.13	5.80	5.47
Rory McIlroy	5.52	5.00	5.26
Kobe Bryant	4.96	5.53	5.25
Maria Sharapova	5.34	4.88	5.11
Tiger Woods	3.94	5.82	4.88
Danica Patrick	4.29	5.18	4.74
Tom Brady	4.43	4.56	4.50

Note. The values of prestige and distinctiveness represent the mean values of the three-item athlete prestige and distinctiveness scales from Table 1.

in the United States, more participants in the main study may be more familiar with Peyton Manning as opposed to some of the other athletes.

Main Test Methods

The second self-administered web-based survey was conducted with a national sample of sport fans in the United States ($N = 292$) obtained through the Qualtrics Panel Management service. Qualtrics Panel Management provides access to a national database of individuals who are contacted to participate in survey research. Before participating in the survey the potential respondents were provided with screener questions to qualify to take the survey. In addition to being a resident of the United States who was 18 years of age or older, the participants were required to have some level of interest in sports to participate in the study. To measure this interest, the first question in the survey asked potential participants how they would rate their level of interest in sports on a 7-point scale, with 1 being *not interested at all* and 7 being *very interested*. Those who scored three or higher on the scale were permitted to continue with the survey as it was deemed that they had at least somewhat of an interest in sports. Of note, the sample as a whole had a high level of interest in sport ($M = 6.02$).

Following the screener questions, respondents were first asked to list their favorite athlete. As suggested by Kowalczyk and Royne (2013), having participants think about their favorite athlete will capture the personal emotions or the connection one has with the parent brand (i.e., an athlete) when examining brand extensions. While there may be some limitations to this approach, as each athlete will have a unique personality that could influence participants' perceptions of the brand extension, this method was deemed to be the best for this particular study. As mentioned, it has been used in previous research when examining celebrity brand extensions to capture

the personal emotions one has with the parent brand (Kowalczyk & Royne, 2013), and a similar method was also used, for instance, to develop a widely used scale to measure team brand associations (Ross, James, & Vargas, 2006). In addition, from a categorization theory perspective, Loken et al. (2007) would suggest that this approach was important to use in an effort to increase the ability for the participants to access information about the category (i.e., professional athletes) and the ability to retrieve information from memory about the category member (i.e., their favorite athlete). Following the listing of their favorite athlete, and similar to the methods of Walsh and Ross (2010) and Kowalczyk and Royne (2013), the participants were then exposed to two hypothetical scenarios indicating that their favorite athlete was introducing a brand extension (one that was the chosen high-perceived-fit extension of sportswear and one that was the chosen low-perceived-fit extension of salad dressing). For instance, for the low-fit salad dressing extension the scenario read,

> Suppose your favorite athlete is introducing a new brand of salad dressing which will be named after the athlete. For example, if your favorite athlete's name is John Smith, the name of the product would be John Smith's Salad Dressing. Keeping this new salad dressing in mind for your favorite professional athlete please answer the following questions below.

Following exposure to the extensions, participants were asked to keep the extensions in mind as they measured the perceived fit of the extensions, attitudes toward the extensions, athlete prestige and distinctiveness, and athlete attachment. While there are various measures of perceived fit and attitudes toward brand extensions, this study adopted the measures used in Kowalczyk and Royne's (2013) study on celebrity brand extensions. Not only did their study use common measurements found in brand extension literature but they were adopted for use with human brands. As such, they were determined to be most appropriate to apply to this study, which is providing a first examination of athlete brand extensions. Specifically, perceived fit was measured by responding to the following: the product is a good fit with <insert athlete>, the product is a logical fit with <insert athlete>, and the product is appropriate to be related with <insert athlete> (Keller & Aaker, 1992). Attitudes toward the extensions were measured with the following statements: this product is good, I have a favorable attitude toward this product, and I have positive feelings toward this product (Batra & Homer, 2004). The items to measure athlete attachment included the following: I would experience an emotional loss if I had to stop being a <insert athlete> fan, when someone criticizes <insert athlete> it feels like a personal insult, and if a story in the media criticized <insert athlete> it would affect me negatively (Carlson & Donavan, 2013). Finally, the items for athlete prestige and distinctiveness were the same as used in the pretest. Each of these items was measured individually for the high-perceived-fit brand extension of sportswear and the low-perceived-fit brand extension of salad dressing and was measured using a 7-point scale anchored by *strongly disagree* (1) and *strongly agree* (7).

Similar to the procedure that was conducted for the participants' favorite athlete, the participants were then exposed to two hypothetical scenarios indicating that one of the Top 10 most marketed athletes who scored high on levels of prestige and distinctiveness in the pretest (i.e., Peyton Manning) would be introducing a sportswear and salad dressing extension. After exposure to both of the Manning extension scenarios, perceived fit of the extensions, attitudes toward the extensions, athlete prestige and distinctiveness, and athlete attachment were once again measured. Following data collection, PLS path modeling was conducted utilizing the statistical package R to address RQ1 and RQ2. PLS was used to test the influence athlete prestige, distinctiveness, and attachment has on both perceived fit of the extensions and consumer attitudes toward the favorite athlete and Peyton Manning brand extensions. In addition, PLS is an effective tool to examine casual relationships when there may not be enough a priori theoretical evidence to support predictive claims (Chin, 1998). That is, PLS allows a researcher to let the data, as opposed to preexisting theory, decide the relationship; it is appropriate to use when there is not enough confidence in existing theory to make predictions or assumptions about the data (Chin, 1998; Vivek & Sudharani-Ravindran, 2008).

Main Test Results

Initially, 443 individuals were recruited to participate in the survey. After data screening, the final sample consisted of 292 completed surveys for an effective response rate of 65.91%. The sample consisted of 174 males (59.6%) and 118 females (40.4%) with an average age of 39.09 years old. The majority of the respondents classified themselves as being White/Caucasian ($n = 202$; 69.2%), followed by African American ($n = 30$, 10.3%), Hispanic ($n = 28$, 9.6%), and Asian ($n = 25$; 8.6%). The education of the participants varied as 16.5% ($n = 48$) held a high school diploma, 27.8% ($n = 81$) attended some college, 39.1% ($n = 114$) earned a college degree, and 15.2% held a master's degree or higher ($n = 44$). Finally, household income of the participants was fairly evenly distributed with 22.3% ($n = 65$) making less than $30,000, 21.3% ($n = 62$) between $30,000 and $50,000, 29.5% ($n = 86$) between $50,000 and $80,000, 10.6% ($n = 31$) between $80,000 and $100,000, and 16.2% ($n = 47$) making $100,000 or more.

While the scales used in this study have been proven to be reliable in previous research (e.g., Carlson & Donavan, 2013; Kowalczyk & Royne, 2013), their reliability in this setting was also examined. All of the scales were found to meet the minimum Cronbach alpha levels of .70 suggested by Nunnally and Bernstein (1994) with the levels ranging from .767 for the measurement of favorite athlete prestige to a high of .960 for the measurement of the perceived fit for the salad dressing extension for Peyton Manning. In addition, examinations took place to ensure instances of multicollinearity, heteroscedasticity, and autocorrelation were not present. To detect potential instances of multicollinearity, the variance inflation factors (VIFs) for each predictor were examined. The VIFs of the predictors in this study ranged from a low of 1.483 for the predictor of athlete attachment when examining the Peyton Manning brand extensions to a high of 3.416 when examining athlete distinctiveness for the Peyton Manning brand extensions. As it has been commonly suggested that the largest VIFs should be less than 10 to satisfy the assumption that predictor variables are not highly correlated, it was determined that there were no issues with multicollinearity (Ho, 2006; Myers, 1990). To determine whether heteroscedasticity was present, the scatter plots of the standardized residuals regressed on the predicated value were examined, and no apparent issues were present, thus leading to the assumption of homoscedasticity of variance. To test whether autocorrelation was present, the Durbin–Watson test statistics were examined (Durbin & Watson, 1951), which ranged from 1.774 to 2.078. Utilizing the calculated Durbin–Watson critical values, and the assumption that values close to two represent nonautocorrelation, all of the calculated values fell within the critical values, which led to the determination that there was no autocorrelation between the residuals.

Following the tests of the assumptions and reliability, PLS path modeling was performed in the statistical package R in order to address RQ1 and RQ2 and to determine the relationship the exogenous variables of athlete prestige, distinctiveness, and attachment have on the endogenous variables of perceived fit and attitudes toward the brand extensions. In total, four path modeling analyses were performed. The first two PLS analyses were performed for the participants' favorite athlete brand extensions in which athlete prestige, distinctiveness, and attachment were set as the exogenous variables and perceived fit and attitudes toward the brand extension were set as the endogenous variables for both the sportswear and the salad dressing extension (i.e., perceived fit and attitudes toward the sportswear extension, perceived fit and attitudes toward the salad dressing extension). The same two PLS analyses were then performed for the Peyton Manning brand extensions. To determine the significance of each of the exogenous variables' paths, a bootstrapping procedure with 200 resamples was conducted with a 95% confidence interval used to determine significance at α = .05 (Chin, 1998).

The first PLS analysis analyzed the degree to which perceived fit and attitudes toward the sportswear extension for the participant's favorite athlete would be affected by athlete prestige, distinctiveness, and attachment. The results suggest that athlete prestige, distinctiveness, and

attachment all had a significant effect on perceived fit and attitudes toward the favorite athlete sportswear extension (see Table 4 and Figure 1). Further analysis indicated that 46.4% of the variance in perceived fit was attributed to the three exogenous variables with athlete prestige (β = .332) having the strongest influence on fit, followed by distinctiveness (β = .240) and athlete attachment (β = .226). Regarding attitudes toward the favorite athlete sportswear extension, athlete prestige (β = .378), distinctiveness (β = .229), and attachment (β = .220) were all significant and accounted for 50.3% of the variance in attitudes.

The next PLS analysis explored the relationship between athlete prestige, distinctiveness, and attachment on perceived fit and attitudes toward the favorite athlete's salad dressing extension (see Table 4 and Figure 2). This

Table 4   Partial Least Squares Path Coefficients for the Favorite Athlete Brand Extensions

Variable	Sportswear perceived fit β	Sportswear perceived fit CI	Sportswear attitudes β	Sportswear attitudes CI	Salad dressing perceived fit β	Salad dressing perceived fit CI	Salad dressing attitudes β	Salad dressing attitudes CI
Athlete prestige	.332*	[.197, .484]	.378*	[.249, .517]	.274*	[.120, .412]	.264*	[.111, .408]
Athlete distinctiveness	.240*	[.088, .413]	.229*	[.093, .364]	−.050	[−.192, .107]	.064	[−.081, .107]
Athlete attachment	.226*	[.068, .350]	.220*	[.092, .358]	.369*	[.265, .488]	.302*	[.168, .423]
R^2	.464		.503		.280		.294	

Note. CI = 95% confidence interval; bootstrap technique (n = 200).

*p < .05.

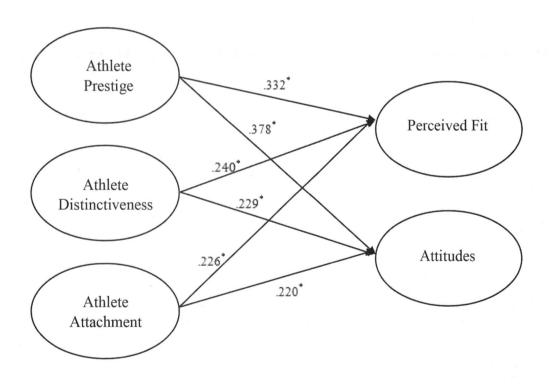

Note. * p < .05

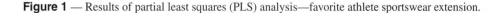

Figure 1 — Results of partial least squares (PLS) analysis—favorite athlete sportswear extension.

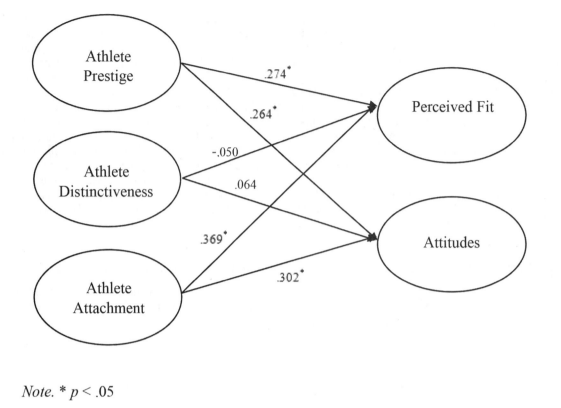

Note. * p < .05

Figure 2 — Results of partial least squares (PLS) analysis—favorite athlete salad dressing extension.

analysis indicated that attachment (β = .369) and prestige (β = .274) had a significant effect on fit, while in contrast to the sportswear extension, distinctiveness did not produce a significant effect. In this instance, attachment and prestige accounted for 28.0% of the variance in perceived fit of the salad dressing extension for the participants' favorite athlete. The influence the variables had on the attitudes toward the favorite athlete's salad dressing extension were similar. Specifically, attachment (β = .302) and prestige (β = .264) had a significant effect on attitudes toward the extension and accounted for 29.4% of the variance.

To see if there are differences in perceived fit and attitudes toward athlete brand extensions of an individual's favorite athlete versus simply a potentially well-known athlete, the same PLS path modeling analyses outlined above were also performed for the Peyton Manning sportswear and the Peyton Manning salad dressing extensions. First, PLS path modeling was conducted to analyze the degree to which perceived fit of the Peyton Manning sportswear extension would be influenced by athlete prestige, distinctiveness, and attachment (see Table 5 and Figure 3). The results determined that only prestige (β = .645) had a significant effect on fit and that prestige accounted for 45.7% of the variance in extension fit. In this case, and different from the fit of the favorite athlete's sportswear extension, distinctiveness and attachment were not significant. When examining attitudes toward the Peyton Manning sportswear extension, prestige,

distinctiveness, and attachment were all significant. The model indicates that 55.5% of the variance in attitudes toward the extension were attributed to prestige (β = .483), attachment (β = .197), and distinctiveness (β = .171).

The final PLS analysis assessed the effect athlete prestige, distinctiveness, and attachment had on perceived fit, and attitudes toward, the Peyton Manning salad dressing extension (see Table 5 and Figure 4). When examining perceived fit of the extension, athlete attachment (β = .530) was found to have a significant effect on fit, which accounted for 40.2% of the variance. Prestige and distinctiveness were not found to be significant in this instance. In comparison with the perceived fit of the favorite athlete's salad dressing extension, prestige was a significant predictor in that instance. Similar to this finding, attachment (β = .389) also had a significant effect on attitudes toward the extension. However, in this instance, distinctiveness (β = .234) was also significant, while prestige was not. The two significant variables in this model accounted for 38.1% of the variance in attitudes toward the Peyton Manning salad dressing extension.

Discussion

Product Category Fit

As this was one of the first attempts to examine athlete brand extensions, the results add considerably to the

Table 5   Partial Least Squares Path Coefficients for the Peyton Manning Brand Extensions

Variable	Sportswear perceived fit		Sportswear attitudes		Salad dressing perceived fit		Salad dressing attitudes	
	β	CI	β	CI	β	CI	β	CI
Athlete prestige	.645*	[.467, .812]	.483*	[.359, .623]	.002	[−.189, .148]	.086	[−.052, .249]
Athlete distinctiveness	.036	[−.148, .212]	.171*	[.018, .322]	.156	[−.009, .358]	.234*	[−.053, .393]
Athlete attachment	.002	[−.090, .101]	.197*	[.109, .274]	.530*	[.421, .650]	.389*	[.269, .492]
R^2	.457		.555		.402		.381	

Note. CI = 95% confidence interval; bootstrap technique ($n = 200$).

*$p < .05$.

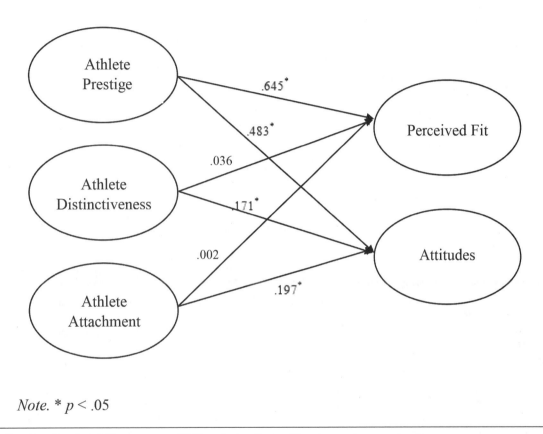

Note. * $p < .05$

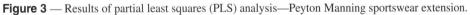

Figure 3 — Results of partial least squares (PLS) analysis—Peyton Manning sportswear extension.

study of athlete brands and brand extensions and provide a number of theoretical and practical implications. First, previous research has indicated that sport-related brand extensions such as sport camps and clothing are generally perceived to be a stronger fit with professional sport team brands when compared with potential brand extensions that do not have a connection to sport (Papadimitriou et al., 2004). The results of our study support Papadimitriou et al.'s (2004) findings while extending them to the setting of professional athletes as the parent brand. For example, it was determined that athletic clothing, shoes, sport camps, sporting goods stores, sports training facilities, and sport energy drinks had the greatest perceived fit with the image of a professional athlete. However, products such as salsa, cosmetics, salad dressing, car wash, and furniture stores all had very low levels of perceived fit. This finding is likely due to the fact that the sport-related products share similar product attributes or associations with professional athletes, whereas there is a disconnect between the image of the products that were not a fit and the image of a parent athlete brand (Aaker & Keller, 1990; Bhat & Reddy, 2001; Broniarczyk & Alba, 1994). These findings would support the tenets of categorization theory as consumers are classifying like products or services (i.e., an athlete and products/services related to sport) as sharing similar attributes, and they are making summary judgments regarding the fit between an athlete and

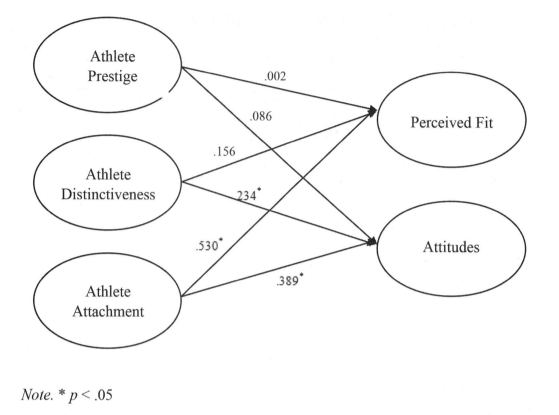

Note. * *p* < .05

Figure 4 — Results of partial least squares (PLS) analysis—Peyton Manning salad dressing extension.

the product categories based on these shared attributes (Loken, 2006; Loken et al., 2007).

As previous research has indicated that perceived fit between the parent brand and the brand extension is an important determinant of brand extension success (e.g., Bhat & Reddy, 2001; Bottomley & Holden, 2001; Loken & John, 1993; Walsh & Lee, 2012), it is therefore recommended from a practical perspective that athletes first consider introducing brand extensions that have some connection to sport. However, if an athlete were to use his or her brand name to introduce a brand extension product or service that does not have a direct connection to sport, it would be in the athlete's best interest to try to market the extension using a sport-related theme. For example, in this study fast-food restaurants had a low level of perceived fit with the image of professional athletes (*M* = 2.44). If an athlete were to determine that he or she was going to open a fast-food restaurant, the athlete could market it as a sports-themed fast-food restaurant with the food or meals named after sports plays (e.g., the Home Run burger), sport imagery in their advertising and in the restaurant, and so forth. Doing so may help in establishing brand extension authenticity (Spiggle et al., 2012) and allow for meaning transfer to take place (McCracken, 1989) and for category inferences to be made (Loken et al., 2007) despite the extension's product category's being viewed as having low levels of perceived fit with an athlete brand.

High-Perceived-Fit Sportswear Extension

In addition to examining what product categories may be a perceived fit for a professional athlete brand, this study also offers a theoretical contribution by providing initial insight on how athlete prestige, distinctiveness, and attachment influence perceived fit and attitudes toward athlete brand extensions. When examining the sportswear extension, athlete prestige was found to be the most influential predictor of both perceived fit of the sportswear extension and of the attitudes the participants held for this particular type of extension. This was true for the sportswear extension for the participant's favorite athlete and was even a more significant individual factor for the Peyton Manning sportswear extension. In other words, if an athlete is highly respected, has a good reputation, or is seen as a status symbol, consumers are more likely to see the fit between that athlete and a sport-related extension, and they are also more likely to have favorable attitudes toward the extension. The athlete's level of prestige is even more important to brand extension success if the athlete who introduces the extension is not considered to be one of the consumer's favorite athletes. This supports previous brand extension research that indicates that the image or the perceived quality of the parent brand will impact consumer evaluation of a brand extension (e.g., Bottomley & Doyle, 1996; Bottomley & Holden, 2001; Walsh & Ross, 2010). In addition, how unique a consumer believes the athlete is when compared with other players in their sport (i.e., distinctiveness) and how attached they are to the athlete also had a significant effect on perceived fit of their favorite athlete's sportswear extension and the attitudes they had toward the Peyton Manning sportswear extension, albeit not as impactful an effect as prestige. These findings support the notion that during the categorization process consumers who have some level of attachment toward the parent brand will be more likely to positively evaluate brand extensions of the parent brand (Fedorikhin et al., 2008; Loken, 2006).

Practically, these results would suggest that an athlete's image, reputation, and status may be the most important factor in establishing fit of, and impacting attitudes toward, an athlete brand extension that has high levels of perceived fit or a connection to sport, while distinctiveness and attachment will also play an important but secondary role in this particular setting. Therefore, athletes who are highly regarded in their particular sport may have a greater chance of success when introducing extensions that are a perceived fit with an athlete's brand image such as sportswear, sport camps, sporting goods stores, and so forth.

Low-Perceived-Fit Salad Dressing Extension

Contrary to the sportswear extension where athlete prestige was found to be the most significant predictor of perceived fit and attitudes toward the extension, athlete attachment was found to be the most significant predictor of these factors for the salad dressing extension. This was also true for both the participant's favorite athlete and for Peyton Manning. Therefore, for brand extensions in which there may not be a direct logical connection between the image of an athlete and the image of the new product or service, the success of the extension may rely on how emotionally attached an individual is to the particular athlete who introduces the product. Similar to the high-fit extensions, this would again support previous research outside of sport that has found that those with a strong emotional connection to the parent brand are more likely to support brand extensions (Fedorikhin et al., 2008) and during the categorization process this attachment is having an impact on the evaluation of the brand extension (Loken, 2006). In addition, within sport-related research, team identification, which includes elements of emotional attachment, has been determined to have a positive impact on evaluations of team-related brand extensions (Apostolopoulou, 2002; Ross, Walsh, & Shreffler, 2014 ; Walsh & Lee, 2012; Walsh & Ross, 2010).

In addition to attachment, prestige was found to have a significant influence on fit and attitudes toward the salad dressing extension for the participant's favorite athlete, while it was not found to be a significant factor for the Peyton Manning salad dressing brand extension. This is not surprising as those who are attached to a particular athlete are also more likely to have positive opinions of the athlete, and it also provides some support for research

indicating that brands with high levels of prestige are more likely to be extendable into product categories with varying levels of fit (Park et al., 1991). Practically, these findings would suggest if athletes are going to introduce brand extensions that have low levels of perceived fit with an athlete brand, then they should offer these extensions in markets where there are high concentrations of fans for that particular athlete. For example, if an athlete had a successful career with a particular team, it may be easier for that athlete to introduce extensions in that team's city or market because of the potential to have a number of fans who have some level of attachment to the athlete and, as such, would be more likely to have positive evaluations of the athlete's brand extensions.

However, the positive impact attachment had on evaluation of the athlete brand extensions does contradict the research on celebrity brand extensions conducted by Kowalczyk and Royne (2013). When examining celebrity brand extensions, they found that attachment to the celebrity, which was measured via celebrity worship, actually had a negative impact on perceived fit and attitudes toward brand extensions introduced by an individual's favorite celebrity (Kowalczyk & Royne, 2013). In the current study, the findings suggest that athlete attachment did not have a negative impact on extension evaluation but rather was a significant positive predictor of fit and attitudes in all but one instance. As has been noted in previous sport brand extension research that has found that consumers respond to team sport–related extensions differently than they do extensions for general consumer-based goods (Walsh & Ross, 2010; Walsh et al., 2012), this finding would suggest that there are also some unique factors that may influence evaluation of athlete brand extensions when compared with how consumers evaluate extensions from other types of celebrities. Specifically, this may suggest that the categorization and meaning transfer process used for athlete brand extensions is more likely to result in positive category inferences' being developed for athlete brand extensions as compared with extensions for other celebrities, particularly when the individuals are emotionally attached to the athlete parent brand.

Limitations and Future Research

This study adds considerably to the literature on brand extensions and athlete brands as it is one of the first to examine the factors that influence perceived fit and attitudes toward athlete brand extensions. While exploratory in nature, the findings of this study add an important element to the sport brand extension literature, therefore allowing sport marketing scholars to conduct future research in this vein that makes casual claims. While PLS path modeling was used in this study, future research may use the foundational information uncovered in this study to make predictions and use structural equation modeling as a data analysis technique to examine causation among variables that may further influence athlete brand extension success and the athlete parent brand. Furthermore, as this study did provide an initial examination of this topic, there are a number of opportunities for future research and some potential limitations to address.

First, this study used the participant's favorite athlete and one athlete who had high levels of prestige and distinctiveness. As such, there may have been strong and positive preexisting attitudes toward both athletes that could have an impact on the participants' evaluations of the athletes and the brand extensions. Future research could potentially examine athletes who may not have as high levels of attachment, prestige, and distinctiveness in an effort to compare the results of the current study with those of research using athletes with varying levels of attachment and perceived image. In addition, while emotional attachment was examined in this study, future studies could focus on examining the impact that cognitive elements of athlete identification (Carlson & Donavan, 2013; Carlson, Donavan, & Cumiskey, 2009) have on consumer evaluation of athlete brand extensions.

Another potential area of study would be to examine the effects that the extensions have on the parent athlete brand. In the main test of this study athlete prestige, distinctiveness, and attachment were measured following the participants' exposure to the hypothetical brand extensions. As previous research has suggested that brand extensions that are not a perceived fit with the parent brand could potentially dilute parent brand image (e.g., Loken & John, 1993, Walsh & Lee, 2012), there is some potential that the measures of athlete prestige, distinctiveness, and attachment may have been impacted by the exposure to the brand extensions. While this effect has not been found in previous sport brand extension research (e.g., Walsh & Ross, 2010; Walsh et al., 2012), it is worth examining in future research if athlete brand extensions may have a negative, or positive, impact on the athlete's brand.

Examining brand extensions from athletes who participate in different sports may also provide a good point of comparison. For instance, it may be possible that athletes who participate in different sports may be more prone to introduce certain types of extension products or services based on the characteristics of the sport they play (e.g., a "rugged" sport such as football vs. a "country-club" sport such as golf). The athletes' own individual personality characteristics and brand image may also impact the perceived fit of different brand extension product categories. This points to future research focusing on examining specific athletes as opposed to allowing the study participants to think about their favorite athlete and examining those results from a holistic perspective. For example, New England Patriots star tight end Rob Gronkowski has a brand extension called the Gronk Party Bus, which is a limo party bus service that is available for rental to the public. An extension such as this is not going to be a good fit for most athletes. However, Gronkowski is well-known for his party lifestyle because of the media's focus on this, evidenced by the Showtime television program *Inside the NFL*'s airing a segment on the Gronk Bus. In fact, the Gronk Party Bus website promotes the bus by saying, "Easily put the Gronk has designed the superlative party bus and wants you to have the time of your life just like he does after winning Super Bowls" ("About the Gronk Bus," n.d.). Future research should focus on examining athletes with differing personalities to understand how athlete brand personality will impact extensions they may introduce.

This study used a nationwide sample of participants. As many athletes may introduce brand extensions in the markets in which they currently play, or played in the past, future research should examine athletes from a particular market or location and survey the fans in that area in an effort to understand how they respond to brand extensions introduced by "local" athletes or athletes who may play for their favorite team. In doing so, it would also be beneficial to examine the fit and attitudes consumers have for actual brand extensions as the current study used hypothetical scenarios. In addition, this study used athletes who were all still active in their particular sport at the time of data collection. As many time athletes will not introduce brand extensions until they retire, future research could examine consumer attitudes and fit of brand extensions of retired athletes to see if consumers respond differently when the extension is introduced by a retired athlete as opposed to an athlete who is still participating in their sport. Finally, while understanding brand extension fit and attitudes is important, examining behavioral intentions such as intent to purchase these athlete brand extensions should be an important next step in this line of research.

References

Aaker, D.A. (1991). *Managing* brand *equity*. New York, NY: Free Press.

Aaker, D.A., & Keller, K.L. (1990). Consumer evaluations of brand extensions. *Journal of Marketing, 54,* 27–41. doi:10.2307/1252171

About the Gronk Bus. (n.d.). Retrieved from http://www.the-gronkbus.com/about/

Apostolopoulou, A. (2002). The effect of brand strength and perceived fit on the success of brand extensions [Abstract]. *17th Annual North American Society for Sport Management Conference Abstracts.* Canmore, Alberta, Canada, 4.

Arai, A., Ko, Y.J., & Ross, S. (2014). Branding athletes: Exploration and conceptualization of athlete brand image. *Sport Management Review, 17,* 97–106. doi:10.1016/j.smr.2013.04.003

Baker, A., & Boyd, T. (1997). *Out of bounds: Sports, media and the politics of identity.* Bloomington: Indiana University Press.

Batra, R., & Homer, P.M. (2004). The situational impact of brand image beliefs. *Journal of Consumer Psychology, 14,* 318–330. doi:10.1207/s15327663jcp1403_12

Bhat, S., & Reddy, S.K. (2001). The impact of parent brand attribute associations and affect on brand extension evaluation. *Journal of Business Research, 53,* 111–122. doi:10.1016/S0148-2963(99)00115-0

Bottomley, P., & Doyle, J. (1996). The formation of attitudes towards brand extensions: Testing and generalizing Aaker and Keller's model. *International Journal of Research in Marketing, 13,* 365–377. doi:10.1016/S0167-8116(96)00018-3

Bottomley, P., & Holden, S. (2001). Do we really know how consumers evaluate brand extensions? Empirical generalizations based on secondary analysis of eight studies. *Journal of Marketing Research, 38,* 494–500. doi:10.1509/jmkr.38.4.494.18901

Broniarczyk, S.M., & Alba, J.W. (1994). The importance of the brand in brand extension. *Journal of Marketing Research, 31,* 214–228. doi:10.2307/3152195

Carlson, B.D., & Donavan, D.T. (2013). Human brands in sport: Athlete brand personality and identification. *Journal of Sport Management, 27,* 193–206. doi:10.1123/jsm.27.3.193

Carlson, B.D., Donavan, D.T., & Cumiskey, K.J. (2009). Consumer-brand relationships in sport: Brand personality and identification. *International Journal of Retail & Distribution Management, 37,* 370–384. doi:10.1108/09590550910948592

Chin, W.W. (1998). The partial least squares approach for structural equation modeling. In G.A. Marcoulides (Ed.), *Modern methods for business research* (pp. 295–336). Mahwah, NJ: Erlbaum.

Cohen, J.B., & Basu, K. (1987). Alternative models of categorization: Toward a contingent processing framework. *The Journal of Consumer Research, 13,* 455–472. doi:10.1086/209081

Cushnan, D. (2014). The world's most marketed athletes. *Sports Pro.* Retrieved from http://www.sportspromedia.com/notes_and_insights/the_worlds_most_marketed_athletes

Durbin, J., & Watson, G.S. (1951). Testing for serial correlation in least squares regression II. *Biometrika, 38,* 159–177. doi:10.1093/biomet/38.1-2.159

Fedorikhin, A., Park, C.W., & Thomson, M. (2008). Beyond fit and attitude: The effect of emotional attachment on consumer responses to brand extensions. *Journal of Consumer Psychology, 18,* 281–291. doi:10.1016/j.jcps.2008.09.006

Ho, R. (2006). *Handbook of univariate and multivariate data analysis and interpretation with SPSS.* Boca Raton, FL: Chapman and Hall. doi:10.1201/9781420011111

John, D.R., Loken, B., & Joiner, C. (1998). The negative impact of extensions: Can flagship products be diluted? *Journal of Marketing, 62,* 19–32. doi:10.2307/1251800

Jones, M., & Schumann, D. (2000). The strategic use of celebrity athlete endorsers in Sports Illustrated: An historic perspective. *Sport Marketing Quarterly, 9,* 65–75.

Keller, K.L. (1993). Conceptualizing, measuring, and managing customer-based brand equity. *Journal of Marketing, 57*(1), 1–22. doi:10.2307/1252054

Keller, K.L., & Aaker, D.A. (1992). The effects of sequential introduction of brand extensions. *Journal of Marketing Research, 29,* 35–50. doi:10.2307/3172491

Kowalczyk, C.M., & Royne, M.B. (2013). The moderating role of celebrity worship on attitudes toward celebrity brand extensions. *Journal of Marketing Theory and Practice, 21,* 211–220. doi:10.2753/MTP1069-6679210206

Kristiansen, E., & Williams, A. (2015). Communicating the athlete as a brand: An examination of LPGA star Suzann Pettersen. *International Journal of Sport Communication, 8,* 371–388. doi:10.1123/IJSC.2015-0066

Loken, B. (2006). Consumer psychology: Categorization, inferences, affect, and persuasion. *Annual Review of Psychology, 57,* 453–485. doi:10.1146/annurev.psych.57.102904.190136

Loken, B., Barsalou, L.W., & Joiner, C. (2007). Categorization theory and research in consumer psychology: Category representation and category-based inference. In C.P. Haugtvedt, F. Karges, & P.M. Herr (Eds.), *Handbook of consumer psychology* (pp. 133–163). Hillsdale, NJ: Erlbaum.

Loken, B., & John, D.R. (1993). Diluting brand beliefs: When do brand extensions have a negative impact? *Journal of Marketing, 57*(3), 71–84. doi:10.2307/1251855

Loken, B., Joiner, C., & Houston, M.J. (2010). Leveraging a brand through brand extension: A review of two decades of research. In B. Loken, R. Ahluwalia, & M.J. Houston (Eds.), *Brand and brand management: Contemporary research perspectives* (pp. 11–41). New York, NY: Taylor & Francis.

McCracken, G. (1989). Who is the celebrity endorser? Cultural foundations of the endorsement process. *The Journal of Consumer Research, 16,* 310–321. doi:10.1086/209217

Myers, R.H. (1990). Classical and modern regression with applications. Boston, MA: Duxbury Press.

Nunnally, J.C., & Bernstein, I.H. (1994). *Psychometric theory.* New York, NY: McGraw-Hill.

Papadimitriou, D., Apostolopoulou, A., & Loukas, I. (2004). The role of perceived fit in fans' evaluation of sports brand extensions. *International Journal of Sports Marketing & Sponsorship, 6,* 27–44. doi:10.1108/IJSMS-06-01-2004-B006

Park, C.W., Milberg, S., & Lawson, R. (1991). Evaluation of brand extensions: The role of product feature similarity and brand concept consistency. *The Journal of Consumer Research, 18,* 185–193. doi:10.1086/209251

Punyatoya, P. (2013). Consumer evaluation of brand extension for global and local brands: The moderating role of product similarity. *Journal of International Consumer Marketing, 25,* 198–215. doi:10.1080/08961530.2013.780857

Rosch, E. (1975). Cognitive representation of semantic categories. *Journal of Experimental Psychology. General, 104,* 192–233. doi:10.1037/0096-3445.104.3.192

Ross, S.D. (2006). A conceptual framework for understanding spectator-based brand equity. *Journal of Sport Management, 20,* 22–38.

Ross, S.D., James, J.D., & Vargas, P. (2006). Development of a scale to measure team brand associations in professional sport. *Journal of Sport Management, 20,* 260–279. doi:10.1123/jsm.20.2.260

Ross, S., Walsh, P., & Shreffler, M. (2014). The impact of need for uniqueness, loyalty proneness, and identification on the likelihood of brand extension purchases. *Global Sport Business Journal, 2*(2), 28–42.

Sood, S., & Keller, K.L. (2012). The effects of brand name structure on brand extension evaluations and parent brand dilution. *JMR, Journal of Marketing Research, 49,* 373–382. doi:10.1509/jmr.07.0418

Spiggle, S., Nguyen, H.T., & Caravella, M. (2012). More than fit: Brand extension authenticity. *Journal of Marketing Research, 49,* 967–983. doi:10.1509/jmr.11.0015

Sujan, M., & Tybout, A.M. (1988). Applications and extensions of categorization research in consumer behavior. *Advances in Consumer Research. Association for Consumer Research (U. S.), 15*(1), 50–54.

Stone, G., Joseph, M., & Jones, M. (2003). An exploratory study on the use of sports celebrities in advertising: A content analysis. *Sport Marketing Quarterly, 12,* 94–102.

Thomson, M. (2006). Human brands: Investigating antecedents to consumers' strong attachments to celebrities. *Journal of Marketing, 70*(3), 104–119. doi:10.1509/jmkg.70.3.104

Vivek, N., & Sudharani-Ravindran, D. (2008). An empirical study on the impact of environmental uncertainty on the supply chain integration of a firm. *The ICAFI Journal of Supply Chain Management, 5*(1), 27–37.

Walsh, P., Chien, C.J., & Ross, S.D. (2012). Sport teams as brand extensions: A case of Taiwanese baseball. *Sport Marketing Quarterly, 21,* 138–146.

Walsh, P., & Lee, S. (2012). Development of a brand extension decision-making model for professional sport teams. *Sport Marketing Quarterly, 21,* 232–242.

Walsh, P., & Ross, S.D. (2010). Examining brand extensions and their potential to dilute team brand association. *Sport Marketing Quarterly, 19,* 196–206.

Williams, A., Walsh, P., & Rhenwrick, I. (2015). A conceptual framework for assessing brand equity in professional athletes. *International Journal of Sport Management, 16,* 1–21.

Yeo, J., & Park, J. (2006). Effects of parent-extension similarity and self regulatory focus on evaluations of brand extensions. *Journal of Consumer Psychology, 16,* 272–282. doi:10.1207/s15327663jcp1603_9

Zhang, S., & Sood, S. (2002). "Deep" and "surface" cues: Brand extension evaluations by children and adults. *The Journal of Consumer Research, 29,* 129–141. doi:10.1086/338207

Journal of Sport Management, 2017, 31, 61-79
https://doi.org/10.1123/jsm.2016-0101
© 2017 Human Kinetics, Inc.

The Role of Interorganizational Relationships on Elite Athlete Development Processes

Popi Sotiriadou
Griffith University

Jessie Brouwers
Tennis Vlaanderen

Veerle De Bosscher
Vrije Universiteit Brussel

Graham Cuskelly
Griffith University

Previous studies acknowledge the importance of sporting organizations' developing partnerships with clubs for athlete development purposes. However, there are no studies that address the way partnerships influence athlete progression and pathways. This study explores interorganizational relationships (IORs) between a tennis federation and tennis clubs in their efforts to improve player development processes. Document analysis and semistructured interviews with representatives from clubs and the Flemish federation were used. The findings show that the federation and the clubs engaged in IORs to achieve reciprocity and efficiency. The federation anticipated gaining legitimacy and asymmetry, and clubs expected to develop stability. Formal and informal control mechanisms facilitated IOR management. The conceptual model discussed in this study shows the types of IOR motives, management, and control mechanisms that drive and influence the attraction, retention/ transition, and nurturing processes of athlete development.

Keywords: elite sport, managing and evaluating elite athlete development, interorganizational relationships, sport clubs, sport organizations, athlete development processes, development of sport

There are many sport organizations involved with the development and success of elite athletes, including national government agencies for sport; Olympic committees; regional/state (RSOs/SSOs) and national sporting organizations (NSOs); or federations, clubs, and private sector organizations (e.g., Phillips & Newland, 2014; Sotiriadou, 2009). Sotiriadou and Shilbury (2009) indicated that RSOs (or SSOs) and NSOs (also referred to as sports federations or national sports governing bodies) are largely responsible for the provision and implementation of elite athlete development programs and pathways at a regional and national level, respectively. However, in many sports, such as triathlon, football (soccer), tennis, and golf, there are athletes who find and follow pathways outside the RSO–NSO structure. These athletes may choose to train in third-party organizations, such as private for-profit companies, private academies, or clubs

(Brouwers, Sotiriadou, & De Bosscher, 2015a, 2015b; Liebenau, 2010; Newland & Kellett, 2012).

Sport clubs increasingly vary in their operations, contribution to sport development, and approach to developing sport (e.g., Wicker & Breuer, 2011). Most clubs' mission is to provide fun, safe, supportive, accessible opportunities for grassroots participation (Sotiriadou, Quick, & Shilbury, 2006). Nevertheless, there are some clubs that offer well-developed, highly competitive programs and support systems that advance an elite development agenda (e.g., Smith & Shilbury, 2004). Hence, clubs can play a significant role in talent development (Brouwers et al., 2015a, 2015b; Liebenau, 2010; Stenling & Fahlén, 2014), which represents the foundation of the sport performance pyramid. In many countries, high sport performance funding is directed to national bodies with little or no funding filtered through to the club level (Sotiriadou, 2009). Therefore, in their efforts to offer strong pathways to talented athletes, clubs are pressured to develop partnerships with a variety of sporting and nonsports organizations (Bloyce, Smith, Mead, & Morris, 2008). Partnerships with sport organizations allow clubs to offer opportunities to talented athletes to develop (Bloyce et al., 2008). However, various studies highlight how little is known about the nature of their relationship (Bloyce et al., 2008; Sotiriadou, 2009), the links between clubs and sport organizations, and the

Popi Sotiriadou and Graham Cuskelly are with the Department of Tourism, Sport and Hotel Management, Griffith University, Gold Coast, QLD, Australia. Veerle De Bosscher is with the Department of Sport Policy and Management, Vrije Universiteit Brussel, Brussels, Belgium. Jessie Brouwers is with the Department of Club Development, Tennis Vlaanderen, Brussels, Belgium. Address author correspondence to Popi Sotiriadou at p.sotiriadou@griffith.edu.au.

potential influence of such partnerships to sport development processes (Mackintosh, 2011). Furthermore, these relationships unfold in different ways depending on the country-specific sport system and structures. Consequently, the relationship between clubs and sport organizations needs to be explored for various reasons.

First, a well-supported club structure can provide a wide range of opportunities and services at a variety of junior (youth) and senior age groups. These opportunities allow movement in and out of the sport system without losing resources or participants (Martindale, Collins, & Daubney, 2005). Second, research on nonprofit organizations shows that it is important to create and nurture relationships to strengthen the clubs and enhance the services they provide (Frisby, Thibault, & Kikulis, 2004). The stronger clubs are more competitive when applying for government grants (Sotiriadou & Wicker, 2013) and more attractive to corporate and private funding sources. Last, understanding the relationship between clubs and RSOs or NSOs is important in successfully sustaining the clubs' motivation and interest in elite athlete development and in maintaining their contribution to elite development pathways.

Interorganizational relationships (IORs) are a useful heuristic from which to understand organizational practices and how and why various sport organizations work jointly to plan and implement specific programs that would allow them to accomplish similar or common goals and objectives (Alexander, Thibault, & Frisby, 2008; Oliver, 1990). This study examines IORs between a regional tennis organization (Tennis Vlaanderen; also referred to as "the federation" in this article) and tennis clubs in Flanders (i.e., the northern, Dutch-speaking region of Belgium; Taks & Kesenne, 2000) and contributes to ongoing discussions on why and how IORs may influence elite athlete development processes. These are dyadic IORs that focus on the interactions between two types of organizations as opposed to interactions between the clubs themselves, or the relationships of the regional tennis organization with other partners in the broader network (such as the Olympic Committee or the national sports administration; Babiak, 2003). The following research question guided this study: How do IORs between the federation and clubs influence elite player development processes?

Conceptual Framework

This study draws on the concept of *elite athlete development processes*. Sotiriadou and Shilbury (2009) defined elite athlete development as a field that

> requires the contribution of various interested groups in an array of specifically designed strategies and programs targeted to those athletes that compete at international level . . . with the potential to create and regenerate involvement from governments, sponsors, participants, spectators, sports supporters and athletes themselves. (p. 146)

This definition denotes how athlete development is a multifaceted field that requires the involvement and collaboration of a range of stakeholders. Furthermore, the word *contribution* in the definition has a significant meaning as it lends itself to various stakeholders' consolidating their efforts to achieve a common goal. In defining the field of sport development, Green (2005) and Sotiriadou, Shilbury, and Quick (2008) argued that elite athlete development is a *process* that addresses athlete entrance, retention, and advancement (Green, 2005) or what Sotiriadou et al. (2008) termed as the "attraction, retention/transition and nurturing" (ARTN) framework. This study is positioned within the realm of sport development to highlight the centrality of IORs within the sport development processes.

There are numerous types of IORs, including partnerships, linkages, or outsourcing services that allow two, or more, organizations to engage in accessing and exchanging tangible (e.g., facilities, financial resources, and technologies) and intangible (e.g., expertise and knowledge) resources (Babiak, 2003; Barnes, Cousens, & MacLean, 2007). These relationships involve "the sharing of power, work, support and/or information with others for the achievement of joint goals or mutual benefits" (Kernaghan, 1993, p. 61). The need to work through and develop partnerships to derive common sport development goals is stressed in Bloyce et al. (2008) and more recently in Mackintosh (2011). However, the application of IORs to the context of high-performance sport and elite athlete development processes is limited. Babiak (2003, 2007, 2009) and Babiak and Thibault (2008, 2009) offer the few existing studies that have examined IORs between a Canadian Sport Centre and its partners including NSOs, Sport Canada, Canadian Olympic Committee, Coaching Association of Canada, private commercial organizations, and other Canadian Sport Centres. These studies examined how a collaborative approach through the establishment of IORs between various partners served as a strategy to offer comprehensive support and resources for elite athletes and coaches, particularly in times of reduced government funding for elite sport.

Interorganizational Relationships

The literature describes three stages in the evolution and implementation of IORs (Alexander et al., 2008; Babiak, 2003; Parent & Harvey, 2009). The initial *formation* stage refers to the determinants, motives, and antecedents to enter a relationship (Babiak, 2007; Oliver, 1990; Parent & Harvey, 2009). The subsequent *management*, or processes, stage reflects the large amount of managerial factors and challenges of the management of a relationship (Babiak & Thibault, 2008, 2009; Frisby et al., 2004; Misener & Doherty, 2013; Parent & Harvey, 2009). Finally, the *evaluation* stage refers to the outcomes and effectiveness of the relationships, as well as the deliverables accrued through the relationship, including products, services, or communications between organizations (Babiak, 2009; Misener & Doherty, 2013, 2014; Parent & Harvey, 2009).

Formation of IORs

According to Oliver (1990), there are key causes, or determinants, that prompt or motivate organizations to form relationships. These determinants include (a) *necessity* (meet necessary legal or regulatory requirements), (b) *asymmetry* (exercise power or control over another organization or its resources), (c) *reciprocity* (pursue common or mutually beneficial goals or interests through cooperation, collaboration, and coordination), (d) *efficiency* (improve internal input/output ratio), (e) *stability* (adaptive response to environmental uncertainty), and (f) *legitimacy* (comply with norms, rules, beliefs, or expectations).

These determinants have been useful in informing sport management studies and elite sport. Specifically, Babiak (2007) examined IOR formation among a Canadian Sport Centre and its partners (e.g., NSOs, Canadian Olympic Committee, corporate partners, and other Canadian Sport Centres). The results showed not only that each partner had different motives for entering a partnership but also had multiple motives to do so. Babiak (2007) concluded that the presence of IOR determinants is often based on resource scarcity and dependence on external sources for funding, as well as institutional forces, power, and control. In addition to the determinants found in mainstream literature (e.g., asymmetry, necessity, efficiency, and stability), *individual-level factors* (i.e., personal values and beliefs, previous history, prior experiences, and personal interactions of key individuals of partner organizations) emerged as a new construct that played an important role in IOR formation within the context of sport organizations (Babiak, 2007). In another study, Alexander et al. (2008) explored a joint initiative between a nonprofit provincial tennis organization and a public sector recreation department that aimed to increase tennis participation. The study showed that necessity, reciprocity, and improved efficiencies motivated the tennis organization to enter the joint initiative, whereas the sport and recreation department sought to offer a more legitimate program to the community. The study concluded that even though motives can differ, conflicts or power struggles can be avoided when partners explain their positions clearly to one another and clarify the values underlying these motives.

Overall, existing studies resonate within the Canadian sport system and reflect the Canadian context. An exception to this represents Parent and Harvey's (2009) study on community-based sport IORs, which integrated North American and European literature to develop a partnership model. In that study, Parent and Harvey (2009) proposed slightly different antecedents to previous studies as essential to the success of a partnership. These antecedents included the project's *purpose* (partnership goals), *environment* (strengths, weaknesses, opportunities, and threats of the general and task environment),

the *nature* of the partner organizations (profit, nonprofit, public), the partners' *motives* (degree of reciprocity of the partners), and their *complementarity and fit* (strategic and cultural fit). Parent and Harvey (2009) argued that partnership *planning* (i.e., actual partnership type, creation of roles and responsibilities, and the development of policy and partnership norms and guidelines) was an essential antecedent.

Management of IORs

Research on IOR management of sport organizations suggests that there are many factors that can contribute to quality IORs and a successful collaboration. These factors include resource and information sharing, objectives and strategies, communication, trust, commitment, consistency, dependability, balance, mutuality, coordination, engagement, authority, responsibility, autonomy, monitoring and reporting, personal contact, relationship management competencies, operational competencies, and relational competencies (e.g., Alexander et al., 2008; Babiak & Thibault, 2008; Lucidarme et al., 2014; Misener & Doherty, 2013, 2014; Parent & Harvey, 2009).

The advent of several IOR management factors led to studies differentiating them based on formal controls and informal (social) processes. *Formal* controls include, for example, outlining objectives and strategies, delineating roles and responsibilities, and developing guidelines and reports (Babiak & Thibault, 2008; Frisby et al., 2004; Huxham & Vangen, 1996). *Informal* (social) processes may include mutual trust, communication, commitment, and engagement (Babiak & Thibault, 2008; Child & Faulkner, 1998; Misener & Doherty, 2013, 2014; Willem & Lucidarme, 2014). Babiak and Thibault (2008) found that informal control processes play a more important role than formal control mechanisms in IOR management in the Canadian sport system. Moreover, they found that IORs are often loosely structured and formal control mechanisms were not extensively used as they appeared to have a negative impact on trust.

The complexity of IOR management is evident in studies that highlight managerial challenges, inadequate managerial processes, and strategic challenges of IORs (Babiak & Thibault, 2009; Frisby et al., 2004). *Managerial challenges* may encompass poor governance; the lack of formalized written rules, policies, guidelines, and planning; the obscurity of roles, responsibilities, and reporting channels; issues with regard to partnerships across sectors; and the lack of human resources to accomplish the duties necessary to sustain IORs (Babiak & Thibault, 2008; Frisby et al., 2004). Even though sport organizations seemingly collaborate, they sometimes compete on different levels for resources, such as money, coaches, and athletes (Babiak & Thibault, 2009). MacLean, Cousens, and Barnes (2011), for instance, found that sport clubs did not organize joint training camps with other clubs out of fear that rival clubs could "steal" or "poach" the best athletes to develop a more competitive team. In their study, Babiak and Thibault (2009) noted the presence of competition between different sport organizations to protect their government funding. This rivalry, or competition, can result in tensions and can be a source of frustration between partners.

Evaluation of IORs

The final process of a partnership is evaluation, a step often overlooked in practice (Parent & Harvey, 2009). Nevertheless, partnership evaluation studies provide insights on key points to consider and available types of evaluation (Babiak, 2009; Misener & Doherty, 2013, 2014; Parent & Harvey, 2009). According to Parent and Harvey's (2009) partnership model, these evaluations include (a) ongoing evaluation of results, (b) evaluation of the short-term effects of programs or other initiatives, (c) evaluation of long-term outcomes/objectives, (d) immediate feedback during an activity, and (e) a summative evaluation at the end of the project. For instance, Babiak (2003) found that outcomes of IORs in the Canadian sports system included resource acquisition, international sporting success of athletes, visibility, increases in the range and coordination of services offered to coaches and athletes, and the creation of social capital. The levels of partners' satisfaction and the degree to which the objectives have been achieved are essential in determining the final evaluation of a partnership (Parent & Harvey, 2009).

A key point in studies on IORs is that the processes of formation, management, and evaluation are interrelated (Alexander et al., 2008; Misener & Doherty, 2013). Misener and Doherty (2013), for instance, noted that the deliverables that sport partners received from IORs were closely aligned to the reasons for forming relationships. Alexander et al. (2008) found that sport partners entered IORs based on motives to improve efficiencies in time and resources, then strived to manage IORs to improve efficiencies, and identified improved efficiencies as a desired outcome. Hence, the formation, management, and evaluation processes can be interwoven.

Overall, the literature suggests the existence of various sport management IOR studies (e.g., Bloyce et al., 2008; Mackintosh, 2011; Parent & Harvey, 2009). However, the majority of research is not centered on partnerships within the elite sports context or talent development processes in particular. Babiak and Thibault's (2008, 2009) framework is used in this study of IORs between tennis clubs and the tennis federation in Flanders to examine the influence of these partnerships on elite athlete development. There are two reasons for drawing upon this framework. First, Babiak and Thibault (2008, 2009) conceptualized their framework in the specific context of elite sport partnerships rather than partnerships at community-level sport. Second, Babiak and Thibault's work was particularly applicable to the research aims of this study and focuses on the "challenges" evident within the elite sport space (e.g., concurrent competition and cooperation of sport organizations on different levels for resources; support and resources for elite athletes and

coaches; power relationships between organizations at different levels in the sport system). These features of their framework allowed us to explore and examine elite sports development partnership in a new sport system and country. For these reasons, Babiak and Thibault's (2008, 2009) framework is used to analyze the findings of this study and to help gain deeper insights into the collected data.

The Elite Tennis System in Flanders

In some countries club interactions with national bodies might be minimal or even inexistent. For example, in Canada and Australia, there are provincial or state sporting organizations that interact with the clubs and, thus, overtake the NSO–club interaction. In smaller countries (e.g., the Netherlands), where regional or provincial sporting organizations are nonexistent (or have very low power), clubs interact directly with the federations. This system dates back to the late 1960s when the three regions of Belgium (Flanders, Wallonia, and the German community) were granted cultural autonomy (Taks & Kesenne, 2000). Each region has its own regulations, laws, sports priorities, and sporting organizations (De Bosscher, 2007). Tennis Vlaanderen (i.e., the federation) is the federation for tennis in Flanders, which sets strategic goals for tennis in Flanders and organizes tennis activities and competitions for players. Belgium has a national tennis organization (i.e., the Royal Belgian Tennis Federation), which is responsible only for the legal representation of Belgium (all three regions) at the International Tennis Federation and has no existing sport administration (De Bosscher, 2007). Each of the three "regional" tennis federations in Belgium carry out all tennis administration related activities, including elite player development, autonomously. Consequently, in Belgium, the tennis federations are in charge of the tasks and activities that are normally a responsibility of an NSO (Winand, Zintz, Bayle, & Robinson, 2010). The elite tennis system in Flanders (as Figure 1 illustrates) includes various stakeholders (i.e., tennis clubs and the federation), athlete development phases (scouting, development, and elite tennis), and relevant programs (e.g., Kids Development Team [KDT], Junior Development Team [JDT], and the Elite Sport School [ESS]). Figure 1 indicates which programs are provided by the federation, Tennis Vlaanderen (white), clubs (gray), or are based on the collaboration between clubs and the federation (half white, half gray).

The federation selects the most talented players between 6 and 12 years of age to participate at the KDT, a player development program that is jointly operated with the clubs. Then, the players between the ages of 12 and 18 years who wish to pursue a professional tennis career could take one of the three directions available. The federation decides and chooses the most talented players to train full-time at a secondary school, the ESS, which the federation has especially designed for tennis players. The centralized support services of the ESS are located in one

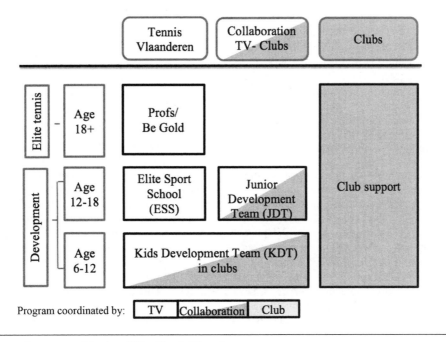

Figure 1 — Elite tennis structure, Flanders. TV = Tennis Vlaanderen.

elite training center. Within this center, selected players train under the guidance of the federation coaches and attend and reside in a boarding school. For players who miss out on the ESS selection criteria, or choose to train at their local club, the federation offers the JDT program. This program enables players to receive some additional support from the federation while they train at their club. The remaining pool of players can follow a development pathway in their clubs. They have the option to remain and train with their club throughout their development stage. After the age of 18, the federation provides a professional support framework (i.e., the Profs/Be Gold program) for players who meet the selection criteria and are on track to reach a senior top 100 world ranking. Players not selected can choose to finance their own support team and train with a private coach or with a local tennis club.

Overall, the federation offers both a centralized (i.e., ESS) and a decentralized (i.e., KDT and JDT) approach to tennis player development that allows the federation to collaborate with clubs in joints programs. In conclusion, the context of player development in Flanders suggests that dyadic IORs exist between the federation and the clubs through existing joint programs (e.g., KDT and JDT) that aim to facilitate elite player development. This study examines the ways relationships between the clubs and the federation influence elite player development processes.

Method

To allow for quality, depth, and richness of data in this exploratory study, a qualitative research approach including document analysis and semistructured interviews

was used. Ethics approval was obtained from the host university to conduct this research (HSL/31/11/HREC).

Selection of IOR Partners

Two types of organizations were selected for this study: the Flemish tennis federation, as the government-funded and coordinating organization for elite player development, and seven tennis clubs that were actively involved in elite player development through player development programs. The joint programs between the club and the federation are only available to clubs with KDT and/or JDT players. Clubs that do not have any players in any of these programs do not engage in player development. Other clubs may have one or two players in each program or only one of the programs available. In selecting clubs for this study, the research team decided that the strongest representation of players in both of the joint programs (i.e., using the number of their combined KDT and JDT players) would be indicative of the clubs that had the stronger engagement with player development processes and would offer deeper insights into the phenomenon under investigation. Furthermore, suggestions from the federation informed the research team and contributed in the final selection of clubs that engage in elite athlete development.

At the time of data collection during 2014, there were 32 clubs that had at least one KDT player (72 KDT players in total). Of these 32 clubs, only 18 had at least one or more JDT players (19 JDT players in total). To enable the research team to explore IORs in all available joint programs, the club head coaches of the 18 clubs with the most players in both programs were contacted, and 7 clubs agreed to participate in the study.

Data Collection

The study design incorporated two sources of data collection: (a) documents from the participating organizations and (b) semistructured interviews with club and federation representatives. Using different types of data (i.e., documents and interviews) offered evidence on various dimensions of the same phenomenon and facilitated data-source triangulation (Yin, 1994) and an accurate description of the IORs.

Documents.   First, publicly available information about the participating organizations, such as websites, strategic plans, promotional materials, and annual reports, was collected and reviewed. Table 1 is an overview of the documents that were used in this study. In total, 360 pages of documents, complemented by webpages of all organizations, were analyzed. A Microsoft Word document was created for each organization where all the details of any type of club–federation interaction were recorded. Using the research question and scope of the study as a guide, these documents were reviewed for details on existing or future relationships between the clubs and the federation. For example, the federation's strategic plan included an analysis of organizational strengths, weaknesses, and goals. One of these goals was "viewing our existing means and know-how (strength), and viewing the limited possibilities of clubs and coaches for elite player development (weakness), the federation will assure its involvement with the development of all talented and elite players (goal)" (Tennis Vlaanderen, 2013b, p. 4). The result of this process generated 45 single-spaced pages of data, which were analyzed manually using *directed* content analysis (Hsieh & Shannon, 2005). During this type of analysis initial coding starts with a theory or relevant research findings and then, during data analysis, the researchers immerse themselves in the data and allow themes to emerge from the data (Hashemnezhad, 2015). These documents, analyzed before the interview transcripts, helped complement the researchers' knowledge and understanding of the phenomenon under investigation and informed the interview guide.

Semistructured interviews.   Second, representatives ($n = 7$) from seven tennis clubs and the Flemish tennis federation ($n = 7$) participated in semistructured interviews. Using purposive sampling (Patton, 2002), the representatives (hereinafter referred to as interviewees) were chosen based on their role and expertise on elite player development (Table 1).

A semistructured interview guide that consisted of two parts was used to collect data. The first part included questions on organizational capacities to develop elite players. This information was necessary to understand organizational capacity to develop elite players and identify in what areas and in what ways clubs may need the federation's input and vice versa. Topics such as availability and condition of training programs, facilities, coaching, and financial support were explored. Moreover, the interviewees were asked to reflect on problems they may have encountered with regard to elite player development. For example, questions included "To what extent can the club/federation develop elite players" or "Which programs are offered to develop elite players?" The second part of the interview included questions on the IORs between clubs and the federation as they related to player development. Specifically, the interviewees were asked about their motives for engaging in IORs, the ways

Table 1   Organizational Representatives Interviewed and Documents Analyzed

Organization	Representative interviewed	Documents/document sources
Tennis federation	Director, elite tennis[a]	Website
	Coordinator, elite tennis[a]	Annual report 2013 (Tennis Vlaanderen, 2013a, 212 pages)
	Head coach, Men's Team[a]	Strategic plan 2009–2012 (Tennis Vlaanderen, 2009, 75 pages)
	Head coach, Women's Team[a]	Strategic plan 2013–2016 (Tennis Vlaanderen, 2013b, 73 pages)
	Coordinator, Kids Development Team[a]	—
	CEO[a]	—
	President[a]	—
Tennis clubs		
Club 1	Head coach (Club 1)	Website
Club 2	Head coach (Club 2)	Website
Club 3	Head coach (Club 3)	Website
Club 4	Head coach (Club 4)	Website
Club 5	Head coach (Club 5)	Website
Club 6	Academy director[b] (Club 6)	Website
Club 7	Academy director (Club 7)	Website

[a]In accordance with ethics clearance, the interviewees from the tennis federation were randomly numbered (TV 1 to TV 7) to protect their identity.
[b]Academy directors are the equivalent to head coaches in larger clubs/academies.

their relationship takes place, and elite athlete development–related outcomes. This included questions such as "What motivates you/your organization to cooperate with the federation/clubs?" "How would you describe the relationship with the federation/clubs?" "How is the relationship managed?" "Is cooperation with the federation/clubs important for player development, and why?" Moreover, interviewees were encouraged to discuss challenges, tensions, and benefits or outcomes of their relationships. The length of the interviews varied from 50 min to 2 hr. The data collected from the clubs and the federation representatives were adequate to reach saturation of themes, which is the point when new categories or variations on existing categories cease to emerge from new data (Soulliere, Britt, & Maines, 2001). Following Sotiriadou and Shilbury's (2010) recommendation, when information became repetitive and added little if anything to the existing categories or codes, the research team knew it was time to cease collecting data or analyzing the category that had reached saturation.

Data Analysis

All the interviews were conducted in Dutch. The second named author researcher, who performed the translation, is bilingual. As such, the three-step process of translating, editing, and proofreading is reliable for creating a translation that is true to the original document. Therefore, the research team did not resort to back-translation services. All interviews were digitally recorded and transcribed verbatim, resulting in 273 pages of single-spaced transcripts. Interview transcripts and the Word documents that resulted from the collected documents were saved in NVivo. NVivo research software was used to organize and code the data (Sotiriadou, Brouwers, & Le, 2014). Data analysis was performed using both (a) a priori concepts informed by the literature on IORs and (b) critically informed reflections on the emerging issues encountered in forming, managing, and evaluating relationships between the clubs and the federation. All the data were carefully read and coded, and each concept was reviewed and discussed among the authors. Two of the authors performed the coding, and the results of the data analysis and emerging concepts were reviewed, compared, and discussed among all authors. Once the research team agreed on the concepts, revisions were made as necessary and the codes were tightened up to the point that maximizes mutual exclusivity and exhaustiveness (Weber, 1990). This process allowed the research team to (a) code the same text in the same way, (b) make valid inferences from the text, and (c) safeguard the reliability and consistency of the classification/coding procedure (Weber, 1990). Next, relationships between the concepts were examined to identify higher order categories. This resulted in three higher order categories for IOR formation including (a) common determinants for the clubs and the federation, (b) federation-specific determinants, and (c) club-specific determinants. For IOR management, the two higher order categories that emerged were (a) formal

and (b) informal control mechanisms. The higher order categories for IOR outcomes and evaluation were (a) elite player development, (b) coach development, and (c) club management/development. The most comprehensive quotations were used to illustrate the findings in the results section. In accordance with ethics clearance, the interviewees from the tennis federation were randomly numbered (TV 1 to TV 7) to protect their identity.

Results on IOR Formation

The emerging themes show that the federation and the clubs had some common determinants that motivated them to form IORs (i.e., individual-level factors, reciprocity, and efficiency). At the same time, there were also a number of organization-specific motivators for IOR formation (i.e., legitimacy and asymmetry for the federation and stability and necessity for the clubs; see Figure 2).

Common Determinants for the Clubs and the Federation

Individual-level factors, such as personal contacts or network of contacts, emerged as important in partnership formation. For example, four club head coaches had contacts within the federation, where they had worked previously. Some of the federation interviewees worked as coaches in the private sector (i.e., clubs), where they created personal values and beliefs that motivated IOR formation between the clubs and the federation. TV 7, for instance, indicated, "I come from a club background myself, maybe that is why I believe so strongly in cooperation with clubs."

The clubs and the federation formed IORs for *reciprocity* and *efficiency*. *Reciprocity* was a main motive for IOR formation as the federation and clubs had player development as a common goal. As such, club–federation partnerships benefit both entities. The following quote from TV 3 illustrates the mutually beneficial relationship and how the federation was open to the idea of cooperation: "We are open to cooperate with clubs that have an elite sport mentality. They make us stronger and we make them stronger. We need to support cooperation and make sure it grows. It will make us all stronger." This reciprocity allowed the federation and clubs to combine their competencies to develop talented players:

> If there are things that they [clubs] do better, then it would be perfect to let them organize those things. The big strength of the federation is that we are subsidized. What we offer here [federation center] to the players costs lots of money in the clubs. So we need to cooperate, let the clubs do what they do well, and we play our role, that works. (TV 5)

Efficiency was also apparent as the federation and clubs expressed the common desire to increase the efficiency of elite player development. However, the two types of organizations expressed efficiency motives

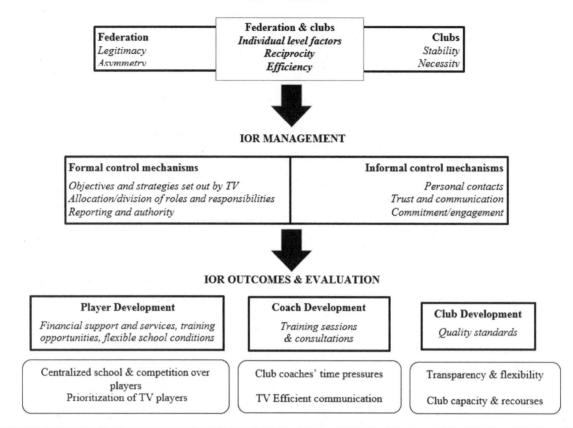

Figure 2 — Formation, management and evaluation of elite athlete interorganizational relationships (IORs). TV = Tennis Vlaanderen.

in different ways. The federation felt the need to intervene with player development at the club level because some of the clubs lacked the capacity to provide quality development programs, or training and coaching. For example, the federation's policy plan mentioned that "viewing the restricted elite sport possibilities of many clubs and coaches, we will ascertain that we are involved with the development of all talented and elite players" (Tennis Vlaanderen, 2013b, p. 4). Specific goals in the federation's plan included "having an open cooperation with the clubs in which the players are central," "optimize the club–TV relationship," and "work together with club coaches as partners in elite sport" (Tennis Vlaanderen, 2013b, p. 4). The open cooperation of the federation with the clubs was operationalized through joint player development programs (such as KDT) that helped strengthen the expertise and skills of club coaches: "With the start of the KDT, the federation gave more responsibility to the clubs and their qualified coaches. The project aims to increase support for talented players at club level through increasing support and assistance for the club coaches" (Tennis Vlaanderen, 2009, p. 56).

At more advanced levels of player development, the federation was of the opinion that clubs struggled to provide the necessary support for elite player development. One federation representative indicated,

> Clubs can offer good support until players are 12 or 14 years old, but the last step of elite player development is too difficult for them. So, we let the clubs do what they do well and then we offer a leading and coordinating role for additional support. (TV 5)

Clubs mentioned the need for (a) group training sessions for players, (b) coaching expertise, and (c) financial assistance. Clubs maintained that collaborating with the federation allowed club players to attend group training sessions where a large number of the best players of the country train together. This was beneficial, as many clubs did not have a sufficient number of talented players of the same age group to train together. The federation invited club coaches to attend group training sessions allowing them to compare and assess players' progress and exchange information with federation coaches. In addition, clubs indicated that cooperation with the federation coaches was useful as the federation has more expertise with the development of top 100 players: "I have never been a top 100 player, but I find it important that if you support an elite player that you involve someone who has reached that level himself and [federation coach] has that experience and gives feedback" (Club 7).

Federation-Specific Determinants

Determinants of partnership formation that were evident for the federation only included *legitimacy* and *asymmetry*. Legitimacy motives were founded on the federation's desire to enhance its reputation and image as a center of expertise. The federation captured these legitimacy considerations as follows:

> In 2008 we made the choice to go down a different path. Back then I had the feeling that we [federation] were acting too much as a club between the other clubs. I mean that we were too busy with developing players that we had in our center, and we overlooked the clubs, other good coaches, and academies that also have the ability to develop elite players. So we took a different philosophy or vision. We said the federation actually needs to be an overarching organization that oversees everything that has to do with elite tennis in Flanders. It is our responsibility to help out the club coaches or academies, so we need to intervene where the club coaches have limitations. (TV 4)

Strategic plans and annual reports further emphasized the federation's desire to profile itself as center of expertise with a leading role in elite player development: "The federation will strive to create an elite sport climate of which each player wants to be part of. [. . .] The federation will assure that KDT serves all club coaches to improve the development of talented players" (Tennis Vlaanderen, 2013a, p. 12).

Asymmetry, in the form of power and control, emerged as an IOR motive for the federation. TV 5 mentioned, "Ideally we have a coordinating or leading role and the clubs work complementary." The federation controlled which players were supported, the types of support offered, and the conditions under which players could train at the federation center. Club 7 mentioned how the federation provided assurances that it is always involved with the development of players who perform well:

> If a child performs well, the federation is involved. If the child does not develop well, it decreases support and slowly support fades. [. . .] The good players that we have in our club automatically qualify for federation support through their good results at tournaments. So, they receive sufficient support from the federation; each player according to his needs be it financial or know-how.

The two strategies that allowed the federation to control the clubs included the "Youth Fund" and the "flexible status" of talented players. Through the Youth Fund, "an incentive fund that stimulates clubs to offer organized and structured player development" (TV 4), the federation awarded quality labels and subsidies to clubs that meet certain criteria (Tennis Vlaanderen, 2013a). TV 4 explained that "one of the criteria for which the clubs receive points, and thus money, is the number of club players that participate in the club tests for talent identification." The federation also played an important role in granting a flexible status to talented players that allowed them to be absent from school to train or participate at international tournaments. The federation had the power to award a flexible status to players and in return required that players meet certain criteria and attend training sessions at the federation.

Club-Specific Determinants

In addition to efficiency and reciprocity, *stability* and *necessity* emerged as important and club-specific determinants for IOR formation. Collaboration with the federation offered clubs stability as the development of talented players in a club environment is expensive for both the club and the players/parents. Club 5, for instance, explained that "tennis will always remain very expensive for players who are not selected to train in the ESS. You really need parents with a good income to pay for the children's tennis development." Clubs were interested in forming IORs with the federation to obtain access to resources including subsidies, international competition support, and player development support. As mentioned earlier, clubs were eligible to receive subsidies if they met certain criteria: "Through the Youth Fund we [clubs] can get subsidies from the federation based on a point system where we get extra points to have KDT players, so we get a bit more subsidies" (Club 3). In addition to direct financial support, the federation could lower the cost for club players to participate at international competitions through providing the opportunity to travel with the federation players and coaches. The excerpt below offers an example comparing the two scenarios:

> If a player can join the federation player group and coach [i.e., join the federation players and coaches in participating in international competitions], he needs to pay Euro[s] 25 per day, everything included. If a club player wants to travel privately, he needs to multiply that by 10 if you look at the total cost, covering the coaches' expenses for flights and accommodation, their time, and so forth. (Club 5)

Necessity emerged as another motive for clubs to enter into IORs with the federation as clubs had to comply with various regulations and meet certain federation requirements. For example, club coaches were required to cooperate with the federation if they wanted their players to obtain a flexible status and funding. As TV 1 explained, "Funding for players with a flexible status is based on how well the club coach cooperates with the federation. Did he attend the coaching education sessions and consultancy sessions? Did he fill out the player reports?" In addition, clubs had to meet certain criteria to receive recognition through quality labels (e.g., youth friendly club, youth friendly club with recognized kids tennis school, or youth friendly club with recognized kids and elite tennis school). These criteria included, for example, the organization of talent selection tests and competitions, club player performances in competitions, or coach education levels of club coaches (Tennis Vlaanderen, 2013a). Club 1 indicated that "obtaining quality labels is important for the image of the club and it facilitates the attraction of players and also sponsors."

Results on IOR Management

This section presents the formal and informal control mechanisms that played a critical role in the management of IORs between the clubs and the federation.

Formal Control Mechanisms

As Figure 2 shows (in italics), formal control mechanisms are used to manage objectives and strategies and division of roles and responsibilities, as well as the process of reporting and authority. The results showed that the federation has set out clear *objectives and strategies* that facilitated the cooperation with the clubs. For example, to increase success in developing elite players, the federation's key objective was to be an "open house" that shares support, expertise, and resources with clubs:

> The federation states in the policy plan that it wants to be an "open house" and I think we [federation] succeed in this more and more. Everybody is welcome here. Players can use our facilities and expertise. [. . .] I really see the added value of our center, especially for players who train in a club or academy, because here they can train with other good players. (TV 4)

To operationalize its open house objective, the federation organized and coordinated various player development programs (e.g., KDT for players ages 6 to 12 and JDT for players ages 12 to 18) that the clubs delivered. These programs emphasized the sharing of resources (e.g., subsidized group training sessions at the federation center with federation coaches, training camps, and travel support to participate at international competitions with federation coaches) and information (e.g., consultation sessions for club coaches). As Club 2 explained, "Club coaches play a very important role in the technical development of KDT players so it is the task of the federation to educate its coaches in technical coaching aspects. The consultation sessions are very important for that."

At the age of 12, the best KDT players are selected to transition into a full-time program at the ESS (see Figure 1), the training center of the federation. The ESS operates in isolation from the clubs and does not involve their cooperation. Club 4 noted that player support is organized and centralized at the ESS: "Financially it is difficult to support elite players at club level whereas at the ESS

everything is organized; tennis training, physio[therapist], strength and conditioning training and travel." In addition, Club 5 mentioned that "the organization with school is much easier as ESS players only need to go to school 18 hours per week. Here [club], players need to go to school full-time minus six hours, that is a lot more difficult."

Player development programs, at different development stages, required *different types of support* (cooperation) from the federation. Club 7 illustrated this as follows:

> For player X who is in the ATP top 200, the federation provides financial support and a coach to travel a couple weeks a year with the player and provides feedback to me [club coach]. For a U14 player the club coach reports to the federation coach so that federation coaches can monitor the player's progress. That is important because I am not specialized in U14 development, I don't know what the player needs to be capable of at the age of 13, 14, [. . .]. The federation coaches know that very well because they have expertise and can compare with other players. The information exchange about player progress is very important.

The results showed a clear division and *allocation of roles and responsibilities* in the IORs between the federation and club coaches. Club 5 stated that clubs "design the programs for the JDT players in dialogue with the federation because the federation provide guidelines on what the training should contain for players of each age and we try to take that into account." Another example of clear management of roles related to the federation coaches' versus the club coaches' roles. While the federation coaches focused on group training sessions where tactics, match situations, and rallying skills with players of the same level were most important, club coaches were responsible for the technical development of the KDT players at club level. In addition, the federation provided feedback on the player's technique via the club coach:

> Feedback on technical progress of the [KDT/JDT] player always goes via the club coach as he has the final responsibility for the player. So, we don't make major technical changes to a players' technique, but we contact the club coach to discuss this. Because, in our opinion, we need to make the club coaches better. (TV 2)

There was evidence that, in return for its support, the federation required that club coaches report on the progress of KDT and JDT players (*reporting and authority*). Club 7 noted that "from the moment that a player receives help from the federation, the club coaches are accountable to the federation based on training schedules, training content and so on." The management of the reporting system demonstrated the federation's authority over the club coaches and KDT/JDT players. For example, TV 7 noted, "The club coaches fill out a document with the training schedule of the KDT players. We [federation] provide guidelines for the weekly and yearly training programs. So in a way we control the clubs." In addition, based on its jurisdiction, the federation had the authority to decide which players were selected for the programs and received support for international competitions. Club 5 noted that "federation coaches decide which players are selected for the KDT, JDT and ESS programs. We [club] can give our opinion, but the final decision is made by the federation."

Informal Control Mechanisms

The informal control mechanisms that emerged were personal contacts, trust and communication, commitment, and engagement. *Personal contacts*, including having a family member or friend who works at the federation, appeared to facilitate the management of IORs. Club 1, for instance, noted, "My son coaches some male players at the federation center so he knows the training programs and completion schedules of the federation players. So we [club] are up-to-date with that." Moreover, Club 1 continued, "The high performance director of the federation is a good friend of mine and [name of federation coach] has played in our club, so I know a lot of people at the federation which makes contact easy." Similarly, Club 7 noted that his sister was one of the head coaches in the federation and he was good friends with another head coach. These personal contacts "encourage the cooperation. So automatically, we have a good communication with the federation." TV 4 explained that "elite tennis is a small world so we [federation] are all closely related [to club coaches]."

It was evident that *trust* was an important informal control mechanism in the management of IORs. The data showed that trust could not be enforced but needed to grow over time. TV 2, for instance, maintained that "they [clubs] need to believe in what we [federation] do, trust us. They should not feel this as if we take their players away. I think that is based on trust." Clear, open, and direct *communication* between the federation and the club coaches emerged as essential to establish trust. Even though the federation maintained that it "has good contact with the club coaches and shows the respect that they [club coaches] deserve for developing good players" (TV 2), some clubs expressed their concerns regarding their trust toward the federation as follows:

> The federation asked one of our players directly to transition to the ESS, without asking me. I learned later about her invitation. The federation really invited her behind my back. We won't keep players here [club] when we don't have the capacity to train them, but sometimes the federation takes our players away when we still have the capacity to coach them. That is very frustrating. (Club 4)

Another important attribute of IOR management was the *commitment* to (and in particular club coaches' *engagement* with) the federation and the federation's initiatives. Clubs noted that they "need to make time

for it (consultancy sessions)" (Club 2). However, TV 7 explained that some "club coaches don't make time for consultation sessions because if they have to give up four hours of coaching at their club to attend a consultation session, they lose 150 Euros. They think about their own income." In response to the issue, TV 4 explained,

> We send email invitations and call them to motivate them. Now we have criteria that club coaches need to meet to be a "KDT-coach": a certain coaching education level, attend consultancy sessions, communicate and report. Otherwise they don't receive recognition as [a] KDT coach. It is a pity that we have to force it like that.

Federation interviewees further indicated that IOR management required their commitment. However, clubs expressed that the federation prioritized its players (*internal priorities*). For instance, Club 4 argued, "The federation is too much focused on its own players. I doubt if the federation knows what is going on in each club." From a federation point of view, TV 4 indicated that "I don't think we could cooperate more with the clubs at the moment. We also have our job, our players here, so we need to make sure we get our work done here first." Also, TV 7 stated that if the federation was to dedicate more time to club players, it would need more personnel.

Results on IOR Outcomes and Evaluation

This section presents the findings on IOR outcomes and overall evaluation as well as emerging tensions in evaluating organizational partnerships and initiatives or joint programs.

Elite Player Development

The overall outcome of the club–federation partnership with respect to player development is captured by TV 3 as follows: "The better we [the federation] cooperate with clubs and coaches, the better for elite player development in Flanders." The joint player programs resulted in improved athlete development outcomes. Specifically, the clubs indicated that the cooperation with the federation helped achieve better quality player development as follows:

> KDT works really well for us and the players. Players really benefit from being part of KDT as they have more opportunities to play with better players and get expert coaching at the federation. The mentality, attitude and training atmosphere it [federation] creates through the KDT really helps to coach and educate the players more professionally. (Club 3)

The interviewees also agreed on the beneficial outcomes of the ESS to player development, including financial support, training partners, centralized support services, and flexible school conditions. Club 2 outlined the benefits of the ESS as follows:

> For [name of player], the choice was very clear. "Go to the Elite Sport School because we can no longer help you here, we don't have training partners and there is no budget from the parents for private coaching."

Even though it was generally accepted that the ESS program was a logical continuation for the best players to further develop, some clubs (in particular the clubs that had the resources to retain and develop players beyond the age of 12) were skeptical about "letting their best players go." It appeared that the centralized services of the ESS were a *source of tension* over the best players for well-resourced clubs capable of developing athletes further, as they perceived the existence of ESS as a way of "handing over" their best players to the federation without receiving any formal recognition for their contribution to player development. Club 6 noted that "unconsciously, there is some competition with the federation. If we see that our best players systematically go to the ESS, then I am almost better off to make them just not good enough so that they are not selected." In their evaluations, four clubs expressed their frustration with the outcomes of the ESS. For example, Club 6 indicated,

> The federation needs to lay out the strategy, but not at the expense of what goes well in the clubs. For example, [name of player] in our club meets the criteria to train at the ESS. But where did she "deserve" these criteria? Here [club]. And who gets the reward? That player . . . she is in very good hands here too and we have facilities to train her further. If all talented club players are invited to train at the ESS, then what's in it for the clubs? Clubs invest time in the better players and when push comes to shove players leave. Clubs do not receive much recognition. So who bears the brunt of having a good player development system in the club? That is actually the clubs themselves. The federation really needs to watch out that it does not obstruct the clubs who can offer equal quality development to players.

All clubs agreed that since the start of the joint programs (KDT and JDT), "the federation opened up itself and lets players develop predominantly in clubs with club coaches, whilst investing more in coaching the club coach to assure quality training" (Club 1). However, the clubs felt that the federation *prioritizes their own players*, and some clubs expressed the opinion that the federation should be more supportive of club players:

> The federation acts like a club that operates next to the other clubs, and that it does not really act like a federation. The federation should take care of all players, also if they chose to train in a club. Even though the federation is opening-up now and tries to cooperate more with clubs, it still doesn't. (Club 4)

Indeed, in their overall evaluation of partnership outcomes, the clubs expressed their hopes with respect to what Club 3 captured best: "I hope that the federation will support more players in the clubs, especially when they go travel for competitions. And hopefully, they will let the players longer in their clubs to develop" (Club 3).

Coach Development

Clubs recognized the benefits of club coaches' being offered opportunities to attend group training sessions of their players as well as participating in consultancy sessions to share information with federation coaches. The following quote illustrates the advantages of coaches' attending group training sessions of their players:

> We are invited to attend some of the group training sessions at the center which is a big advantage because then we can position the level of our players within their age group. I only have one very good U11 player at the club, so attending the group training sessions allows monitoring his progress compared to his age group. Also, I can discuss his [club player] progress with the federation coaches, and then they often discuss technical aspects with us which are always very interesting. (Club 2)

However, participating in consultations was somewhat problematic due to the nature of *coaching at club level*. Club 2, for instance, noted that "the consultancy sessions are really worth it for us . . . the feedback is worth it." However, "Tennis coaching at club level is often a secondary activity for people with another full time job" (TV 4), and other *work commitments* interfere with coaching commitments. TV 4 explained the problematic nature of the club coaches' commitments as follows: "It is difficult to motivate club coaches to come to the federation center." In assessing the situation and in acknowledgment of the restricted club coaches' time, the federation indicated that

> We could not communicate more, but maybe more efficiently. Communication can be done by phone or email, but most important is to meet the player and club coach in person at the federation, so that the player can play and we can discuss the player together. But then the club coaches need to reschedule their club training sessions. So we try to limit this to only a couple times a year. (TV 1)

Club 3 noted how the benefits of coach development and information sharing translate into athlete development as follows: "The more information we can share together, the more visions we can bring together about a player, it all adds value for the development of the player."

Club Management/Development

The use of labels (i.e., points system) appeared to stimulate clubs to meet certain *quality standards*: "The quality labels are good. It indicates what a club stands for and what they do. The way the criteria are made for the clubs is a bit complex, but it is good. It is also not easy to label the clubs" (Club 3). Club 2 added, "Most clubs who have the labels deserve it. And it stimulates to achieve the criteria. You need to invest in that, you need to make sure that your children go play on the Kinder tour, you need to motivate them and their parents." Also, Club 1 added that another benefit of that program for clubs was that "if we have the labels, it is a bit easier to find sponsors."

In evaluating the labels, some criticism also emerged. Even though quality labels appeared to stimulate clubs to meet certain quality standards, there was lack of *transparency* and *flexibility*. Club 7 noted that "how the club develops talented players appears not important to the federation, it is how you tell them you do it, it has to be according to their guidelines, to receive points." Club 6 noted "I think it is ridiculous that the federation cannot show some flexibility so that a player can train extra hours during school time. I think, sometimes the federation is too strict with its rules." This quote is an example that captures the ways in which some clubs were irritated by the federation's power and the necessity to comply with the rules.

Overall, clubs expressed positive views on their partnership with the federation and the ways their relationships have *improved over time*. Club 5 summarized this as follows:

> I think there has been already a positive evolution of the federation. Before it was the clubs against the federation, now it is cooperation. I think the federation should invest even more in the clubs and provide the clubs with support so that the clubs can get even better. If the clubs become better, then the players will become better. . . . if the clubs are stronger, the players can develop longer in their clubs.

The results on overall club satisfaction and partnership assessment varied depending on the club's capacity and resources. Specifically, well-resourced clubs with adequate athlete and coach development expertise expressed a different opinion as to the overall value of their partnerships with the federation than less resourced clubs. TV 1 drew a comparison as follows:

> I think that is a good system for the younger players with younger coaches who don't have much experience, in the smaller clubs. But once you have a good organization, where you have your own reports and aims and programs for the players, the federation reporting is just extra work, and you can question the added value.

It appeared that these partnerships "work well" for clubs that see value in the federation's involvement with player development and could use even more support. However, for the well-resourced clubs the evaluation of their overall partnership was not as favorable:

> Actually, we don't need the federation. I mean, what is their added value for us? Do our players get better when they train a couple times at the federation? It is difficult to measure. Is it a hassle for our players to go train there? Yes definitely. It means additional communication, reporting, while we have a system ourselves that is really good. We need to put our reports in the Dropbox system. (TV 1)

Similarly, the value of the federation's involvement with coach development was met with skepticism: "Those consultations for the coaches . . . there is nothing we did not know yet. We have a lot of expertise here. Our coaches have experience, so maybe we need those consultation sessions less than other coaches at smaller clubs" (TV 1).

Discussion

Developing elite tennis players was a common goal for the federation and clubs, and this reciprocity confirms that convergence of objectives (see Kouwenhoven, 1993) can be a condition for IOR formation. Clubs were interested in accessing financial benefits, gaining club coach expertise, and enabling club players to participate in group training sessions and at international tournaments under the guidance of federation coaches. The importance of obtaining resources in forming IORs is congruent with the findings of Babiak (2007), who argued that resources obtained through partnering can add strategic, functional, and operational value to the organizations. This finding is consistent with previous research (e.g., Alexander et al., 2008; Babiak, 2007), suggesting that organizations seek partnerships with organizations that have more expertise to use external knowledge to increase the efficiency of programs. In its role as the leading and coordinating organization for player development, the federation was also interested in forming IORs with clubs and sharing resources and information aimed at strengthening the clubs' capacity and club coaches' expertise in relation to player development. For the federation, efficiency reflected its ambition to ensure clubs can provide quality player development programs.

The federation's effort to portray itself as an open house, where players can train, get advice, and receive support, represents a strategy used to enhance its image and status and a means to legitimize its position within the sport system in Flanders. Image and reputation are important intangible resources that are derived from combinations of internal investments (the federation's efforts) and external evaluations (club evaluations; Kong & Farrell, 2010). In nonprofit settings, strong image and reputation are linked to higher quality and delivery of services or programs and the creation of a competitive advantage (Boyd, Bergh, & Ketchen, 2010). This stance accurately reflects the definition of legitimacy as a "generalized perception or assumption that the actions of an entity are desirable, proper, or appropriate within some socially constructed system of norms, values, beliefs and definitions" (Suchman, 1995, p. 574). Indeed, evidence in this study supports Suchman's (1995) seminal work on organizational legitimacy, which suggests that organizational efforts to strengthen legitimacy have an effect on how other entities (i.e., clubs) perceive the organization as more meaningful and trustworthy. The federation's efforts for legitimacy is deeply rooted in the traditional hierarchy of sport structures where federations, as governing bodies for sport, are typically superior to clubs in the sport system (Shilbury & Kellett, 2011).

The results illustrate IOR power relationships and the positioning of the two types of organizations in the sport system in Flanders. According to Etzioni's (1964) categorization of power, the federation exercised "utilitarian" power, generated through its financial resources (e.g., equipment, programs, financial support to clubs) and "normative" power formed through symbols of prestige and esteem (e.g., quality labels). Quality labels (e.g., the Youth Fund) emerged as a way for the federation to exercise power and control over clubs, expressing an asymmetry in their relationship. At the same time, it was necessary for clubs to comply with federation regulations and meet certain criteria to receive recognition through the quality labels. Hence, the federation's asymmetry was directly linked to the club's necessity for IOR formation. As predicted theoretically, relationship formation on the contingency of asymmetry "creates interdependencies that necessitate the loss of decision-making latitude and discretion" (Birškytė, 2012, p. 178). Furthermore, the type of quality label determined the amount of subsidies provided to clubs. To achieve stability, clubs tended to comply with the federation's rules and tried to achieve high-quality labels. The emergence of stability as a factor in partnering with the federation is not surprising given that previous research has highlighted the high need for sport clubs to attain resources (Wicker & Breuer, 2011). Particularly at a competitive level, sports can be time and cost intensive, for both the athletes and the sports club (Breuer & Wicker, 2009). Hence, clubs with competitive athletes tend to have higher expenditures for coaches' salaries, training lessons, and competition fees (Wicker, 2011).

The results suggest that the management and evaluation of club–federation IORs revolved around player development programs (e.g., joint player development programs for players under the age of 12). Even though the joint player development programs represented a strategy that promoted harmonious relationships and facilitated elite player development, the federation's centralized program (i.e., the ESS) for players over the age of 12 was a source of tension for clubs that felt capable of continuing to develop these players yet their players would transition to the ESS. Specifically, some clubs expressed their frustration in losing their best players to the ESS without receiving any recognition for their time and effort in player development. An interesting finding from a study on the effectiveness of ESS in Flanders (De Bosscher, De Knop, & Vertonghen, 2016) revealed that ESS athletes highly commended the quality of club coaches and coaching services offered at club level

instead of the ESS. Similar to MacLean et al.'s (2011) findings on basketball clubs' losing their best players to rival clubs, the current study highlighted that these tensions can also be evident between clubs and the federation, articulated through clubs' concerns over losing their best players to train in the ESS. This centralized program appeared to create friction in IORs as it is likely that these clubs lost trust in the federation to develop players after the age of 12. This collaboration–competition dichotomy was evident in Babiak's (2007) finding that reciprocity stimulated cooperation and at the same time having the same goal caused conflict, power, and control issues. Babiak and Thibault (2009) also noted that even though organizations in the Canadian sport system collaborated, they also competed on different levels for resources, including athletes.

Clear division of roles was an essential approach in coordinating IORs. Specifically, the federation and the clubs were clear in relation to the joint programs and the role of club coaches in those programs as the parties responsible for the development of talented players. In the division of roles, the federation was clearly responsible for offering guidance, feedback, and consultancy to club coaches and players, which facilitated the coordination of IORs. Clearly defined roles and responsibilities imply a well-managed relationship (e.g., Babiak & Thibault, 2008, 2009; Frisby et al., 2004) and accountability. In addition, written reports were a way of formally exchanging information and sharing knowledge on programs and aspects of athlete progress. Division of roles, responsibilities, and reporting mechanisms are typical traits of highly formalized sport organizations (Theodoraki & Henry, 1994). Organizational structures characterized by formalized procedures, roles, and programs and specialized roles for volunteers are indicative of "the Boardroom" design archetype (Kikulis, Slack, & Hinings, 1992). In the boardroom domain, the acceptance of public/government funds places greater pressure on recipients to satisfy the government's interest in the development of elite athletes and their performance at international competitions. Consequently, organizations are evaluated in terms of the bureaucratic practices they have in place and the support they provide for domestic and high-performance sport program units (Macintosh & Whitson, 1990). By implication, federations focus exclusively on their national high-performance sport programs and introduce more professional control over the direction of their organization. This further explains the asymmetry in club–federation relationships.

There was evidence that formalization enabled the federation to be explicit about its structure and requirements in relation to elite athlete development. However, formalization was also a source of frustration for club coaches who had difficulties complying with several reporting requirements. Lucidarme et al. (2014) suggested that when working with volunteers, or people that have another full-time job and engage in a partnership after work hours, there is less time to commit in that partnership. Hence, it is likely that when club coaches have another full-time job, their availability to commit to the federation's training sessions, consultancies, and reporting requirement is restricted. Moreover, the results showed that club coaches often prioritized the operation of their own club. Similarly, the federation indicated the need to focus its resources on its own players first, before providing support to external players. Based on the results, prioritizing their internal goals may be explained on the basis of the federation's call for additional personnel to foster its cooperation with club coaches. Hence, there may be room for both types of organization to manage their IORs better and improve their player development outcomes.

Theoretical and Practical Considerations

From a theoretical point of view, this paper complements existing studies (e.g., Alexander et al., 2008; Frisby et al., 2004; Misener & Doherty, 2012, 2014) as it extends the application of IORs to elite athlete development (e.g., Babiak, 2007). In particular, this paper contributes to the ongoing discussion on the ways IORs enable sport organizations to achieve common goals, in this instance, elite athlete development. Figure 2 is a preliminary presentation of player development IORs between a federation and tennis clubs. This dyadic examination of IORs enabled the depiction of IOR motives for forming relationships and the mechanisms used to manage these relationships (see Figure 2). It also allowed the identification of the positive role that joint programs and clear divisions of roles have on elite athlete development. Joint athlete development programs allowed the clubs and the

federation to work together, exchange information, and increase efficiencies in their operations (Oliver, 1990).

Sotiriadou, Brouwers, and De Bosscher (2016) explained that despite some variations across countries, clubs, national and state organizations, as well as education and private providers are all key partners in elite pathways and create an integrated network of IOR partners. Figure 3 shows that at the heart of IORs between the NSO and the clubs are the ARTN *athlete development outcomes* (Green, 2005; Sotiriadou et al., 2008). This study demonstrated that for sport organizations to achieve these outcomes and maximize effectiveness in athlete development, there is a need for cooperation, consultation, and involvement from both types of organizations. Specifically, Figure 3 shows that there are three categories of *motives* that can drive the formation of IORs. These are the motives that drive the NSO to form partnerships with clubs, the motives that drive clubs to work with the NSO, and motives common to both types of organizations. These categories of formation motives (or antecedents to IOR formation) lead into two types of *management control mechanisms*: formal and informal. Control mechanisms can either facilitate or potentially hinder athlete development progression in three key areas: coach development, club development, and player development. In particular, partnerships are particularly useful during the *attraction*, *retention*, and *transition* processes of athlete development. Hence, it is concluded that IORs between the NSO and clubs/academics can result in efficiencies in athlete development. Efficiencies occur in spite of situations (e.g., centralization of key services, prioritization of internal athletes, and time pressures of

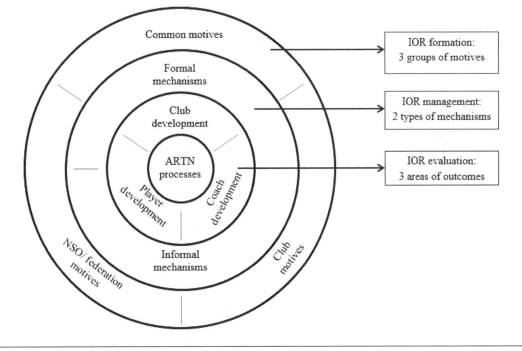

Figure 3 — The influence of interorganizational relationship (IOR) on the attraction, retention/transition, and nurturing (ARTN) processes of athlete development. NSO = national sporting organization.

coaches) where partners (e.g., well-resourced clubs) are confronted with issues (e.g., losing elite players to the ESS, being unable to nurture them beyond a certain age) that represent barriers or potential areas of conflict in relation to effective athlete progression within the ARTN processes. This finding reiterates that the final stage of athlete development (the *nurturing* process in the ARTN) in the system is occurring at a higher level (e.g., national) and to a degree controlled by NSOs.

The findings in this study pinpoint the influence that the centralized services the federation offered to clubs has had on the evaluation for IORs. Specifically, well-resourced clubs expressed dissatisfaction in their overall evaluation as centralized training, poaching of athletes, and compulsory coaching consultancy sessions were of a lesser value to them. These findings offer new knowledge in the area of managing elite sport because they link (a) sport development outcomes to organizational capacity and (b) organizational capacity to the centralized approach in managing elite sports. It can be concluded that, in the case of Flanders, a centralized system can present a barrier to elite athlete development for the most resource-capable clubs. These findings help augment a growing body of literature on managing high-performance sport. Specifically, in their study on the organizational capacity of five sport systems (including Flanders), Truyens, De Bosscher, and Sotiriadou (2016) examined the role of organizational resources and demonstrated that different sport systems have diverse resource configurations, especially in relation to program centralization, athlete development, and funding prioritization.

Various formal and informal control mechanisms (e.g., Babiak & Thibault, 2008) illustrated the ways these organizations interact and the challenges they encounter. These interactions and challenges represent various managerial and practical implications. Given that the clubs' capacities to deliver player development pathways vary, federations should gain knowledge of the clubs' and club coaches' capacity to develop athletes and aim to tailor their support and manage their partnerships on that premise. For example, clubs with only a few KDT players might need more group training sessions at the federation center than clubs with many KDT players that can occasionally organize their own high-level group training.

This knowledge and adaptation of IORs based on clubs' capacity to deliver players at various development stages is significant for another reason. The club–federation IORs for developing players under the age of 12 (e.g., joint program KDT) were in principle harmonious. However, their IORs became strained as tensions emerged when clubs felt undermined and lost their best players to the ESS. These clubs received no recognition for developing players who met selection criteria to train at the ESS. This tension and lack of recognition could potentially undermine the drive for these clubs to stay interested and engaged with player development. In response, federations might have to consider allowing players to train longer at well-resourced clubs with their club coach, and invest more in providing external support to the clubs

(e.g., financial), club coaches (e.g., consultancy sessions), and players (e.g., international tournament support and group training), instead of centralizing the best players at the ESS from the age of 12. Moreover, a rewards system (e.g., subsidies, equipment, or training support) that enhances club capacities to deliver player development outcomes may be an essential strategy to manage IORs tensions and encourage clubs to continue enabling elite player development. Clubs that have the resources to develop elite players might welcome some flexibility from the federation to implement player development programs more autonomously.

Conclusion and Future Research Directions

The examination of IORs between local tennis clubs and a tennis federation provided insights into their roles, actions, and interactions (Andersen et al., 2015) within the elite player development system in Flanders. Even though the results of this study may be relevant to other sports similar to tennis (e.g., middle to late specialization, commercialized sports, or sports where clubs engage in athlete development), it is important to interpret the findings with caution as the focus of this study was on a specific sport within a specific sport system. Hence, it is likely that in other sports or countries IOR formation and management between clubs and the federation may vary widely. As Kikulis et al. (1992) argued, investigations of a set of organizations "require a consideration of the unique organizational interactions and the context in which they have developed" (p. 348). For instance, early specialization sports (e.g., gymnastics) might require federations to set up elite athlete development–related IORs with clubs at an earlier stage of athlete development. Similarly, there are sports where athletes transition from another activity (e.g., transition from gymnastics to diving or aerial skiing). It is likely that the club–federation IORs for the organizations to which athletes transfer might be less prominent or important for athlete development. Therefore, as Kikulis et al. (1992) predicted, future research should continue exploring sport-specific IOR interactions and context.

A further consideration is the potential limitations that examining a relatively small region (Flanders, the Dutch-speaking community of Belgium) may present to this study. Flanders covers an area of 13,522 km^2 and has a population of 6.2 million (Belgian Federal Government, 2013). Hence, Flanders is a small region in comparison with some tennis champion powerhouses including Spain, France, and the United States. It is likely that the geographic proximity between clubs and the federation in Flanders facilitates a coordinated approach to player development and the implementation of joint programs. In the case of Flanders, it is relatively easy to organize group training session, and coach consultancy sessions do not require excessive travel, management, or coordination other than clear communication. In larger countries, IOR formation and management may present challenges due to distance and access to, and costs associated with, transportation or travel time. In addition, the presence of RSOs or SSOs in larger or federated countries (e.g., Canada and Australia) means that IORs may not be dyadic, and thus, may be more difficult to manage (Alexander et al., 2008). Therefore, future research is recommended to examine how IORs may facilitate elite athlete development in larger countries, how these countries overcome challenges related to distance, and the involvement of more than two partner organizations.

Last, this study offers insights into IOR formation and management at a certain point in time. Pressures for clubs to manage athlete development in a professional and efficient way can lead to increasing their expertise and capacities (Sotiriadou & Wicker, 2013). As clubs improve the quality of player development programs, their coaches gain more expertise and knowledge. As larger numbers of clubs achieve high standards, it is likely that interactions with the federation will change over time. Therefore, federations might need to adapt their joint programs and support to the clubs according to the growing athlete development capacities of clubs. Moreover, the federation might need to consider the role and operation of its ESS as tensions between the federation and clubs are likely to grow when more clubs can provide high quality player development programs and developmental continuity for players over the age of 12. Hence, as Alexander et al. (2008) suggested, it is important to explore the ways IORs evolve over time. A study of this nature would allow sport organizations to revisit the management of IORs over time and adapt accordingly.

In this study, joint elite athlete development programs and transparency in roles and responsibilities represent the cornerstones of federation-club cooperation. IORs appear to operate under a fine line as a frequently harmonious cooperation can be tainted when organizations prioritize their own interests. The federation's centralized services can also disturb IOR balance as clubs lose successful athletes to the training center, without recognition of their contributions and with no real opportunities to offer development continuity to their athletes. To strategically foster IORs, clubs' interest and motivation to continue their elite development contribution is essential because undermanaged partnerships between federations and clubs can result in losing the clubs as a key stakeholder in elite player development.

References

Alexander, T., Thibault, L., & Frisby, W. (2008). Avoiding separation: Sport partner perspectives on a long-term inter-organisational relationship. *International Journal of Sport Management and Marketing, 3*, 263–280. doi:10.1504/IJSMM.2008.017192

Andersen, S.S., Houlihan, B., & Ronglan, L.T. (2015). Systems and the development of elite athletes. In S.S. Andersen, B. Houlihan, & L.T. Ronglan (Eds.), *Managing elite sport systems: Research and practice* (pp. 3–15). New York, NY: Routledge.

Babiak, K. (2003). *Examining partnerships in amateur sport: The case of a Canadian National Sport Centre* (Unpublished doctoral dissertation). University of British Columbia, Vancouver, Canada.

Babiak, K. (2007). Determinants of interorganizational relationships: The case of a Canadian nonprofit sport organization. *Journal of Sport Management, 21*, 338–376.

Babiak, K.M. (2009). Criteria of effectiveness in multiple cross-sectoral interorganizational relationships. *Evaluation and Program Planning, 32*, 1–12. doi:10.1016/j.evalprogplan.2008.09.004

Babiak, K., & Thibault, L. (2008). Managing inter-organisational relationships: The art of plate spinning. *International Journal of Sport Management and Marketing, 3(3)*, 281–302. doi:10.1504/IJSMM.2008.017193

Babiak, K., & Thibault, L. (2009). Challenges in multiple cross-sector partnerships. *Nonprofit and Voluntary Sector Quarterly, 38(1)*, 117–143. doi:10.1177/0899764008316054

Barnes, M., Cousens, L., & MacLean, J. (2007). From silos to synergies: A network perspective of the Canadian sport system. *International Journal of Sport Management and Marketing, 2*, 555–571. doi:10.1504/IJSMM.2007.013967

Belgian Federal Government. (2013). Statistics Belguim. Retrieved from http://statbel.fgov.be/nl/statistieken/cijfers/bevolking/structuur/woonplaats/oppervlakte_dichtheid/

Birškytė, L. (2012). Fostering inter-organisational relationships as a way to increase efficiency in tax administration. *Intelektinė Ekonomika (Intellectual Economics), 6(2)*, 174–188.

Bloyce, D., Smith, A., Mead, R., & Morris, J. (2008). "Playing the Game (Plan)": A figurational analysis of organizational change in sports development in England. *European Sport Management Quarterly, 8*, 359–378. doi:10.1080/16184740802461637

Boyd, B.K., Bergh, D.D., & Ketchen, D.J. (2010). Reconsidering the reputation–performance relationship: A resource-based view. *Journal of Management, 36*, 588–609. doi:10.1177/0149206308328507

Breuer, C., & Wicker, P. (2009). Leistungs- und Hochleistungssport im Sportverein. In C. Breuer (Ed.), *Sportentwicklungsbericht 2007/2008: Analyse zur Situation der Sportvereine in Deutschland.* Cologne, Germany: Sportverlag Strauß.

Brouwers, J., Sotiriadou, P., & De Bosscher, V. (2015a). An examination of the stakeholders and elite player development pathways in tennis. *European Sport Management Quarterly, 15*, 454–477. doi:10.1080/16184742.2015.1067239

Brouwers, J., Sotiriadou, P., & De Bosscher, V. (2015b). Sport-specific policies and factors that influence international success: The case of tennis. *Sport Management Review, 18*, 343–358. doi:10.1016/j.smr.2014.10.003

Child, J., & Faulkner, D. (1998). *Strategies of cooperation.* London, UK: Oxford Press.

De Bosscher, V. (2007). *Sports policy factors leading to international sporting success* (Doctoral dissertation). Brussels, Belgium: VUBPRESS.

De Bosscher, V., De Knop, P., & Vertonghen, J. (2016). A multidimensional approach to evaluate the policy effectiveness of elite sport schools in Flanders. *Sport in Society, 19,* 1596–1621.

Etzioni, A. (1964). *Modern organizations.* Englewood Cliffs, NJ: Prentice-Hall.

Frisby, W., Thibault, L., & Kikulis, L. (2004). The organizational dynamics of under-managed partnerships in leisure service departments. *Leisure Studies, 23,* 109–126. doi:10.1080/0261436042000224482

Green, B.C. (2005). Building sport programs to optimize athlete recruitment, retention, and transition: Toward a normative theory of sport development. *Journal of Sport Management, 19*(3), 233–253

Hashemnezhad, H. (2015). Qualitative content analysis research: A review article. *Journal of ELT and Applied Linguistics, 3*(1), 54–62.

Hsieh, H.F., & Shannon, S.E. (2005). Three approaches to qualitative content analysis. *Qualitative Health Research, 15*(9), 1277–1288. doi:10.1177/1049732305276687

Huxham, C., & Vangen, S. (1996). Working together: Key themes in the management of relationships between public and nonprofit organizations. *International Journal of Public Sector Management, 9,* 5–17. doi:10.1108/09513559610153863

Kernaghan, K. (1993). Partnership and public administration: Conceptual and practical considerations. *Canadian Public Administration, 36,* 57–76. doi:10.1111/j.1754-7121.1993.tb02166.x

Kikulis, L.M., Slack, T., & Hinings, B. (1992). Institutionally specific design archetypes: A framework for understanding change in national sport organizations. *International Review for the Sociology of Sport, 27,* 343–368. doi:10.1177/101269029202700405

Kong, E., & Farrell, M. (2010). *The role of image and reputation as intangible resources in non-profit organisations: A relationship management perspective* (p. 245). In E. Tsui, Proceedings of the 7th International conference on intellectual capital, knowledge management and organizational learning. Hong Kong Polytechnic University, China.

Kouwenhoven, V. (1993). The rise of the public private partnership: A model for the management of public-private cooperation. In J. Kooiman (Ed.), *Modern governance: New government-society interactions* (pp. 119–130). London, UK: Sage.

Liebenau, L. (2010). *Sport development pathways for amateur golfers: The case study of Queensland* (Unpublished honour's thesis). Bond University, Australia.

Lucidarme, S., Marlier, M., Cardon, G., De Bourdeaudhuij, I., & Willem, A. (2014). Critical success factors for physical activity promotion through community partnerships. *International Journal of Public Health, 59,* 51–60. doi:10.1007/s00038-013-0527-5

Macintosh, D., & Whitson, D. (1990). *The game planners: Transforming Canada's sport system.* Montreal, Canada: McGill-Queen's University Press.

Mackintosh, C. (2011). An analysis of County Sports Partnerships in England: The fragility, challenges and complexity of partnership working in sports development. *International Journal of Sport Policy and Politics, 3,* 45–64. doi:10.1080/19406940.2010.524809

MacLean, J., Cousens, L., & Barnes, M. (2011). Look who's linked with whom: A case study of one community basketball network. *Journal of Sport Management, 25,* 562–575. doi:10.1123/jsm.25.6.562

Martindale, R.J.J., Collins, D., & Daubney, J. (2005). Talent development: A guide for practice and research within sport. *Quest, 57,* 353–375. doi:10.1080/00336297.2005.10491862

Misener, K.E., & Doherty, A. (2012). Connecting the community through sport club partnerships. *International Journal of Sport Policy and Politics, 4,* 243–255. doi:10.1080/19406940.2012.674962

Misener, K., & Doherty, A. (2013). Understanding capacity through the processes and outcomes of interorganizational relationships in nonprofit community sport organizations. *Sport Management Review, 16,* 135–147. doi:10.1016/j.smr.2012.07.003

Misener, K., & Doherty, A. (2014). In support of sport: Examining the relationship between community sport organizations and sponsors. *Sport Management Review, 17,* 493–506. doi:10.1016/j.smr.2013.12.002

Newland, B., & Kellett, P. (2012). Exploring new models of elite sport delivery: The case of triathlon in the USA and Australia. *Managing Leisure, 17,* 170–181. doi:10.1080/13606719.2012.674393

Oliver, C. (1990). Determinants of interorganizational relationships: Integration and future directions. *Academy of Management Review, 15,* 241–265.

Parent, M.M., & Harvey, J. (2009). Towards a management model for sport and physical activity community-based partnerships. *European Sport Management Quarterly, 9,* 23–45. doi:10.1080/16184740802461694

Patton, M.Q. (2002). *Qualitative evaluation and research methods.* London, UK: Sage.

Phillips, P., & Newland, B. (2014). Emergent models of sport development and delivery: The case of triathlon in Australia and the US. *Sport Management Review, 17,* 107–120. doi:10.1016/j.smr.2013.07.001

Shilbury, D., & Kellett, P. (2011). *Sport management in Australia: An organisational overview.* Crows Nest, Australia: Allen & Unwin.

Smith, A.C.T., & Shilbury, D. (2004). Mapping cultural dimensions in Australian sporting organisations. *Sport Management Review, 7*(2), 133–165. doi:10.1016/S1441-3523(04)70048-0

Sotiriadou, K. (2009). The Australian sport system and its stakeholders: Development of cooperative relationships. *Sport in Society, 12,* 842–860. doi:10.1080/17430430903053067

Sotiriadou, P., Brouwers, J., & De Bosscher, V. (2016). High performance development pathways. In E. Sherry, N. Schulenkorf, & P. Phillips (Eds.), *Managing sport development: An international approach* (pp. 64–76). New York, NY: Routledge.

Sotiriadou, P., Brouwers, J., & Le, T.A. (2014). Choosing a qualitative data analysis tool: A comparison of NVivo and

Leximancer. *Annals of Leisure Research, 17*, 218–234. doi:10.1080/11745398.2014.902292

Sotiriadou, K., Quick, S., & Shilbury, D. (2006). Sport for some: Elite versus mass participation. *International Journal of Sport Management, 7*, 50–66.

Sotiriadou, P., & Shilbury, D. (2009). Australian elite athlete development: An organisational perspective. *Sport Management Review, 12*(3), 137–148. doi:10.1016/j.smr.2009.01.002

Sotiriadou, P., & Shilbury, D. (2010). Using grounded theory in sport management research. *International Journal of Sport Management and Marketing, 8*(3–4), 181–202. doi:10.1504/IJSMM.2010.037503

Sotiriadou, K., Shilbury, D., & Quick, S. (2008). The attraction, retention/transition, and nurturing process of sport development: Some Australian evidence. *Journal of Sport Management, 22*, 247–272. doi:10.1123/jsm.22.3.247

Sotiriadou, P., & Wicker, P. (2013). Community sports clubs' responses to institutional and resource dependence pressures for government grants. *Annals of Leisure Research, 16*, 297–314. doi:10.1080/11745398.2013.853338

Soulliere, D., Britt, D.W., & Maines, D.R. (2001). Conceptual modeling as a toolbox for grounded theorists. *The Sociological Quarterly, 42*, 253–269. doi:10.1111/j.1533-8525.2001.tb00033.x

Stenling, C., & Fahlén, J. (2014). Same same, but different? Exploring the organizational identities of Swedish voluntary sports: Possible implications of sports clubs' self-identification for their role as implementers of policy objectives. *International Review for the Sociology of Sport.* Advance online publication.

Suchman, M.C. (1995). Managing legitimacy: Strategic and institutional approaches. *Academy of Management Review, 20*, 571–610.

Taks, M., & Kesenne, S. (2000). The economic significance of sport in Flanders. *Journal of Sport Management, 14*, 342–365. doi:10.1123/jsm.14.4.342

Tennis Vlaanderen. (2009). Strategic plan 2009–2012. Brussels, Belgium: [Author].

Tennis Vlaanderen. (2013a). Jaarverslag 2013 [Annual report 2013]. Brussels, Belgium: [Author].

Tennis Vlaanderen. (2013b). Strategic plan 2013–2016. Brussels, Belgium: [Author].

Theodoraki, E.I., & Henry, I.P. (1994). Organisational structures and contexts in British national governing bodies of sport. *International Review for the Sociology of Sport, 29*, 243–265. doi:10.1177/101269029402900302

Truyens, J., De Bosscher, V., & Sotiriadou, P. (2016). An analysis of countries' organizational resources, capacities and resource configurations in athletics. *Journal of Sport Management.* doi:10.1123/jsm.2015-0368

Weber, R.P. (1990). *Basic content analysis* (2nd ed.). Newbury Park, CA: Sage. doi:10.4135/9781412983488

Wicker, P. (2011). Willingness-to-pay in non-profit sports clubs. *International Journal of Sport Finance, 6*, 155–169.

Wicker, P., & Breuer, C. (2011). Scarcity of resources in German non-profit sport clubs. *Sport Management Review, 14*, 188–201. doi:10.1016/j.smr.2010.09.001

Willem, A., & Lucidarme, S. (2014). Pitfalls and challenges for trust and effectiveness in collaborative networks. *Public Management Review, 16*, 733–760. doi:10.1080/14719037.2012.744426

Winand, M., Zintz, T., Bayle, E., & Robinson, L. (2010). Organizational performance of Olympic sport governing bodies: Dealing with measurement and priorities. *Managing Leisure, 15*(4), 279–307. doi:10.1080/13606719.2010.508672

Yin, R.K. (1994). *Case study research: Design and methods* (2nd ed.). Newbury Park, CA: Sage.

Journal of Sport Management, 2017, 31, 80-95
https://doi.org/10.1123/jsm.2016-0044
© 2017 Human Kinetics, Inc.

Consumers' Perceived Value of Sport Team Games—A Multidimensional Approach

Thilo Kunkel

Temple University

Jason Patrick Doyle

Griffith University

Alexander Berlin

Friedrich Schiller University of Jena

Consumers' evaluations of their favorite sport team's contests are influenced by the value that the team provides to them. The current research contributes to the sport management literature through conceptualizing and measuring the dimensions that influence the perceived value consumers link with their favorite sport team's games and testing the explanatory ability of this perceived value on their satisfaction with, and commitment toward, the team. Five semistructured expert interviews were conducted to conceptualize perceived value dimensions and measurement items. Next, a multidimensional Consumers' Perceived Value of Sport Games scale (CPVSG) was developed and tested across two studies with football (soccer) consumers ($N_1 = 225$; $N_2 = 382$) in Germany. Results from confirmatory factor and structural equation modeling analyses indicate that five dimensions—functional, social, emotional, epistemic, and economic value—reflect perceived value dimensions that consumers associate with sport team games. Results also indicated these perceived value dimensions were predictive of consumers' satisfaction with, and commitment toward, their favorite team. Thus, this research adds to the literature by providing the multidimensional CPVSG scale and demonstrating its value in explaining variance in attitudinal outcome variables.

Keywords: consumer value, satisfaction, commitment, perceived value

Sport teams face strong competition from each other as well as from alternate entertainment options that compete for consumer attention (Mullin, Hardy, & Sutton, 2007). Teams need to attract and retain enough fans so they generate sufficient operating revenue to remain sustainable (James, Kolbe, & Trail, 2002). Given the ever-increasing number of sport- and nonsport-related entertainment activities available today, teams need to adopt a consumer-oriented approach and demonstrate value to consumers to remain competitive. Within the

sport context, a game between two teams represents the core product (or service), which is an important source of income (Mason, 1999). Research illustrates that the top 20 football (soccer) teams in Europe receive approximately 20% of their annual revenue from game-day attendance (Deloitte, 2014). Consumer attendance at games also impacts revenues derived from merchandise and sponsorship sales, further illustrating the role that the core product plays in contributing to overall organizational performance (Mason, 1999).

Sport research has begun to evidence the link between the perceived value consumers attribute to team games and attitudinal and behavioral outcomes (e.g., Byon, Zhang, & Baker, 2013; Cronin, Brady, & Hult, 2000; Hightower, Brady, & Baker, 2002; Kwon, Trail, & James, 2007; Wakefield, 1995). Although such research has provided a number of contributions to knowledge surrounding sport consumer value perceptions, there is a need to advance understandings by adopting broader conceptualizations of the value attached to sport team games. Specifically, research to date has preferred to use

Thilo Kunkel is with the School of Sport, Tourism and Hospitality Management & Fox School of Business, Temple University, Philadelphia, PA. Jason Patrick Doyle is with the Department of Tourism, Sport and Hotel Management, Griffith Business School, Griffith University, Nathan Campus, Brisbane, Australia. Alexander Berlin is with the Department of Sports Economics and Health Economics, Friedrich Schiller University of Jena, Jena, Germany. Address author correspondence to Thilo Kunkel at thilo.kunkel@temple.edu.

a unidimensional conceptualization of perceived value, providing an opportunity for further work that captures the broader domains that contribute to consumer value perceptions within the sport context.

Consumers' perceived value has been conceptualized in two ways: as a one-dimensional construct or as a multidimensional construct (cf. Graf & Maas, 2008; Sánchez-Fernández & Iniesta-Bonillo, 2007). The one-dimensional approach treats consumers' perceived value as a cognitive trade-off between perceived quality and perceived costs (e.g., Dodds, Monroe, & Grewal, 1991; Sweeney, Soutar, & Johnson, 1999; Zeithaml, 1988). This conceptualization focuses on the functional aspects of perceived value, assuming consumers are rational and make consumption decisions solely based on the price of the product or service they are consuming (Sánchez-Fernández & Iniesta-Bonillo, 2007). While this approach may be appropriate for research on fast-moving consumer goods, defining value purely from a cost assessment perspective does not adequately reflect the nature of the sport consumption experience. Sport consumption is highly emotive (Mullin et al., 2007) and motivated by a range of facets (e.g., Funk, Filo, Beaton, & Pritchard 2009; Funk & James, 2001), where even perennially unsuccessful teams have been shown to possess loyal consumers who evaluate the team positively on at least some dimension (e.g., Bristow & Sebastian, 2001; Doyle, Lock, Funk, Filo, & McDonald, in press; Lock, Funk, Doyle, & McDonald, 2014). Thus, the value domains linked to sport consumption are multifaceted and require further exploration (Lee, Trail, Kwon, & Anderson, 2011).

Although mainstream marketing literature has adapted comprehensive multidimensional approaches to examine consumer value perceptions (e.g., Sweeney & Soutar, 2001), sport researchers have generally used simplistic one-dimensional approaches (cf. Cronin et al., 2000; Hightower et al., 2002). To address this identified gap, a concise multidimensional Consumers' Perceived Value of Sport Games (CPVSG) scale was developed to investigate the influence of the perceived value of team games on consumers' satisfaction with, and commitment toward, their favorite team. The research integrates brand association, sport motive, and service quality literature streams to address the following research question: *What is the relationship between consumers' perceived value of sport games and their attitudes toward their favorite sport teams?*

Literature Review

Theoretical Framework

The theory of consumption values (Sheth, Newman, & Gross, 1991) provides a multidimensional conceptualization of consumers' perceived value and is the guiding framework we use to explore the perceived value of sport team games. The theory outlines that a consumer's overall value perceptions are derived from five dimensions—functional value, social value, emotional value, epistemic value, and conditional value. Sheth et al. (1991) proposed the five dimensions influenced consumer attitudes and decision-making yet operated independently from one another. This theorization expanded on the unidimensional conceptualization of value and provided greater variability for researchers to account for the various ways in which consumers evaluate products and services and how these evaluations shape subsequent attitudes and behaviors.

Sweeney and Soutar (2001) used the theory of consumption values as a basis to develop the multidimensional PERVAL (Perceived Value) scale, consisting of four distinct value domains. However, unlike Sheth et al. (1991), Sweeney and Soutar suggested the four value dimensions were interrelated as consumers' perceptions of one dimension (e.g., functional value) may influence their perceptions of another dimension (e.g., economic value). Within the PERVAL, Sweeney and Soutar also argued that the conceptual functional value dimension consisted of two dimensions—quality and price—and that the theorized conditional and epistemic dimensions were not applicable for inclusion in their scale development research. Conditional value was eliminated on conceptual grounds because it represented an outcome of the functional, social, and emotional dimensions. Similarly, epistemic value was not considered because the study was conducted in the context of "durable goods" for which epistemic value was not applicable. However, it was suggested that epistemic value represented a valid dimension in some consumption settings, in particular when products or services are examined that require specific knowledge or expertise (Sweeney & Soutar, 2001).

In contrast with Sheth et al. (1991), Sweeney and Soutar (2001), as noted above, argued that functional value conceptually consisted of two dimensions—price and quality. This conceptualization has been adopted in subsequent research, including studies assessing consumers' perceived value of sportswear (Chi & Kilduff, 2011). In the theory of consumption values (Sheth et al., 1991), the dimension of functional value contains aspects of performance, reliability, durability, and price. Sweeney and Soutar drew upon supporting literature to argue that performance, reliability, and durability represented perceived quality, rather than perceived value (Dodds et al., 1991, Zeithaml, 1988). Accordingly, it was proposed perceived price represented another dimension, because "quality and price are held to have separate influences on perceived value; quality having a positive and price a negative effect" (Sweeney & Soutar, 2001, p. 206). Therefore, price was separated from functional value to represent the economic value consumers derive from a product or service. As a result, Sweeney and Soutar's final multidimensional PERVAL scale contained the four dimensions—functional value, economic value, social value, and emotional value.

We draw upon the conceptual similarities that exist between the theory of consumption values (Sheth et al., 1991) and existing scale development work on consumer value perceptions (e.g., PERVAL; Sweeney & Soutar,

2001) to conceptualize the value domains linked with the consumption of sport team games. This approach is consistent with Lee et al. (2011), who suggested the PERVAL scale could be adapted and modified to better fit the sport context and called for the development of more robust measurement tools. Here, we conceptually align with Sweeney and Soutar (2001) in the belief that the dimensions are interrelated, as perceptions surrounding one dimension may influence another. We also exclude conditional value from our conceptualization, as it functions as an outcome of other dimensions, and include price and quality as two separate dimensions (Sweeney & Soutar, 2001). In addition, we acknowledge the exclusion of epistemic value from the PERVAL was as a result of the context in which that scale was developed. Due to theoretical and practical considerations, we therefore include epistemic value in this research because sport teams represent complex entities toward which consumers can have varying levels of knowledge and expertise (e.g., Sheth et al., 1991; Sweeney & Soutar, 2001). Therefore, the proposed conceptualization of consumers' perceived value of sport team games contains five dimensions—functional value, economic value, social value, emotional value, and epistemic value.

Functional Value

Functional value represents the utility derived from the perceived quality and expected performance of sport team games (Sweeney & Soutar, 2001). Previous research indicates sport consumers who attribute various forms of value to their sport consumption experience higher levels of satisfaction (Brady, Vorhees, Cronin, & Bourdeau, 2006; Cronin et al., 2000) and commitment (Hightower et al., 2002). These studies indicate three main aspects influence consumers' perceptions of functional value—the service environment, related service personnel, and the performance of the team. First, the service environment includes consumers' perception of the stadium where the game takes place (Hightower et al., 2002; Hill & Green, 2000, 2012; Wakefield, Blodgett, & Sloan, 1996). Second, service personnel are the employees with whom the consumer interacts while consuming the game (Theodorakis & Alexandris, 2008). Third, the performance of the team refers to perceptions of how the team functions during the match (Brady et al., 2006). Overall, the service environment, related service personnel, and the performance of the team have been linked with positive consumer behavior related to sport teams and are therefore conceptualized as three factors representing consumers' functional value of sport team games.

Social Value

Social value represents the utility derived from the ability of sport team game consumption to enhance social self-capital (Sweeney & Soutar, 2001). Sheth et al. (1991) proposed the social value of a product is derived from its ability to connect consumers to relevant social groups.

It has been demonstrated that the consumption of sport team games provides individuals with opportunities to connect with relevant social groups (Doyle, Filo, Lock, Funk, & McDonald, 2016; Gibson, Willming, & Holdnak, 2002; Katz & Heere, 2013; Lock, Taylor, & Darcy, 2011; Lock, Taylor, Funk, & Darcy, 2012; McDonald, Milne, & Hong, 2002; Melnick, 1993; Pons, Mourali, & Nyeck, 2006; Wann, 1995) as attending sport events provides consumers with chances for social bonding and enhanced peer group acceptance (cf. Funk et al., 2009; Melnick, 1993; Pons et al., 2006). Thus, socialization has been identified as a core motive explaining why consumers follow sport teams (Funk et al., 2009) and as a brand association consumers link with sport teams (Gladden & Funk, 2001, 2002). Furthermore, the social value that consumers derive from sport teams has been shown to influence their loyalty toward the team (Bauer, Stokburger-Sauer, & Exler, 2008) and game consumption (Wakefield, 1995).

Emotional Value

Emotional value represents the utility derived from the feelings or affective states that consuming the sport team's games generates (Sweeney & Soutar, 2001). Thus, emotional value refers to what consumers feel when they consume products and services (cf. Keller, 1993; Sheth et al., 1991) and, therefore, includes hedonic aspects of the consumption experience. Sport teams are able to initiate strong emotional responses compared with other products and services (Mullin et al., 2007) and, therefore, satisfy consumers' emotional needs. In particular, two main consumer motives that trigger affective emotions have been identified to influence their behavior. These two motives are excitement (Wann, 1995) and escape or diversion (Funk et al., 2009; Gladden & Funk, 2002; Trail, Robinson, Dick, & Gillentine, 2003; Wann, 1995). Therefore, it is conceptualized that these motives initiate actions targeted to satisfy consumers' needs (Heckhausen & Heckhausen, 2006). The outcome of these actions represents the perceived emotional value consumers link to the consumption of sport team games. Therefore, excitement and escape have been conceptualized as two factors representing consumers' emotional value of sport team games.

Epistemic Value

Epistemic value represents the utility derived from the capacity of a sport team's game to arouse curiosity, provide novelty, and satisfy a desire for knowledge (cf. Sheth et al., 1991). Epistemic aspects that relate to sport teams have been identified in previous studies. For example, Gladden and Funk (2002) demonstrated that a consumer's knowledge, together with importance and affect, represented his or her attitude toward a sport team. Sport in particular is an area where epistemic value may represent an outcome that can satisfy consumers' needs, given the plethora of player names, different rules, technical aspects, and tactical details that are involved in sport events. Therefore, consumers' knowledge and their level of expertise with the sport team can influence their purchase intentions (cf. Trail & James, 2001).

Economic Value

Economic value represents the utility derived from sport team games due to the reduction of its perceived short-term and long-term costs (Sweeney & Soutar, 2001). The economic value attributed to a product or service is influenced by the price in relation to the quality of the product or service (cf. Dodds et al., 1991; Zeithaml, 1988). Economic value research has been conducted in the sport context, with findings revealing economic value perceptions have a positive relationship with sport consumer decision making (e.g., Wakefield, 1995). Elsewhere, Hightower et al. (2002) demonstrated that perceived economic value positively influenced consumers' intentions to attend games of their favorite team in the future.

Multidimensional Conceptualization

Based on the above review, the multidimensional conceptualization of consumption values (Sheth et al., 1991; Sweeney & Soutar, 2001) has been adopted to inform our development of a multidimensional consumers' perceived value scale relevant for sport consumers. Specifically, five value dimensions were theoretically identified as relevant to sport team games: functional, social, emotional, epistemic, and economic. These five dimensions are theoretically represented by eight factors, as depicted in Figure 1. Therefore, the first purpose of this research is to examine the proposed multidimensional

conceptualization of consumers' perceived value of sport team games. Thus, Hypothesis 1 was developed:

Hypothesis 1: Consumers' perceived value of sport games is reflected by five value dimensions: functional value, social value, emotional value, epistemic value, and economic value.

Conceptually, consumers' perceived value of games is interrelated with their attitudes toward the team, as the games represent the core product of the teams (cf. Sheth et al., 1991). Thus, the second purpose of this research was to identify the relationship between consumers' perceived value of games and attitudes toward their favorite team. An attitude represents "a psychological tendency that is expressed by evaluating a particular entity with some degree of favor or disfavor" (Eagly & Chaiken, 1993, p. 1). Two attitudinal outcomes that have been identified as particularly relevant to professional spectator sport are consumers' satisfaction with (e.g., Hightower et al., 2002), and commitment toward (e.g., Pritchard, Havitz, & Howard, 1999), their favorite team.

Satisfaction is defined as "both an evaluative and emotion-based response to a service encounter" (Cronin et al., 2000, p. 204). Organizations often use satisfaction to measure their brand performance (Anderson & Sullivan, 1993) because satisfaction has been linked with desirable outcomes, such as word-of-mouth recommendations and future consumption (e.g., Yoshida & James, 2010). Commitment is defined as "an enduring desire to maintain a valued relationship" (Moorman, Zaltman, & Deshpande, 1992, p. 316). In this case, commitment represents a consumer's emotional connection with a sport team and is characterized by the persistence and resistance to change this connection (Pritchard et al., 1999).

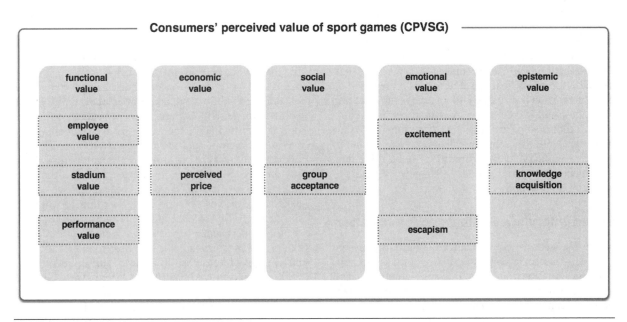

Figure 1 — Conceptualization of value dimensions.

Consumers' perceived value of a service has been identified to influence their overall satisfaction in related entertainment settings including tourism and restaurant experiences. For example, Ryu, Lee, and Kim (2012) demonstrated perceived value influenced satisfaction with a restaurant consumption experience, while Bajs (2015) demonstrated consumers' perceived value influenced their overall satisfaction with a tourist destination. Elsewhere, Williams and Soutar (2009) identified that consumers' perceived value of a four-wheel-drive adventure tour in Australia explained 62% of the variance of their satisfaction with the tour. In addition, Westerbeek and Shilbury (2003) argued value perceptions directly and indirectly influence the overall satisfaction sport consumers feel toward sport services, a proposition that has received partial support from subsequent research revealing a positive relationship between perceived value and intentions to revisit the location of a large sport event (Jin, Lee, & Lee, 2013). Given commitment and satisfaction are important attitudinal outcomes that may be influenced by consumers' perceived value of sport team games, two hypotheses were developed:

> *Hypothesis 2*: Consumers' perceived value of attending sport games has a positive association with their commitment toward their favorite team.

> *Hypothesis 3*: Consumers' perceived value of attending sport games has a positive association with their satisfaction with their favorite team.

Method

To address the purpose of the research and examine the three hypotheses, we conducted two studies. Throughout this process we followed a three-step process to develop a multidimensional consumer value scale and test its predictive ability. This process was guided by an established approach recommended by Churchill (1979) and Rossiter (2002). In the first step, we conceptualized a multidimensional consumer value scale based on the literature review and results of five semistructured interviews with experienced sport marketing scholars. In the second step, we collected data from 225 sport spectators to test the conceptualized scale and demonstrate its predictive ability (Study 1). In the third step, we collected data from a further 382 sport spectators to verify the scale (Study 2).

Expert Interview: Scale Conceptualization

In the first step, we conceptualized a multidimensional CPVSG. This scale consisted of five dimensions representing functional, economic, social, emotional, and epistemic value. To confirm the identified value dimensions, we conducted five semistructured interviews with sport marketing experts, each lasting for approximately 30 min. We first asked the experts to explain what they believed represented value from the sport consumer perspective. This commentary confirmed that value consisted of dimensions broader than a unidimensional economic exchange.

Next, we presented the conceptualized five dimensions of the scale and asked the experts to evaluate the relevance of each dimension. The experts again agreed that sport team games provide consumers with value that exceeds value for money and gave suggestions for modification of the proposed scale. The experts recommended examining two value dimensions (functional value and emotional value) with separate factors reflecting their higher order value dimensions, which we have subsequently presented in Figure 1. Furthermore, the experts recommended that rather than eliminating economic value as researchers have done in other fields (e.g., Williams & Soutar, 2009, only examined functional, social, emotional, and epistemic value in a tourism context), we should investigate all five proposed dimensions, in particular because the economic value dimension most closely represents traditional unidimensional value conceptualizations. Other discussions centered on the inclusion of the epistemic value dimension, yet its inclusion was recommended to align with the theoretical framework and recommendations made to examine this dimension in high-involvement product and service categories (Sweeney & Soutar, 2001). Overall, the experts supported the inclusion of all five dimensions, rating each individual dimension as an important aspect of value linked to sport games.

Second, to identify potential scale items, we reviewed existing spectator sport scales that captured the five dimensions. Relevant scales were identified in the sport attendance motivation (e.g., Robinson, Trail, & Kwon, 2004; Wann, 1995), brand image (e.g., Bauer et al., 2008; Gladden & Funk, 2001), service quality (e.g., Brady & Cronin, 2001; Brady et al., 2006; Wakefield et al., 1996), and consumer value (Lee et al., 2011) literature. Using this process, we identified or self-developed 78 unique items that measured the eight factors representing the five proposed value dimensions.

Third, to reduce the number of scale items and ensure face validity, we again consulted with the five sport management experts who provided comments during Step 1. Each expert was given a list containing the items, factors, and value dimensions and asked to allocate the items to one of the eight factors representing the five value dimensions or to indicate if they did not match any of the factors. The experts were also asked to comment on the item wording to improve the face validity of each item. Items were rated on a 5-point Likert scale (1 = *does not reflect dimension at all*; 5 = *reflects dimension very well*), and items with an average of below 4 (80% threshold; Polit & Beck, 2006) were removed. Overall, 37 items were deemed to be ambiguous or scored below the 80% threshold and were, therefore, removed from the list. The final list of items contained 41 items, which were used in the two studies.

Study 1: Scale Conceptualization and Testing

Procedures

In the second step, we collected quantitative data to test the conceptualized scale. To do so, we recruited participants from online fan forums targeting the German Bundesliga, which is the premier football (soccer) competition in Germany with a reported average attendance of 43,534 during the 2014–2015 season (Weltfussball.de, 2015a). To collect data, we applied a netnographic approach and followed established guidelines for research of this type (e.g., Kozinets, 2002). In the first step, we introduced ourselves to the moderator of a fan forum related to the Bundesliga and asked for permission to approach forum members to act as the sample for the research. After permission was granted, we created an account on the forum and posted invitations to participate in the survey. The invitations included a link to a website that contained an online questionnaire hosted by eQuestionnaire.

Materials

The questionnaire included 41 items to measure the eight factors representing the five value dimensions, items designed to measure the outcome variables of commitment and satisfaction, and items designed to collect demographic information from participants. Items that remained after data analysis are presented in Table 1. Psychological commitment was examined with the following three items adapted from Mahony, Nakazawa, Funk, James, and Gladden (2002) and Kunkel, Funk, and Hill (2013): (a) "I am very committed to my favorite team," (b) "There is nothing that could change my commitment toward my favorite team," and (c) "I would defend my favorite team in public even if this caused problems." Satisfaction was examined with the following three items: (a) "All in all, I am satisfied with my favorite team," (b) "My favorite team meets my expectations," and (c) "Visiting a game of my favorite team is an ideal experience to other leisure activities (e.g., cinema, theatre, or other sporting event)" (Homburg, Koschate, & Hoyer, 2005).

Table 1   Items, Factor Loadings, and Mean Scores of Study 1 and Study 2

Dimension and item	Study 1 M	Study 1 Factor loading	Study 2 M	Study 2 Factor loading
Functional				
Empl_1 The employees of my favorite team are being friendly.	5.12	.82	5.75	.76
Empl_2 The employees of my favorite team are taking actions to address my needs.	4.44	.80	5.16	.91
Stad_1 I am impressed with the stadium/arena of my favorite team.	5.52	.88	5.95	.89
Stad_2 The stadium of my favorite team is designed well.	5.31	.96	5.86	.78
Perf_1 My favorite team performs well.	4.56	.70	5.25	.87
Perf_2 At my favorite team I can see good games.	4.76	.93	5.33	.92
Economic				
Eco_1 Tickets at my favorite team are reasonably priced.	4.81	.92	5.63	.90
Eco_2 Tickets at my favorite team offer value for money.	4.93	.85	5.84	.71
Social				
Soc_1 Attending a game of my favorite team makes me feel like I belong to a special group.	3.22	.72	3.43	.73
Soc_2 Attending games of my favorite team make others accept me more.	4.85	.84	4.77	.85
Emotional				
Exc_1 Attending games of my favorite team is exciting.	6.38	.68	6.18	.74
Exc_2 I enjoy the excitement associated with attending games of my favorite team.	5.88	.81	6.12	.83
Esc_1 Attending games of my favorite team allows me to forget about my problems.	5.87	.79	5.14	.80
Esc_2 Attending games of my favorite team takes me away from my daily routines.	5.50	.84	6.02	.76
Epistemic				
Epi_1 Attending games of my favorite team helps me to learn about the tactical aspects of Football.	4.24	.77	4.48	.88
Epi_2 Attending games of my favorite team helps me to learn about the technical aspects of Football.	4.56	.90	4.71	.90

Note. Empl = Employee; Stad = Stadium; Perf = Performance; Eco = Economic; Soc = Social; Exc = Excitement; Esc = Escape; Epi = Epistemic.

Participants

Participants were 225 fans of various teams competing in the Bundesliga. The majority of participants were male (88.4%) with an average age of 29.7 years. Participants were highly educated (65% with college or university degree) and attended an average of 13.06 (SD = 6.1) home games and 5.19 (SD = 4.3) away games of their favorite team in the previous season. Thus, the sample was composed of highly engaged consumers of the Bundesliga. Although participants may not be representative of all Bundesliga consumers (e.g., the less engaged), they demonstrate similar characteristics to samples derived from previous fan forum research (e.g., Koenigstorfer, Groeppel-Klein, & Kunkel, 2010; Kunkel, Funk, & King, 2014; Lock, Darcy, & Taylor, 2009). In addition, the focus of this study was on the psychographic relationships of the value dimensions. Therefore, the sample was considered to appropriately serve the purpose of Study 1.

Data Analysis

Data were analyzed using SPSS 21 and MPlus 6.1 software. Data analysis of mean scores for the value dimension items indicated that data were positively skewed and, therefore, violated the assumption of normal distribution. This was not surprising given that participants of this research were consumers of online fan forums who generally are committed fans (Koenigstorfer et al., 2010). Therefore, we used the Satorra–Bentler correction to account for the nonnormal distribution of data in subsequent tests (Curran, West, & Finch, 1996). The small number of fans represented in this sample of each of the 18 teams in the first Bundesliga make traditional measurement invariance tests (e.g., Cheung & Rensvold, 2002) impractical; therefore, we used analysis of variance tests to demonstrate that fans of different teams did not significantly differ in their level of fandom, $F(18, 207) = 2.18$, $p = .057$; number of home games attended, $F(18, 207) = 0.919$, $p = .47$; and number of away games attended, $F(18, 207) = 1.76$, $p = .12$. Consequently, we proceeded with pooling the sample.

We used confirmatory factor analysis (CFA) with maximum likelihood estimation and the Satorra–Bentler correction to analyze the reliability and validity of the conceptualized scale. Several fit indices (χ^2/df, RMSEA, SRMA, FL) were used to examine the validity of the scale. Furthermore, we followed Hair, Black, Babin, and Anderson's (2010) recommendations to ensure convergent validity and removed items with factor loadings below .50. Overall, we tested eight factors, representing the five conceptualized value dimensions. Consistent with our conceptual approach described earlier, the economic value, social value, and epistemic value dimensions were represented by a single factor. Meanwhile, emotional value was represented by excitement (Exc) and escape (Esc), and the functional dimension was represented by factors assessing perceptions of employee interaction (Empl), the service environment (Stad), and performance on the field (Perf).

Each construct was measured with two items to provide a concise measurement tool, in the interests of providing benefits to both researchers and practitioners. This decision was informed by the suggestions of previous research that has used two items to measure constructs as a means of achieving parsimony while retaining the ability to assess for reliability (e.g., Funk et al., 2009; Walsh, Shiu, & Hassan, 2014). Concise scales also reduce the risk for response bias caused by fatigue because of the inclusion of too many items, and they allow for the inclusion of other measures related to the research interest while still keeping the survey at a reasonable length (Richins, 2004; Stanton, Sinar, Balzer, & Smith, 2002), which will benefit both researchers and practitioners when using the CPVSG scale in future research projects.

Results

We followed a stepwise approach in assessing the scale and testing its predictive ability on outcome variables (Homburg & Giering, 1996). First, we assessed the eight individual factors. The mean scores of the items, except one item measuring social value, ranked above the midpoint of 4.0, and CFA results ($\chi^2 = 98.70$; $df = 76$; $\chi^2/df = 1.29$, $p = .04$; RMSEA = .036; comparative fit index [CFI] = .98; Tucker–Lewis index [TLI] = .97; and standardized root mean square residual [SRMR] = .033) indicated a good model fit for the eight factors (Hair et al., 2010). All indicator reliability (IR) scores exceeded .40 (Homburg & Giering, 1996). Mean scores and factor loading for the eight-factor solution from Study 1 are presented in Table 1. Average variance extracted (AVE) scores for all constructs met the recommended .50 threshold, and all Cronbach's alpha scores exceeded values of .70, providing support for the internal consistency of the eight constructs (Nunnally & Bernstein, 1994). Discriminant validity between the eight dimensions was confirmed with AVE scores exceeding the squared correlations between constructs (Hair et al., 2010). The correlation matrix for the eight constructs is presented in Table 2.

Second, we assessed how well the eight factors reflected the five conceptualized value dimensions. Fit indices ($\chi^2 = 154.05$; $df = 89$; $\chi^2/df = 1.73$, $p < .01$; RMSEA = .057; CFI = .95; TLI = .94; and SRMR = .059) indicated a good model fit for the five value dimensions. Third, we scrutinized the overall scale and tested the loading of the five value dimensions on a higher order perceived value construct. Consumers' perceived value of sport team games was reflected by functional value (IR = .91), economic value (IR = .70), social value (IR = .54), emotional value (IR = .86), and epistemic value (IR = .39). Fit indices ($\chi^2 = 169.55$; $df = 94$; $\chi^2/df = 1.80$, $p < .01$; RMSEA = .060; CFI = .95; TLI = .93; and SRMR = .066) provided an acceptable model fit. The five-dimension solution is presented in Figure 2.

Fourth, we tested the association between consumers' perceived value of team games and two outcome variables. Consumers' perceived value of their favorite team's games ($\beta = .57$) explained 32% of the variance of

Table 2   Eight Constructs Correlation Matrix, Study 1

	AVE	1	2	3	4	5	6	7	8
1. Stad	.85	1	.18	.06	.10	.25	.06	.12	.15
2. Perf	.69	.42	1	.29	.08	.38	.06	.07	.27
3. Eco	.78	.25	.54	1	.05	.36	.11	.15	.28
4. Soc	.61	.23	.29	.32	1	.12	.45	.03	.09
5. Exc	.56	.50	.62	.60	.35	1	.37	.06	.23
6. Esc	.64	.23	.24	.33	.67	.61	1	.03	.09
7. Epi	.70	.18	.25	.16	.39	.26	.35	1	.08
8. Empl	.66	.39	.52	.53	.31	.48	.31	.29	1

Note. Values below the diagonal are correlation estimates. Values above the diagonal are squared correlation estimates. AVE = average variance extracted.

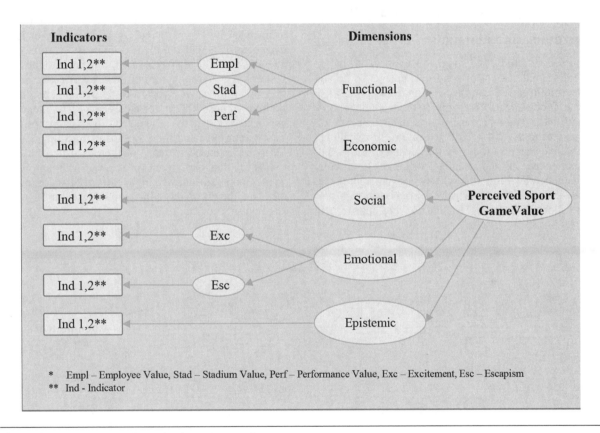

Figure 2 — Specification of perceived sport game value.

consumers' satisfaction with this team. Fit indices (χ^2 = 227.02; df = 124; χ^2/df = 1.83, $p < .01$; RMSEA = .061; CFI = .93; TLI = .92; and SRMR = .074) indicated an acceptable model fit. Consumers' perceived value of their favorite team's games ($\beta = .44$) explained 20% of the variance of their commitment toward this team. Fit indices (χ^2 = 209.18; df = 124; χ^2/df = 1.68, $p < .01$; RMSEA = .055; CFI = .94; TLI = .93; and SRMR = .071) indicated an acceptable model fit.

Last, the relationships between the five individual value dimensions and the two outcome variables were examined to provide deeper insights into the importance

of each dimension. Fit indices for the relationship between the value dimensions and satisfaction indicated an acceptable model fit (χ^2 = 179.402; df = 115; χ^2/df = 1.55, $p < .01$; RMSEA = .050; CFI = .96; TLI = .95; and SRMR = .053). Results indicate functional value (β = .67, $p < .001$) had a significant positive relationship with consumers' satisfaction, whereas economic value ($\beta = -.18$, $p = .06$), social value ($\beta = -.04$, $p = .50$), and epistemic value ($\beta = -.12$, $p = .06$) had nonsignificant negative relationships with the satisfaction of the sample. Emotional value ($\beta = .13$, $p = .43$) had a nonsignificant relationship with consumers' satisfaction. Overall, 39%

of the variance of consumers' satisfaction with their favorite team was explained by the model. Fit indices for the relationship between the value dimensions and commitment indicated an acceptable model fit (χ^2 = 170.937; df = 115; χ^2/df = 1.47, p < .01; RMSEA = .046; CFI = .96; TLI = .95; and SRMR = .050). Results indicate functional value (β = .45, p < .001), social value (β = .26, p = .029), economic value (β = .27, p = .007), and emotional value (β = .37, p = .028) had significant positive relationships with consumers' commitment. Epistemic value (β = .036, p = .72) had a nonsignificant relationship with consumers' commitment. Overall, 28% of the variance of consumers' commitment with their favorite team was explained by the model. Results are presented in Figure 3.

Study 2: Scale Confirmation

Procedures and Materials

In the second study, we sought to confirm the scale using a second sample of sport consumers. To do so, we recruited participants who attended a game of a German football team competing in the second division of the Bundesliga, which had an average attendance of 29,945 during the 2014–2015 season (Weltfussball.de, 2015b). We chose to focus on the second division and game attendees instead of online consumers to provide greater generalizability to results by complementing the sample used in Study 1, which focused on the top-tier of the sport in Germany. Attendees were approached

randomly at the game to provide their e-mail address and participate in the online questionnaire. In total, 693 people provided their e-mail addresses and were sent an invitation to complete the survey the following day. The invitations included a link to a website that contained an online questionnaire hosted by eQuestionnaire. The questionnaire contained the same items used in Study 1. Errors recording or entering correct e-mail addresses led to 105 emails being returned. Of the 588 successfully submitted emails, 423 were opened and completed to varying degrees. After a data cleaning process removing incomplete surveys, 382 completed questionnaires were retained for analysis.

Participants

The majority of participants were male (80.6%) with an average age of 37 years. Again, participants were highly educated (55% with a college or university degree) and attended an average of 11.4 (SD = 6.1) home games and 2.8 (SD = 3.4) away games of their favorite team in the previous season. With regard to the seating area in the stadium, almost 40% preferred less expensive areas that are located close to the designated supporter groups. This information revealed the participants in Study 2 were older and attended matches of their favorite team less frequently than participants in Study 1. Although Study 2 participants still showed high levels of behavior toward the team, they were more likely to represent the average German soccer fan.

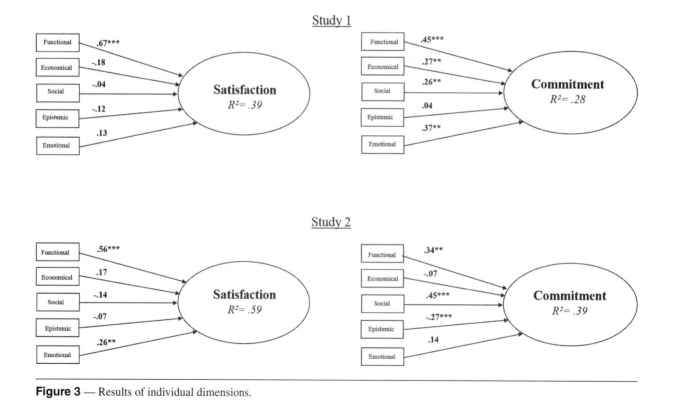

Figure 3 — Results of individual dimensions.

Results

We followed the same stepwise approach as described in Study 1. First, we assessed the eight individual factors. The mean scores of the items, except one item measuring social value, ranked above the midpoint of 4.0, and CFA results ($\chi^2 = 126.01$; $df = 76$; $\chi^2/df = 1.66$, $p = .01$; RMSEA = .042; CFI = .98; TLI = .96; and SRMR = .031) indicated a good model fit for the eight factors. Mean scores and factor loading for the eight-factor solution from Study 2 are presented in Table 1. AVE scores for all constructs met the recommended .50 threshold, and all Cronbach's alpha scores exceeded values of .70, providing support for the internal consistency of the eight constructs. Discriminant validity between the eight dimensions was confirmed with AVE scores exceeding the squared correlations between constructs. The correlation matrix for the eight constructs is presented in Table 3.

Second, we assessed how the eight factors reflected the five conceptualized value dimensions. Fit indices ($\chi^2 = 162.17$; $df = 89$; $\chi^2/df = 1.82$, $p = .01$; RMSEA = .046; CFI = .97; TLI = .96; and SRMR = .045) indicated a good model fit for the five value dimensions. Third, we scrutinized the overall scale and tested the loading of the five value dimensions on a higher order perceived value construct. Consumers' perceived value of sport team games was reflected by functional value (IR = .91), economic value (IR = .77), social value (IR = .74), emotional value (IR = .86), and epistemic value (IR = .63). Fit indices ($\chi^2 = 208.86$; $df = 94$; $\chi^2/df = 2.21$, $p < .001$; RMSEA = .057; CFI = .95; TLI = .94; and SRMR = .058) indicated an acceptable model fit.

We tested the association between consumers' perceived value of their favorite team games and two outcome variables. Consumers' perceived value of their favorite team's games ($\beta = .77$) explained 58% of the variance of consumers' satisfaction with this team. Fit indices ($\chi^2 = 274.02$; $df = 124$; $\chi^2/df = 2.20$, $p < .01$; RMSEA = .056; CFI = .94; TLI = .93; and SRMR = .061) indicated an acceptable model fit. Consumers' perceived value of their favorite team's games ($\beta = .57$) explained 33% of the variance of consumers' commitment toward this team. Fit indices ($\chi^2 = 264.72$; $df = 124$; $\chi^2/df = 2.12$, p

$< .01$; RMSEA = .055; CFI = .94; TLI = .93; and SRMR = .059) indicated an acceptable model fit.

Next, the relationship between the five individual value dimensions and the two outcome variables was tested. Fit indices for the relationship between the value dimensions and satisfaction indicated an acceptable model fit ($\chi^2 = 204.229$; $df = 115$; $\chi^2/df = 1.77$, $p < .01$; RMSEA = .045; CFI = .96; TLI = .95; and SRMR = .045). Results indicate functional value ($\beta = .56$, $p < .001$) and emotional value ($\beta = .26$, $p = .007$) had significant positive relationships with consumers' satisfaction, whereas social value ($\beta = -.14$, $p = .15$) and epistemic value ($\beta = -.07$, $p = .31$) had nonsignificant negative relationships with consumers' satisfaction. Economic value ($\beta = .17$, $p = .06$) had a nonsignificant relationship with consumers' satisfaction. Overall, 59% of the variance of consumers' satisfaction with their favorite team was explained by the model. Fit indices for the relationship between the value dimensions and commitment indicated an acceptable model fit ($\chi^2 = 203.774$; $df = 115$; $\chi^2/df = 1.77$, $p < .01$; RMSEA = .045; CFI = .96; TLI = .95; and SRMR = .045). Results indicate functional value ($\beta = .34$, $p = .002$) and social value ($\beta = .45$, $p < .001$) had significant positive relationships with consumers' commitment, whereas epistemic value ($\beta = -.27$, $p < .001$) had a significant negative relationship with commitment. Economic value ($\beta = -.07$, $p = .52$) and emotional value ($\beta = .14$, $p = .22$) had nonsignificant relationships with consumers' commitment. Overall, 39% of the variance of consumers' commitment with their favorite team was explained by the model.

Discussion

This research contributes to the sport management literature related to sport team games. In *Hypothesis 1*, we stated that consumers' perceived value of sport team games is reflected by five value dimensions—functional value, social value, emotional value, epistemic value, and economic value. Based on existing literature and interviews with sport management experts, functional value was represented by three constructs, and emotional

Table 3   Eight Constructs Correlation Matrix, Study 2

	AVE	1	2	3	4	5	6	7	8
1. Stad	.70	1	.21	.21	.11	.11	.11	.10	.10
2. Perf	.80	.46	1	.46	.25	.25	.24	.23	.24
3. Eco	.64	.46	.68	1	.23	.32	.32	.14	.23
4. Soc	.62	.34	.50	.48	1	.36	.36	.40	.12
5. Exc	.61	.34	.50	.57	.60	1	.48	.20	.12
6. Esc	.61	.33	.49	.57	.60	.69	1	.19	.12
7. Epi	.79	.32	.48	.38	.64	.45	.44	1	.11
8. Empl	.70	.32	.49	.48	.36	.36	.35	.34	1

Note. Values below the diagonal are correlation estimates. Values above the diagonal are squared correlation estimates. AVE = average variance extracted.

value consisted of two constructs. The social, epistemic, and economic value components were conceptualized as one-dimensional constructs. CFA results of both studies indicated the eight factors fit the five conceptualized value dimensions well, and the five dimensions reflected consumers' overall perceived value of their favorite sport team's games. Results indicate consumers' perceived value is not a unidimensional construct, and consumers do not only assess sport teams from a utilitarian value perspective. Furthermore, although researchers doubted the relevance of functional and economic aspects for sport consumers (e.g., Bauer et al., 2008), results of this research indicate that functional and economic aspects are also relevant to consumers' perceived value of sport team games, which is in line with research indicating sport fans' emotions influence their behavior (Kwak, Kim, & Hirt, 2011). Overall, findings indicate that consumers' perceived value of sport team games should be regarded as a multidimensional construct, and results of both studies supported Hypothesis 1.

In *Hypothesis 2*, we stated that consumers' perceived value of their favorite sport team's games had a positive association with their commitment toward their favorite team. Results of Study 1 and Study 2 indicate consumers' perceived value of sport team games explained 20% and 33% of the variance of consumers' commitment toward their favorite team, respectively. In *Hypothesis 3*, we stated that consumers' perceived value of their favorite team's games had a positive association with their satisfaction with their favorite team. Results of Study 1 and Study 2 indicate consumers' perceived value explained 32% and 58% of the variance of consumers' satisfaction with their favorite team, respectively. In both studies, the explanatory power of consumers' perceived value of sport team games had a stronger relationship to consumers' satisfaction with their favorite team than their commitment toward the team. This finding is consistent with previous research that has identified a strong relationship between perceived value and satisfaction (Bajs, 2015; Ryu et al., 2012; Williams & Soutar, 2009). Overall, these results support the expected relationship between consumer value perceptions and both psychological outcome variables, as suggested by Sheth et al. (1991). Therefore, the predictive ability of the conceptualized multidimensional consumers' perceived value scale has been supported.

The differences between Study 1 and Study 2 in the explained variance of outcome variables may be explained through contextual differences. Study 1 was conducted with a heterogeneous group of consumers of all teams within the Bundesliga, and it can be expected that consumers of traditionally successful teams have different value perceptions of games than consumers of less successful teams. Therefore, combining consumers of all teams within a league may have reduced the predictive ability of the scale. Study 2 was conducted with a more homogeneous group of game attendees of one team within the Bundesliga's second division, and thus the ability of the scale to predict outcome variables may

have been stronger than in Study 1. Overall, although the predictive ability of the perceived value dimensions for sport teams shows differences in their strength between contexts, their structure seems to be consistent and, hence, they can be used to explain outcome variables related to sport teams. Therefore, results of both studies supported Hypothesis 2 and Hypothesis 3.

In relation to the specific dimensions and their influence on the outcome variables, results from both studies outlined the importance of the functional dimension. Functional value was significantly related to satisfaction and commitment in both samples. This highlights the importance of the service environment in influencing sport consumer behavior, supporting and extending previous work (Brady et al., 2006; Hightower et al., 2002; Hill & Green, 2000, 2012; Theodorakis & Alexandris, 2008; Wakefield et al., 1996). Social value represented an important predictor of commitment in both studies but did not have a significant relationship for satisfaction in either. This suggests that attendance at sport events is influenced by socializing agents, but these same agents do not influence satisfaction with the actual game, adding to existing work in this area (Funk et al., 2009). The epistemic dimension and commitment held a significantly negative relationship in Study 2, suggesting that the more someone wanted to learn about the team, the less he or she was committed. This is logical as more committed fans are likely to have more knowledge about the sport and the team; therefore, epistemic value may be more important to less committed fans, as knowledge generates associations linked to the team, which influences fan commitment and behavior (e.g., Funk & James, 2001).

Last, and perhaps most importantly, economic value was only a significant predictor of commitment in Study 1 and did not explain a significant proportion of variance in satisfaction in either study. These results indicate sport consumers' value perceptions are less impacted by economic considerations. However, respondents preferred lower cost sections within the stadium, indicating economic considerations may be more important when the cost inhibits the consumer from attending games. Overall, this supports the conceptualization that consumers' value perceptions are influenced by factors that extend past economic considerations (Lee et al., 2011), extending previous sport research (Cronin, et al., 2000; Hightower et al., 2002) and providing a platform for future work.

Contributions

The current research advances knowledge in the sport literature by providing a conceptually sound and practically useful multidimensional scale capturing consumers' perceived value of sport team games. We extended simplistic one-dimensional consumer value approaches (e.g., Cronin et al., 2000; Hightower et al., 2002) by conceptualizing that consumers' perceived value of attending sport team games exceeds solely economically driven or value-for-money evaluations. We also extended previous research by providing an improved consumers' perceived value scale that has specific relevance to the sport context (e.g., Lee et al., 2011). The conceptualized multidimensional approach captures the different aspects of consumption, such as the performance-based, educational, and excitement factors of team games, which contribute to consumers' overall value perceptions in regard to sport team games.

This research indicates that the five distinct, yet related, value dimensions—functional value, social value, emotional value, epistemic value, and economic value—are reflective of consumers' overall perception of the value of their favorite sport team's games. The conceptualized multidimensional approach of consumers' perceived value of sport team games is predictive of consumers' commitment toward, and satisfaction with, their favorite sport team. This indicates that consumers' perceived value of games is an antecedent to team-related attitudes. Therefore, for consumers to develop a strong attitude toward their favorite team, such as feeling committed and satisfied, they need to perceive that consumption of the team's games, representing the core product, provides value to them on some dimension. Given the multidimensional conceptualization, the overall value perceived by consumers can be derived from various sources that extend beyond solely economic aspects (cf. Williams & Soutar, 2009). Thus, the conceptualized approach may be beneficial to account for individual preferences that may vary between consumers or contexts (e.g., Sweeney & Soutar, 2001).

Practical Implications

Sport organizations can use the CPVSG scale to gain a better understanding of the value consumers link with their core product. From this work, sport management practitioners are provided with a concise set of 16 items that measure the five dimensions of consumers' perceived value. The scale provides practitioners with a succinct measurement tool that reduces the risk for response bias caused by fatigue because of the inclusion of too many items (e.g., Richins, 2004). Furthermore, the scale allows practitioners to test additional constructs of interest while still keeping the survey at a reasonable length (e.g., Stanton et al., 2002; Walsh et al., 2014). Knowledge of the impact of each dimension enables practitioners to initiate actions to increase consumers' perceived value of games and subsequently influence their attitudes toward the team. Developing an understanding of the perceptions surrounding each dimension also enables sport organizations to invest in marketing efforts that seek to maintain dimensions that are perceived well by consumers, and to enact campaigns designed to improve perceptions surrounding dimensions that contribute low levels of value. For instance, should consumers perceive that the epistemic value of consuming their favorite team's matches is low, the team may wish to distribute a game-day program containing tactical information and statistics about the team and individual players to increase

this value attribute. Other marketing strategies that sport teams may benefit from using are detailed below.

Results of this research revealed functional value was an important predictor of attitudinal variables in both samples, indicating marketers should focus on enhancing perceptions fans hold about the team's personnel and the service environment to increase their value perceptions. Results also reveal marketers should focus on enhancing perceptions of social value to enhance consumer commitment and emotional value to boost perceptions of commitment and satisfaction. Sport organizations may also use this research to implement management or marketing actions to influence consumers' perceived value of team games. For example, to increase the functional value of sport team games, practitioners can aim to improve the service quality at the stadium (cf. Hill & Green, 2000, 2012), which may include offering healthy concession options or providing Wi-Fi at the stadium. To increase the emotional value of sport team games, practitioners can implement light shows or other special effects to stimulate emotional responses (e.g., Kwak et al., 2011). To increase the social value of sport team games, practitioners can host social events for fans to engage with other fans or encourage fans to form their own unique communities by providing them with support and resources to facilitate gatherings before, during, and after the game (e.g., Gibson et al., 2002). To increase the epistemic value of sport team games, practitioners can stage tactical discussions or roundtables with former players or coaches or use other well-educated fans to educate less involved fans of the team (e.g., Kunkel, Doyle, & Funk, 2014). To increase the economic value of sport team games, practitioners can promote special games with group discounts or bundle packages with merchandise (e.g., Funk & James, 2001). Overall, given the positive association between consumers' perceived value of games and outcome variables, practitioners are able to subsequently increase consumers' commitment toward and satisfaction with the team by augmenting the perceived value dimensions linked with the consumption of their core product.

Limitations and Future Research

Four main limitations of this research indicate opportunities for future research. The main limitations of this research were the focus on one sport in one country, the self-selection of participants that may not be representative of the consumer populace, the cross-sectional nature and the focus on purely attitudinal constructs, and the focus on existing literature. First, the generalizability of this research to other sports or countries requires further investigation. The scale was tested within the context of German professional football, and the differences in the predictive abilities of the scale between Study 1 (conducted with participants supporting 18 different teams) and Study 2 (conducted with participants supporting one specific team) indicate that results were contextually influenced. Therefore, the stability and predictive ability of the scale requires further empirical investigation, both within the context of professional football and within other sports. Ideally, future research will also consider wide-ranging contexts across varying sports (e.g., basketball, rugby), levels of professionalism (e.g., amateur, collegiate), and countries (e.g., United States, Australia). Research should also test the predictive ability of the dimensions in conjunction with available segmentation procedures (e.g., Bouchet, Bodet, Bernache-Assollant, & Kada, 2010; Doyle, Kunkel, & Funk, 2013) to further understand the diverse cohorts that exist within sport consumer populations.

Second, participants of both studies may not accurately represent the average German football consumer. Participants in both studies were likely more highly involved with their favorite team than the average consumer as they were recruited from online fan forums in Study 1 (e.g., Koenigstorfer et al., 2010) or at the stadium in Study 2. Participants also reported a relatively high average attendance at football games, indicating a strong involvement with the team. In the future, researchers and practitioners may benefit from surveying participants with lower levels of involvement to gain a comprehensive overview of the value their potential consumer-base links with attending team games. Research of this type may be useful in determining the value domains most important to fostering positive value perceptions among groups possessing different psychological connections (e.g., Funk & James, 2001).

Third, both outcome variables—commitment toward, and satisfaction with, the team—represent attitudinal constructs. Future cross-sectional and longitudinal research could investigate the influence of perceived value on behavioral outcomes, such as merchandise purchasing or game attendance. In addition, future longitudinal research could investigate how management and marketing actions influence consumers' perceived value and subsequent behavior. Cross-lagged panel models or latent growth models could be used to examine the development and change of perceived value and its influence on future behavior (e.g., Kunkel, Doyle, Funk, Du, & McDonald, 2016). Given that these investigations are time and resource intensive, potential collaborations with industry partners, such as sport teams or sponsors, may be beneficial to support these future research endeavors.

Fourth, this research is focused on the value consumers associate with sport team games, but the value consumers receive from following sport teams exceeds the immediate experience at games. While the direct experience at games may provide value that is associated with the team, such as the social or emotional benefits derived from attending games, the game experience is generally not processed and interpreted in a vacuum and is affected by the personal relevance that consumers link to following the team (Heere et al., 2011). Team identification literature (Heere & James, 2007; Lock et al., 2014) may provide a solid foundation to evaluate the affective value derived from following a team. Similarly, following teams provides value to consumers through their function of community representation (e.g., Heere et al., 2011) and through mechanisms that foster esteem (Kwon, Trail, & Donghun, 2008). Using the contingent valuation method may be beneficial to examine the associated social benefits of following teams (e.g., Walker & Mondello, 2007) as it has been shown to be a viable method for sport properties (Drayer & Shapiro, 2011). Overall, future research is encouraged to investigate the value perceptions of consumers with consideration given to the influence of additional variables (e.g., team identification) to extend our work.

Conclusion

This research enhances our understanding of the perceived value construct in the spectator sport context. Previous research has conceptualized perceived value as a simplistic value-for-money unidimensional construct. The present research indicates perceived value is more complex, and a multidimensional conceptualization is required in a spectator sport context. Consequently, a multidimensional conceptualization of consumers' perceived value of sport team games was developed. Results of two studies demonstrated the predictive ability of the developed multidimensional scale on consumers' commitment toward and satisfaction with their favorite team. Last, this research provides practitioners with a theoretically sound and concise scale capturing five distinct consumer value dimensions, which can be used to inform the development of marketing actions.

Acknowledgments

The authors are grateful to Prof. Daniel C. Funk, Prof. Frank Daumann, and participants of the European Association for Sport Management conference for feedback on earlier versions of this article.

References

Anderson, E.W., & Sullivan, M.W. (1993). The antecedents and consequences of customer satisfaction for firms. *Marketing Science, 12,* 125–143. doi:10.1287/mksc.12.2.125

Bajs, I.P. (2015). Tourist perceived value, relationship to satisfaction, and behavioral intentions: The example of the Croatian tourist destination Dubrovnik. *Journal of Travel Research, 54,* 122–134. doi:10.1177/0047287513513158

Bauer, H.H., Stokburger-Sauer, N.E., & Exler, S. (2008). Brand image and fan loyalty in professional team sport: A refined model and empirical assessment. *Journal of Sport Management, 22,* 205–226. doi:10.1123/jsm.22.2.205

Bouchet, P., Bodet, G., Bernache-Assollant, I., & Kada, F. (2010). Segmenting sport spectators: Constructing and preliminary validation of the Sporting Event Experience Search (SEES) scale. *Sport Management Review, 14,* 1–12.

Brady, M.K., & Cronin, J.J., Jr. (2001). Customer orientation: Effects on customer service perceptions and outcome behaviors. *Journal of Service Research, 3,* 241–251. doi:10.1177/109467050133005

Brady, M.K., Vorhees, C.M., Cronin, J., & Bourdeau, B.L. (2006). The good guys don't always win: The effect of valence on service perceptions and consequences. *Journal of Services Marketing, 20,* 83–91. doi:10.1108/08876040610657011

Bristow, D., & Sebastian, R. (2001). Holy cow! Wait 'til next year! A closer look at the brand loyalty of Chicago Cubs baseball fans. *Journal of Consumer Marketing, 18,* 256–275. doi:10.1108/07363760110392976

Byon, K.K., Zhang, J.J., & Baker, T.A. (2013). Impact of core and peripheral service quality on consumption behavior of professional team sport spectators as mediated by perceived value. *European Sport Management Quarterly, 13,* 232–263. doi:10.1080/16184742.2013.767278

Cheung, G.W., & Rensvold, R.B. (2002). Evaluating goodness-of-fit indexes for testing measurement invariance. *Structural Equation Modeling, 9,* 233–255. doi:10.1207/S15328007SEM0902_5

Chi, T., & Kilduff, P.D. (2011). Understanding consumer perceived value of casual sportswear: An empirical study. *Journal of Retailing and Consumer Services, 18,* 422–429. doi:10.1016/j.jretconser.2011.06.004

Churchill, G. (1979). A paradigm for developing better measures of marketing constructs. *JMR, Journal of Marketing Research, 16,* 64–73. doi:10.2307/3150876

Cronin, J., Brady, M.K., & Hult, T.M. (2000). Assessing the effects of quality, value, and customer satisfaction on consumer behavioral intentions in service environments. *Journal of Retailing, 76,* 193–218. doi:10.1016/S0022-4359(00)00028-2

Curran, P.J., West, S.G., & Finch, J.F. (1996). The robustness of test statistics to nonnormality and specification error in confirmatory factor analysis. *Psychological Methods, 1,* 16–29. doi:10.1037/1082-989X.1.1.16

Deloitte. (2014). Football money league 2014. Manchester, UK: Sports Business Group, Deloitte.

Dodds, W.B., Monroe, K.B., & Grewal, D. (1991). Effect of price, brand and store information on buyers' product evaluations. *JMR, Journal of Marketing Research, 28,* 307–319. doi:10.2307/3172866

Doyle, J.P., Filo, K., Lock, D., Funk, D.C., & McDonald, H. (2016). Exploring PERMA in spectator sport: Applying positive psychology to examine the individual-level benefits of sport consumption. *Sport Management Review, 19,* 506–519. doi:10.1016/j.smr.2016.04.007

Doyle, J.P., Kunkel, T., & Funk, D.C. (2013). Sports spectator segmentation: Examining the differing psychological connections amongst spectators of leagues and teams. *International Journal of Sports Marketing & Sponsorship, 14,* 20–36. doi:10.1108/IJSMS-14-02-2013-B003

Doyle, J.P., Lock, D., Funk, D.C., Filo, K., & McDonald, H. (in press). "I was there from the start": The identity maintenance strategies used by fans to combat the threat of losing. *Sport Management Review.* doi:10.1016/j.smr.2016.04.006

Drayer, J., & Shapiro, S.L. (2011). An examination into the factors that influence consumers' perceptions of value. *Sport Management Review, 14,* 389–398. doi:10.1016/j.smr.2010.11.001

Eagly, A.H., & Chaiken, S. (1993). *The psychology of attitudes.* Fort Worth, TX: Harcourt, Brace, Jovanovich.

Funk, D.C., Filo, K., Beaton, A.A., & Pritchard, M. (2009). Measuring the motives of sport event attendance: Bridging the academic-practitioner divide to understanding behavior. *Sport Marketing Quarterly, 18,* 126–138.

Funk, D.C., & James, J.D. (2001). The psychological continuum model: A conceptual framework for understanding an individual's psychological connection to sport. *Sport Management Review, 4,* 119–150. doi:10.1016/S1441-3523(01)70072-1

Gibson, H.J., Willming, C., & Holdnak, A. (2002). "We're Gators . . . not just Gator fans": Serious leisure and University of Florida football. *Journal of Leisure Research, 34,* 397–425.

Gladden, J.M., & Funk, D.C. (2001). Understanding brand loyalty in professional sport: Examining the link between brand associations and brand loyalty. *International Journal of Sports Marketing & Sponsorship, 3,* 54–81. doi:10.1108/IJSMS-03-01-2001-B006

Gladden, J.M., & Funk, D.C. (2002). Developing an understanding of brand associations in team sport: Empirical evidence from consumers of professional sport. *Journal of Sport Management, 16,* 54–81. doi:10.1123/jsm.16.1.54

Graf, A., & Maas, P. (2008). Customer value from a customer perspective: A comprehensive review. *Journal für Betriebswirtschaft, 58,* 1–20. doi:10.1007/s11301-008-0032-8

Hair, J., Black, W., Babin, B., & Anderson, R. (2010). *Multivariate data analysis: With readings* (7th ed.). New York, NY: Prentice-Hall.

Heckhausen, J., & Heckhausen, H. (2006). *Motivation und Handeln* (3rd ed.). Heidelberg, Germany: Springer. doi:10.1007/3-540-29975-0

Heere, B., & James, J.D. (2007). Stepping outside the lines: Developing a multi-dimensional team identity scale based on social identity theory. *Sport Management Review, 10,* 65–91. doi:10.1016/S1441-3523(07)70004-9

Heere, B., Walker, M., Yoshida, M., Ko, Y.J., Jordan, J.S., & James, J.D. (2011). Brand community development through associated communities: Grounding community measurement within social identity theory. *Journal of Marketing Theory and Practice, 19,* 407–422. doi:10.2753/MTP1069-6679190404

Hightower, R., Brady, M.K., & Baker, T.L. (2002). Investigating the role of the physical environment in hedonic service consumption: An exploratory study of sporting events. *Journal of Business Research, 55,* 697–707. doi:10.1016/S0148-2963(00)00211-3

Hill, B., & Green, B.C. (2000). Repeat attendance as a function of involvement, loyalty, and the sportscape across three football contexts. *Sport Management Review, 3,* 145–162. doi:10.1016/S1441-3523(00)70083-0

Hill, B., & Green, B.C. (2012). Repeat participation as a function of program attractiveness, socializing opportunities, loyalty and the sportscape across three sport facility contexts. *Sport Management Review, 15,* 485–499. doi:10.1016/j.smr.2012.03.006

Homburg, C., & Giering, A. (1996). Konzeptualisierung und Operationalisierung komplexer Konstrukte: Ein Leitfaden für die Marketingforschung. *Marketing: ZFP, 18,* 3–24.

Homburg, C., Koschate, N., & Hoyer, W.D. (2005). Do satisfied customers really pay more? A study of the relationship between customer satisfaction and willingness to pay. *Journal of Marketing, 69,* 84–96. doi:10.1509/jmkg.69.2.84.60760

James, J.D., Kolbe, R.H., & Trail, G.T. (2002). Psychological connection to a new sport team: Building or maintaining the consumer base? *Sport Marketing Quarterly, 11,* 215–225.

Jin, N., Lee, H., & Lee, S. (2013). Event quality, perceived value, destination image, and behavioral intention of sports events: The case of the IAAF World Championship, Daegu, 2011. *Asia Pacific Journal of Tourism Research, 18,* 849–864. doi:10.1080/10941665.2012.711336

Katz, M., & Heere, B. (2013). Leaders and followers: An exploration of the notion of scale-free networks within a new brand community. *Journal of Sport Management, 27,* 271–287. doi:10.1123/jsm.27.4.271

Keller, K.L. (1993). Conceptualizing, measuring, managing customer-based brand equity. *Journal of Marketing, 57,* 1–22. doi:10.2307/1252054

Koenigstorfer, J., Groeppel-Klein, A., & Kunkel, T. (2010). The attractiveness of national and international football leagues—Perspectives of fans of "star clubs" and "underdogs." *European Sport Management Quarterly, 10,* 127–163. doi:10.1080/16184740903563406

Kozinets, R.V. (2002). The field behind the screen: Using netnography for marketing research in online communities. *JMR, Journal of Marketing Research, 39,* 61–72. doi:10.1509/jmkr.39.1.61.18935

Kunkel, T., Doyle, J.P., & Funk, D.C. (2014). Exploring sport brand development strategies to strengthen consumer involvement with the product—The case of the Australian A-League. *Sport Management Review, 17,* 470–483. doi:10.1016/j.smr.2014.01.004

Kunkel, T., Doyle, J.P., Funk, D.C., Du, J., & McDonald, H. (2016). The development and change of brand associations and their influence on team loyalty over time. *Journal of Sport Management, 30,* 117–134. doi:10.1123/jsm.2015-0129

Kunkel, T., Funk, D.C., & Hill, B. (2013). Brand architecture, drivers of consumer involvement, and brand loyalty with professional sport leagues and teams. *Journal of Sport Management, 27,* 177–192. doi:10.1123/jsm.27.3.177

Kunkel, T., Funk, D.C., & King, C. (2014). Developing a conceptual understanding of consumer-based league brand associations. *Journal of Sport Management, 28,* 49–67. doi:10.1123/jsm.2011-0153

Kwak, D.H., Kim, Y.K., & Hirt, E.R. (2011). Exploring the role of emotions on sport consumers' behavioral and cognitive responses to marketing stimuli. *European Sport Management Quarterly, 11,* 225–250. doi:10.1080/16184742.2011.577792

Kwon, H., Trail, G.T., & James, J.D. (2007). The mediating role of perceived value: Team identification and purchase intention of team-licensed apparel. *Journal of Sport Management, 21,* 540–554. doi:10.1123/jsm.21.4.540

Kwon, H.H., Trail, G.T., & Donghun, L. (2008). The effects of vicarious achievement and team identification on BIRGing and CORFing. *Sport Marketing Quarterly, 17,* 209–217.

Lee, D., Trail, G.T., Kwon, H.H., & Anderson, D.F. (2011). Consumer values versus perceived product attributes: Relationships among items from the MVS, PRS, and PERVAL scales. *Sport Management Review, 14,* 89–101. doi:10.1016/j.smr.2010.05.001

Lock, D., Darcy, S., & Taylor, T. (2009). Starting with a clean slate: An analysis of member identification with a new sports team. *Sport Management Review, 12,* 15–25. doi:10.1016/j.smr.2008.09.001

Lock, D., Funk, D.C., Doyle, J.P., & McDonald, H. (2014). Examining the longitudinal structure, stability, and dimensional interrelationships of team identification. *Journal of Sport Management, 28,* 119–135. doi:10.1123/jsm.2012-0191

Lock, D., Taylor, T., & Darcy, S. (2011). In the absence of achievement: The formation of new team identification. *European Sport Management Quarterly, 11,* 171–192. doi:10.1080/16184742.2011.559135

Lock, D., Taylor, T., Funk, D.C., & Darcy, S. (2012). Exploring the development of team identification. *Journal of Sport Management, 26,* 283–294. doi:10.1123/jsm.26.4.283

Mahony, D.F., Nakazawa, M., Funk, D.C., James, J.D., & Gladden, J.M. (2002). Motivational factors influencing the behavior of J. League spectators. *Sport Management Review, 5,* 1–24. doi:10.1016/S1441-3523(02)70059-4

Mason, D.S. (1999). What is the sports product and who buys it? The marketing of professional sports leagues. *European Journal of Marketing, 33,* 402–419. doi:10.1108/03090569910253251

McDonald, M.A., Milne, G.R., & Hong, J. (2002). Motivational factors for evaluating sport spectator and participant markets. *Sport Marketing Quarterly, 11,* 100–113.

Melnick, M.J. (1993). Searching for sociability in the stands: A theory of sports spectating. *Journal of Sport Management, 7,* 44–60. doi:10.1123/jsm.7.1.44

Moorman, C., Zaltman, G., & Deshpande, R. (1992). Relationships between providers and users of market research: The dynamics of trust within and between organizations. *JMR, Journal of Marketing Research, 29,* 314–329. doi:10.2307/3172742

Mullin, B.J., Hardy, S., & Sutton, W.A. (2007). *Sport marketing* (3rd ed.). Champaign, IL: Human Kinetics.

Nunnally, J.C., & Bernstein, I.H. (1994). *Psychometric theory* (3rd ed.). New York, NY: McGraw-Hill.

Polit, D.F., & Beck, C.T. (2006). The Content Validity Index: Are you sure you know what's being reported? Critique and recommendations. *Research in Nursing & Health, 29,* 489–497. doi:10.1002/nur.20147

Pons, F., Mourali, M., & Nyeck, S. (2006). Consumer orientation toward sporting events. *Journal of Service Research, 8,* 276–287. doi:10.1177/1094670505283931

Pritchard, M.P., Havitz, M.E., & Howard, D.R. (1999). Analysing the commitment-loyalty link in service contexts. *Journal of the Academy of Marketing Science, 27,* 333–348. doi:10.1177/0092070399273004

Richins, M.L. (2004). The material values scale: Measurement properties and development of a short form. *The Journal of Consumer Research, 31,* 209–219. doi:10.1086/383436

Robinson, M., Trail, G., & Kwon, H. (2004). Motives and points of attachment of professional golf spectators. *Sport Management Review, 7,* 167–192. doi:10.1016/S1441-3523(04)70049-2

Rossiter, J.R. (2002). The C-OAR-SE procedure for scale development in marketing. *International Journal of Research in Marketing, 19,* 305–335. doi:10.1016/S0167-8116(02)00097-6

Ryu, K., Lee, H., & Kim, W.G. (2012). The influence of the quality of the physical environment, food, and service on restaurant image, customer perceived value, customer satisfaction, and behavioral intentions. *International Journal of Contemporary Hospitality Management, 24,* 200–223. doi:10.1108/09596111211206141

Sánchez-Fernández, R., & Iniesta-Bonillo, Á.M. (2007). The concept of perceived value: A systematic review of the research. *Marketing Theory, 7,* 427–451. doi:10.1177/1470593107083165

Sheth, J.N., Newman, B.I., & Gross, B.L. (1991). *Consumption values and market choices: Theory and application.* Cincinnati, OH: College Division South-Western.

Stanton, J.M., Sinar, E.F., Balzer, W.K., & Smith, P.C. (2002). Issues and strategies for reducing the length of self-report scales. *Personnel Psychology, 55,* 167–194. doi:10.1111/j.1744-6570.2002.tb00108.x

Sweeney, J.C., & Soutar, G.N. (2001). Consumer perceived value: The development of a multiple item scale. *Journal of Retailing, 77,* 203–220. doi:10.1016/S0022-4359(01)00041-0

Sweeney, J.C., Soutar, G.N., & Johnson, L.W. (1999). The role of perceived risk in the quality–value relationship: A study in a retail environment. *Journal of Retailing, 75,* 77–105. doi:10.1016/S0022-4359(99)80005-0

Theodorakis, N.D., & Alexandris, K. (2008). Can service quality predict spectators' behavioral intentions in professional soccer? *Managing Leisure, 13,* 162–178. doi:10.1080/13606710802200852

Trail, G.T., & James, J.D. (2001). The Motivation Scale for Sport Consumption: Assessment of the scale's psychometric properties. *Journal of Sport Behavior, 24,* 108–127.

Trail, G.T., Robinson, M.J., Dick, R.J., & Gillentine, A.J. (2003). Motives and points of attachment: Fans versus spectators in intercollegiate athletics. *Sport Marketing Quarterly, 12,* 217–227.

Wakefield, K.L. (1995). The pervasive effects of social influence on sporting event attendance. *Journal of Sport and Social Issues, 19,* 335–351. doi:10.1177/019372395019004002

Wakefield, K.L., Blodgett, J.G., & Sloan, H.J. (1996). Measurement and management of the sportscape. *Journal of Sport Management, 10,* 15–31. doi:10.1123/jsm.10.1.15

Walker, M., & Mondello, M.J. (2007). Moving beyond economic impact: A closer look at the contingent valuation method. *International Journal of Sport Finance, 2,* 149–160.

Walsh, G., Shiu, E., & Hassan, L.M. (2014). Replicating, validating, and reducing the length of the consumer perceived value scale. *Journal of Business Research, 67,* 260–267. doi:10.1016/j.jbusres.2013.05.012

Wann, D.L. (1995). Preliminary validation of the Sport Fan Motivation Scale. *Journal of Sport and Social Issues, 19,* 377–396. doi:10.1177/019372395019004004

Weltfussball.de. (2015a). *Bundesliga 2014/2015 Zuschauer Heimspiele.* Retrieved October 27, 2015, from http://www.weltfussball.de/zuschauer/bundesliga-2014-2015/1/

Weltfussball.de. (2015b). *2. Bundesliga 2014/15 Zuschauer Heimspiele.* Retrieved October 27, 2015, from http://www.weltfussball.de/zuschauer/2-bundesliga-2014-2015/1/

Westerbeek, H., & Shilbury, D. (2003). A conceptual model for sport services marketing research: Integrating quality, value and satisfaction. *International Journal of Sports Marketing & Sponsorship, 5,* 3–23. doi:10.1108/IJSMS-05-01-2003-B002

Williams, P., & Soutar, G.N. (2009). Value, satisfaction and behavioral intentions in an adventure tourism context. *Annals of Tourism Research, 36,* 413–438. doi:10.1016/j.annals.2009.02.002

Yoshida, M., & James, J.D. (2010). Customer satisfaction with game and service experiences: Antecedents and consequences. *Journal of Sport Management, 24,* 338–361. doi:10.1123/jsm.24.3.338

Zeithaml, V.A. (1988). Consumer perceptions of price, quality, and value: A means-end model and synthesis of evidence. *Journal of Marketing, 52,* 2–22. doi:10.2307/1251446

Journal of Sport Management, 2017, 31, 96-110
https://doi.org/10.1123/jsm.2016-0115
© 2017 Human Kinetics, Inc.

Human Kinetics
ARTICLE

Prioritizing Sponsorship Resources in Formula One Racing: A Longitudinal Analysis

Joe Cobbs
Northern Kentucky University

B. David Tyler
Western Carolina University

Jonathan A. Jensen
University of North Carolina at Chapel Hill

Kwong Chan
Northeastern University

Accessing and exploiting organizational resources are essential capabilities for competitive sport organizations, particularly those engaged in motorsports, where teams lacking resources frequently dissolve. Corporate sponsorship represents a common method for resource acquisition, yet not all sponsorships equally benefit the sponsored organization. Sponsorship utility can be dependent on institutional dynamics such as league governance that produces competitive disparities. Through this study we extend the resource-based view to assert that sponsorships vary in their propensity to contribute to team survival, warranting prioritization in sponsorship strategy based on access to different sponsor resources. To empirically investigate the influence of a variety of sponsorships, survival analysis modeling was used to examine 40 years of corporate sponsorship of Formula One racing teams. One finding from the longitudinal analysis was that sponsorships offering financial or performance-based resources enhance team survival to a greater degree than operational sponsorships. However, such prioritization is subject to team experience, changes in institutional monetary allocation, and diminishing returns.

Keywords: motorsports, survival analysis, marketing strategy, resource-based view, resource priority, competitive advantage

In the charity, arts, entertainment, and sport industries, corporate sponsorship has flourished as a structured exchange mechanism whereby the industries' organizations can access heterogeneous resources from commercial partners in return for promotional affiliation and enhancement (Meenaghan, 2001). Sponsorship represents an important platform for interorganizational research in sports for several reasons. Scholars have recognized the potential for a sponsorship alliance to differentiate and add financial value to a sponsoring firm's brand while serving as a primary method of resource acquisition for sponsored sport organizations (Jensen, Cobbs, & Turner, 2016). For example, since 1995, Shell has provided the Ferrari Formula One (F1) racing team with diverse resources such as financial investment, petroleum products, and technological performance expertise. In exchange, Ferrari provides Shell with the F1 product testing, knowledge, and sponsorship resources to meet Shell's promotional objectives of creating awareness for Shell's premium products, sustaining its perceived position as a technology leader, solidifying key stakeholder relationships via event hospitality, and encouraging purchase through themed point-of-sale promotions (Verity, 2002).

Moreover, because corporate sponsorship is an institutionalized support mechanism ubiquitous throughout sport and its various segments, engagement in this type of interorganizational alliance spans a myriad of connected industries, organizations, activities, and managers (Crowley, 1991). Yet, the managerial aspects of sponsorship alliances have received scant attention in an otherwise maturing body of research (Cornwell, 2008). Similar to other alliances, the resources exchanged within a sponsorship are heterogeneous and not necessarily related to a sustainable competitive advantage (Amis, Pant, & Slack, 1997). Since Amis and colleagues (1997) first used the resource-based view (RBV) to study sponsorship management, scholars building on their work have maintained their investigative focus on the sponsoring firm while

Joe Cobbs is with the Department of Marketing, Economics, and Sports Business, Northern Kentucky University, Highland Heights, KY. B. David Tyler is with the College of Business, Western Carolina University, Cullowhee, NC. Jonathan A. Jensen is with the Department of Exercise and Sport Science, University of North Carolina at Chapel Hill, Chapel Hill, NC. Kwong Chan is with the Department of Marketing, Northeastern University. Address author correspondence to Joe Cobbs at cobbsj1@nku.edu.

ignoring the influence on the sponsored sport organization (e.g., Fahy, Farrelly, & Quester, 2004; Jensen et al., 2016; Papadimitriou & Apostolopoulou, 2009). In this paper, we advance the RBV agenda in sport by evaluating the heterogeneity of resources accessed by the sponsored sport organization in relation to its competitive survival.

Finally, the growing popularity of sponsorship alliances as a mechanism for resource exchange is evidenced by the rapid expansion of corporate sponsorship investment, which reached an estimated worldwide expenditure of US$55.3 billion in 2015 (International Events Group, 2015). Given these factors, empirical research to test how sponsorships offering divergent resources impact the longevity of sponsored sport organizations is broadly relevant and important to the sports industry as managers make decisions on prioritizing sponsorship solicitation.

Background

The Compelling Context of Formula One Racing

Sport organizations are particularly dependent on sponsorship as a resource necessary for survival in the highly competitive arena of motorsport, such as the National Association for Stock Car Auto Racing (NASCAR), V8 Supercars, and F1 racing, where up to 70% of team budgets are funded by sponsorships (Sylt & Reid, 2008). The ultracompetitive arena of F1 motor racing provides an ideal context within which to study the influence of sponsorship resources on organizational survival. In October of 2014, two different F1 teams (Caterham and Marussia) approached administration, the British equivalent of Chapter 11 bankruptcy (Sylt, 2015). The Marussia team went into administration in late 2014 and missed the final three races of the 2014 F1 season, while the remaining Caterham assets were liquidated at auction in early 2015 (Smith, 2015). The loss of two teams temporarily reduced the starting grid for F1 races to only 18 cars, which posed a management crisis for the sport as the 100-year agreement for the sport's commercial rights between the Fédération Internationale de l'Automobile (FIA) and private equity firm CVC was put in jeopardy of default (Sylt, 2015). Given F1 teams' heavy reliance on sponsorship to fulfill budgetary needs (Sylt & Reid, 2008), a better understanding of sponsorship resource priority could help existing and future teams survive and avoid administration or bankruptcy.

The purpose of this longitudinal study is to prioritize and test the influence of differing categories of sponsorship (in the form of performance, financial, and operational-related alliances) on the survival of sport organizations. To achieve this aim, we employed a survival model utilizing 40 years of data that included the sponsorship alliances between 124 different F1 racing teams and 1,077 supporting commercial sponsors. Survival analysis modeling, commonly used in the health field to examine the determinants of a person's lifetime, is an appropriate method to study how various factors influence the duration to a particular event (Singer & Willett, 2003). In this study, the event of interest is the dissolution of the sport organization or team. In survival analysis, the modeled dependent variable is the hazard rate, which is a function that denotes the probability of the organization experiencing dissolution (Audretsch & Mahmood, 1995). The hazard rate is based on the age and characteristics of an organization (i.e., independent or control variables in the model) in relation to its peers within a particular institutional environment. Therefore, a negative coefficient in a survival analysis model indicates the associated variable reduces the *hazard of dissolution*, or likelihood of the organization's ceasing to exist in a particular year. For example, successfully registering patents may contribute to the survival of sports technology firms such as Sportvision and Hawk-Eye, purveyors of American football's first-down graphic and soccer's goal line technology. If so, we would expect a negative coefficient to be associated with a variable that measures registered patents because such patents reduce the likelihood of sports technology firms' bankruptcy or dissolution.

F1 teams are competitive enterprises that access various categories of resources via corporate sponsorship to enhance performance and in turn, maintain operations on an international scale (Cobbs, Groza, & Pruitt, 2012; Jensen & Cobbs, 2014). Because of the high-profile nature of F1, a team's birth, survival, competitive performance, sponsorship activity, dissolution, and institutional conditions are all publicly documented across global media sources. While scholars have recognized the theoretical diversity of interorganizational alliance resources and suggested situational contingencies to their utility (e.g., Cui, 2013), we can empirically test how a sport organization's access to such resources through sponsorship influences its survival in the dynamic, highly competitive institutional environment of F1 racing.

RBV and Resource Heterogeneity

While the popularity of the RBV has focused attention on the contribution of organizational resources to a sustained competitive advantage (Barney, 1991; Wernerfelt, 1984), the mere sustainability of operations concerns many sport enterprises. In a dynamic, competitive environment, an organization's administrators must continually manage resources in a manner conducive to sustaining operations while organizational learning accumulates. Levitt and March (1988) explain that "organizations are seen as learning by encoding inferences from history into routines that guide behavior" (p. 319). To maintain operations during this process, sports team administrators often formulate interorganizational alliances in the form of corporate sponsorships, which act as a quasi-market mechanism to enable the team to leverage its own core capabilities as bartering chips in relationships with sponsors that facilitate additional resource access (Cobbs et al., 2012). The RBV initially emphasized the characteristics (i.e., rare, valuable, inimitable, nonsubstitutable) and competitive implications of resources internal to the organization (Barney, 1991). Sport strategy theorists later extended the RBV beyond the boundaries of the firm to recognize the potential competitive contribution of interfirm alliances and their associated resources (Amis et al., 1997; Jensen et al., 2016).

While alliances such as sponsorships often have clear short-term benefits in terms of resource access, relying on interorganizational relationships for access to a range of resources entails dependency dilemmas that may be detrimental over time (Pfeffer & Nowak, 1976). Furthermore, an organization's capacity to manage multiple alliances is finite (Cui, Calantone, & Griffith, 2011; Deeds & Hill, 1996), organizational and alliance resources are not homogeneous (Cui & O'Connor, 2012; Grant, 1991), and their utility is subject to dynamic conditions (Cui, 2013). In other words, a certain sponsorship resource (e.g., tire supplier for a racing team) may be particularly valuable in a given set of organizational or institutional conditions (e.g., where teams are responsible for sourcing their own tires), whereas that same resource may be less relevant when such conditions change (e.g., the racing series contracts with a single tire supplier for all competing teams, as happened in F1 in 2011). As a result, ongoing prioritization and maximization of resources is necessary when managing any alliance strategy, including sponsorship solicitation and execution.

According to the RBV, resources are heterogeneously distributed across firms and do not represent identical benefits (Barney, 1991). Grant (1991) identified six general categories of firm resources: financial, physical, human, technological, reputation, and organizational. In empirical contexts emphasizing resource exchange, scholars have routinely reduced the categorization to designations such as technical versus nontechnical (Chan, Kensinger, Keown, & Martin, 1997), marketing versus research (Anand & Khanna, 2000), technological versus marketing (Das, Sen, & Sengupta, 1998), and unilateral support versus bilateral cooperation (Lee, Lee, & Pennings, 2001). In the sports context, Fahy et al. (2004) designated sponsorship resources as tangible and intangible assets and capabilities of the sponsoring firm. However, all of these resource categorizations tend to describe the actual resource or alliance relationship and not necessarily a sponsorship's potential contribution to the sponsored team in relation to its competitive environment. While the RBV emphasizes internally available resources, it is most beneficial for strategy development when considered with the external perspective of the industrial organization (Wernerfelt, 1984; see Truyens, De Bosscher, Heyndels, & Westerbeek, 2014, for a discussion of the industrial organization perspective and the RBV applied to sport). Likewise, certain sponsorship resources may offer a more direct contribution to a team's survival in a particular environment, and that contribution may change with the dynamics of the competitive environment (e.g., adjustments to the league revenue distribution model).

Prior researchers who focused on the competitive environment have applied a "complementarity" or "strategic relatedness" approach to resource application by characterizing the resource exchange within an alliance relationship based on a comparison of each partner's industry or operational context (Chung, Singh, & Lee, 2000; Sarkar, Echambadi, Cavusgil, & Aulakh, 2001; Tsai, 2000). Complementarity with alliance partners offers a distinctive basis for prioritization of complementary resources. Sarkar et al. (2001, p. 360) conceptualize alliance complementarity as a symmetry consisting of "unique and valuable resources available to achieve strategic objectives," which thus enhance "competitive viability." This perspective implies not only that resources are heterogeneously distributed across firms and industries but also that resources retain a strategic dimension relating to their potential utility in competition. In other words, sponsorships provide access to certain resources that may be more or less relevant to a team's survival based on the competition faced in a specific environment. To that end, we propose sponsorship alliance distinctions within this study based on access to three different types of resource categories: performance-based sponsorships, financial sponsorships, and operational sponsorships. While access to each type of resource constitutes a different element of sponsorship strategy, we hypothesize each to deter team dissolution to varying degrees based on resource complementarity within the institutional context of F1 racing.

Hypotheses

Performance-Based Sponsorships

The first sponsorship resource designation—labeled performance-based—is signified by high industry relatedness between sponsorship partners where the complementarity of available resources directly relates to competitive performance. Dyer and Singh (1998) define complementary resources as collectively generating "greater rents than the sum of those obtained from the individual endowments of each (alliance) partner" (pp. 666–667). In the context of F1 racing, such alliances are most common in the form of sponsorships with automobile component manufacturers, aerodynamic engineering firms, or other high tech partnerships focused on enhancing track performance. A sponsor that shares an industry with or operates in an industry strategically related to the team's competitive environment is likely better equipped to offer complementary resources that enhance performance and combat rivals (Varadarajan & Cunningham, 1995). Accessing complementary resources to enhance performance is a foundation of alliance formation (Chung et al., 2000). Likewise, in the expansive literature on sponsorship congruence (for a review, see Fleck & Quester, 2007), sponsor product relevance is one key to high-fit sponsorships (Olson & Thjømøe, 2011).

Bergmann Lichtenstein and Brush (2001) found resources relating directly to the production process to be more salient to entrepreneurs, who typically pursued such resources through interorganizational partnerships in congruent industries. This assertion follows organizational learning theory (Levitt & March, 1988), which includes the tenet that entrepreneurial enterprises can compensate for their liability of newness by gaining relevant industry knowledge through alliances with established firms (Freeman, Carroll, & Hannan, 1983). However, as the entrepreneurial organization accumulates competitive experience over time, the necessity of accessing performance-based resources may diminish (Bergmann Lichtenstein & Brush, 2001). As a result, we anticipate resources exchanged within congruent industry sponsorships to exert a positive influence on a team's performance in head-to-head competition and thereby stave off organizational dissolution, but we expect the survival effect of such sponsorships to diminish as a team accumulates competitive experience:

> **H1a**: A team's performance-based sponsorships are negatively related to the hazard of dissolution.

> **H1b**: As a team gains experience, the negative relationship between dissolution and performance-based sponsorships weakens.

Financial Sponsorships

Financial or monetary resources represent the most ubiquitous designation of firm resource categorization (e.g., Barney, 1995; Grant, 1991), which is not surprising given their versatility. Financial resources not only possess an intrinsic transformative nature but can also symbolize the ultimate aim of many organizations—that being to increase financial wealth. Indeed, this money-making condition is so vital to an entrepreneurial enterprise such as a racing team that the financial numbers test (i.e., how will the business make money?) entails one of the two essential tenets of a viable business model (vs. the organizational narrative test, which asks if the story of the business makes sense; Magretta, 2002). In our context, financial sponsorships involve firms in industries unrelated to either competitive performance or business operations. For example, team sponsors such as Johnnie Walker spirits, Labatt's beer, Pepsi-Cola, and Universal Music Group fit this category, where the sponsors contribute financial resources to the team but do not otherwise contribute resources directly relevant to track performance or business operations (i.e., the subsequent sponsorship category).

Beyond simply creating monetary wealth, financial resources provide an organization with flexibility because their quality of liquidity enables these resources to be quickly exchanged for another resource deemed at the time to be vital to the team; however, Barney (1991) points out financial resources are often not rare and are therefore unlikely to solely generate a sustainable competitive advantage. While accessing financial resources may be imperative to team survival, some researchers have shown that in the early stages of organizational development, financial resources, though relevant, are not as important to the entrepreneur as those resources

relating directly to performance (Bergmann Lichtenstein & Brush, 2001; Brush, Greene, & Hart, 2001). Therefore, we formally hypothesize that access to financial resources through sponsorships contributes to a team's continued existence but suspect such sponsorships are not as vital as performance sponsors:

> **H2a**: A team's financial-based sponsorships are negatively related to the hazard of dissolution.

> **H2b**: The relationship between financial sponsors and dissolution is less intense than the relationship between performance sponsors and dissolution.

Operational Sponsorships

Resources contributing to the ongoing operation of an organization, but that are not strictly monetary or straightforwardly influencing a team's direct competition with rivals, were labeled as operational sponsorships. This category is characterized by the commodity goods and services necessary for the continued functioning of a team and instrumental to accessing further resources (Brush et al., 2001). For most organizations, such resources might include office equipment, Internet access, certain basic employee services, and other administrative capabilities. Similarly, for racing teams this category may include sponsors in the logistics (e.g., FedEx, DHL, Hanjin), human resources (e.g., Adecco, Randstad), or office supply industries (e.g., Brother, IKON). This type of operational resource is typically not the primary basis for competition within an industry and tends to be easier to access given their near universal utilization. As a result, operational resources are not particularly rare, and similar to financial resources, are unlikely to be a source of competitive advantage (Barney, 1991). In addition, these resources lack the flexibility and liquidity of pure financial resources. We therefore formally hypothesize operational sponsorships to contribute to organizational survival but suspect access to such resources is less influential than either performance or financial sponsorships in predicting team dissolution:

> **H3a**: A team's operational sponsorships are negatively related to the hazard of dissolution.

> **H3b**: Operational sponsorships are the least influential to dissolution compared with performance or financial sponsorships.

Sponsorship Management Constraints

Though sponsorships offer a convenient mechanism for interorganizational resource exchange, like individuals, an organization's capacity for managing relationships may be bounded and subject to diminishing returns (McFadyen & Cannella, 2004). Firms possess an alliance management capability that is constrained by factors such as partner evaluation, coordination, and integration costs in time, focus, and monetary investment (Ireland, Hitt, & Vaidyanath, 2002). Managing different types and increasing numbers of sponsorships can strain a team's capability for maximizing returns to the numerous relationships (Rothaermel & Deeds, 2006). Deeds and Hill (1996) describe this phenomenon as arising "because the effectiveness with which the firm can select and manage alliance partners is likely to be negatively related to the number of alliances the firm is managing" (p. 42). Given this cost to managing increasing alliance relationships, too many sponsorships may eventually exhibit diminishing returns and be detrimental to a team's continuity. For example, adding a tenth performance-based sponsor to a racing team's portfolio may not produce marginal benefits equivalent to the second or third performance-based sponsor signed because the team already has nine other performance-based sponsors and must also manage each of these corporate partnerships:

> **H4**: Increasing numbers of (a) performance, (b) financial, and (c) operational sponsorships will exhibit diminishing returns to reducing the hazard of team dissolution.

Method

To test the prioritization of sponsorships offering heterogeneous resources, we employed a survival analysis modeling methodology, also referred to as event history (e.g., Singer & Willett, 2003), in the context of F1 motor racing. In this study, we define the organizational form as a motor racing team competing within the institutional system of F1. By setting the system boundary based on a particular industry (F1), we negate cross-industry discrepancies and emphasize the variance among teams and their particular strategies for navigating a common institutional environment (Miller & Shamsie, 1996; Rao, 1994).

Sample

Given the historical international popularity of F1 racing and the characteristics described above, data on F1 team existence and alliances with sponsoring firms were feasible to compile from the institution's formal organization in 1950 through 2007.[1] We acquired the foundation of the data from the online database ChicaneF1, which provides a comprehensive catalog of historical team and sponsoring firm information (Davies & Lawrence, n.d.). Next, the data were cross-checked with data we obtained from an internal F1 team source to verify reliability (SportsPro Media, 2007). We further consulted historical F1 texts containing pictures of various teams' race cars in an attempt to match visible corporate partner logos on the vehicles with sponsorships compiled in the data (Donaldson, 2002; Schlegelmilch & Lehbrink, 2004). These cross-verification efforts supported the general reliability of the ChicaneF1 team–sponsor data and served to clear up ambiguities where present. To compile historical team performance data, we referenced the official F1 website (Formula One Administration [FOA], n.d.). The resulting data set consisted of 124 separate F1 team organizations,[2] 776 team years,[3] 1,077 sponsoring firms, and 5,054 team–sponsor alliance years.

Dependent Variable

Survival analysis examines event occurrences or changes in a subject or organization's condition over time. In the current study, the data set is longitudinal in annual intervals and cross-sectional in that a multitude of teams are chronicled. The potential outcome conditions in any given time period of the F1 teams studied here are only twofold: operational or nonoperational. While survival may be more difficult to discern when applied to traditional organizations (Freeman et al., 1983), the motor racing context enables delineation based on whether a team competed in a race in a particular season or not. Therefore, we composed a binary survival term coded 1 if a team dissolved in a given year (i.e., did not compete further following that season), and 0 if the team continued in competition following the given year.

From this data, we generated annual hazard rates based on the proportion of the teams at risk with a given level of experience that incur dissolution (Singer & Willett, 2003). This hazard of team dissolution represents the dependent variable in survival analysis (Audretsch & Mahmood, 1995). Essentially, survival analysis produces an age-based hazard function for the population of teams that represents the chronological probability of team failure, given the team has not yet dissolved. The hazard function accounts for both noncensored cases (i.e., teams whose entire life span is represented within the data set) and censored cases (i.e., teams that remain in existence when data set concludes in 2007) in computing probabilities, which is vital to the analysis given that teams still in existence have yet to experience dissolution and are therefore right-censored in the data set. The independent variables then predict probabilities of dissolution, or hazard rates. As a result, a *negative* coefficient to an independent variable signifies a reduced hazard of dissolution or, alternatively, an *increased* probability of survival.

Independent Variables

The primary hypotheses (H1–H3) addressed the nature of resources exchanged between sponsorship partners according to the complementarity between the sponsoring firm's industry[4] and the team's competitive environment (Sarkar et al., 2001). Each team's competitive experience (per H1b) was noted in the number of years of F1 race participation. Before classifying the sponsorships in this context, two researchers developed sponsorship resource designations of (a) performance-based, (b) financial, or (c) operational by studying the relevant literature referenced in the hypotheses outlined above and extensively reviewing the press announcements of over 100 F1 sponsorships. A third researcher and two F1 team sponsorship managers then reviewed these three designations and confirmed their face validity.

We defined performance-based sponsorships as those accessing resources that directly contribute to the team's racing performance on the track, such as Brembo brakes and Pirelli tires. Financial sponsorships offered resources strictly monetary in nature from sponsors in industries unrelated to motorsports or business operations, such as Martini spirits and GoldenPalace casino gaming. Operational sponsorships provided access to resources that contribute to the organizational operations of the team but not team performance in racing competition, such as Allianz commercial insurance and Accenture management consulting.

Next, two researchers independently classified each sponsorship in the data set as primarily performance-based, financial, or operational. The initial intercoder reliability was 89%, and conflicts were subsequently reconciled through discussion and further clarification of the classification descriptions, as well as a review of sponsorship announcements within the relevant industry under evaluation. Upon completion of the sponsorship classifications, we compiled three variables measuring the count of performance, financial, and operational sponsorships for each F1 team in each year of the data set. In total, the data featured 2,781 performance-based sponsorships, 1,318 financial sponsorships, and 955 operational sponsorships.

To test the fourth hypothesis, which predicted diminishing returns to sponsorship resource access, a separate quadratic term for each of the three sponsorship category variables was formulated (Hoang & Rothaermel, 2005). If such an effect existed, we would expect to see a positive coefficient on the quadratic terms, signifying that as the number of sponsorships offering the specified type of resource reached a certain level, incremental sponsorships of that type would positively influence the odds of team dissolution.

Control Variables

On-track performance may affect team survival through both direct and indirect access to resources. Superior race results directly enhance financial resources through prize money allocations, and potential sponsors theoretically desire to align themselves with prestigious others (Stuart, 1998), indicating that generating prestige through superior performance might facilitate additional sponsor-resource access. In these ways, competitive performance seems highly probable to influence team survival. Therefore, we control for the performance of F1 teams both recently and historically. We operationalize recent success through a rolling average of the annual points earned by a team over the previous 5 years.[5] Historical success we derive by an aggregation of the drivers' championships won by a team previous to the current season.

To account for several other factors with the potential to impact team longevity, we compiled four additional control variables. Based on organizational learning theory (Levitt & March, 1988), sponsors' experience in the F1 competitive environment may influence their sponsored team's survival. As a result, we included a variable that summed the years of F1 involvement for all of a team's

sponsors in a particular year. Because sports leagues are not static institutions, we examined adjustments in the governance of F1 during our study's time span and denoted two specific eras using a binary variable. Specifically, team years after 1995 were signified as 1 and years before 1996 we denoted as 0. Following the 1995 season, the governing body of F1 (FIA), the commercial rights holder (Formula One Promotions and Administration), and F1's competing teams renegotiated their operating agreement (i.e., Concorde Agreement), which resulted in a greater distribution of financial resources to the teams based on annual competitive performance (Collings, 2004). Consequently, team points may be more important to survival and financial sponsors less important after 1995. Finally, we include both the number of times in which a team has been sold before a given year and the world gross domestic product (GDP) annual growth rate (U.S. Department of Agriculture Economic Research Service, 2016) as additional covariates relating to the characteristics of a team and the global macroeconomic condition, respectively.

Descriptive statistics and the correlation matrix for the variables appear in Table 1. Unsurprisingly given the large sample size, almost all correlations are statistically significant. However, all variance inflation factors (VIF) are less than 10, which indicates multicollinearity is not overly concerning (O'Brien, 2007).[6]

Model Estimation

Researchers employing survival analysis must determine whether a specified shape of the baseline hazard function is appropriate to their context. The hazard function is based on the chronological shape of the hazard rate and depicts the probability that dissolution will occur after any given duration. As there is no a priori reason to specify a hazard rate functional form in the F1 context (i.e., no exogenous reason to assume that teams are systematically more or less viable at any given period), we use Cox regression (Cox, 1972) to model the data. Although hazard rates are assumed to be proportional between groups in Cox regression and other semiparametric models, this technique is preferred because of its ability to model both time-dependent and continuous covariates. For a detailed description of Cox regression applied in management research, see Brett et al. (2007). For explanation of survival analysis and a call for application in sport management research, see Jensen and Turner (2016). In the current study, continuous variables include global GDP growth; team points; team drivers' championships; alliance partners' experience; and compilations of performance, financial, and operational sponsors by team.

Results

Overall Hazard Function

Analyzing the lifetime of F1 teams utilizing survival analysis modeling results in a computation of the overall hazard rate for the dissolution of an F1 team, which is

Table 1 Descriptive Statistics and Correlations

Variable	M	SD	1	2	3	4	5	6	7	8	9
1. Performance-based sponsors	4.46	5.47									
2. Team experience (years)	11.88	12.12	.46								
3. Financial sponsors	2.14	2.80	.73	.35							
4. Operational sponsors	1.53	2.78	.77	.33	.74						
5. Team sponsors' experience (years)	40.54	52.71	.85	.65	.64	.67					
6. Post-1995 dummy	0.22	0.41	.77	.41	.76	.77	.70				
7. Team points	25.46	35.37	.42	.69	.23	.23	.65	.29			
8. Drivers' championships	1.87	3.10	.33	.86	.14	.14	.57	.22	.81		
9. Team sold	0.04	0.19	.13	.01	.18	.16	.07	.16	-.09	-.10	
10. Global GDP growth (%)	3.11	1.29	-.03	-.07	-.02	-.01	-.05	.03	-.00	-.03	-.03

Note. There are 570 team years and 124 unique teams. Correlations with absolute values equal to or greater than .09 are significant at the $p < .05$ level. GDP = gross domestic product.

the dependent variable. Dating back to 1967, the overall hazard function for F1 teams is 0.12, defined as the conditional probability that an F1 team may fail at any given time (11.69%).

The hazard function can also be computed across various time frames to determine whether teams are more or less likely to fail early or later in the team's life. For example, in Year 1 of an F1 team's experience, the hazard for dissolution is 0.29, which is the conditional probability that an F1 team will fail after only 1 year of existence (i.e., 28.92%). As one might expect, the hazard decreases to 26.79% after the second year, 15.0% after the third, and to only 5.26% after the fourth. A smoothed version of the baseline hazard function visually depicts how the hazard changes over time. As illustrated in Figure 1 and in accordance with the data, the hazard for dissolution is highest in the first decade of existence and slowly drops as the team gains experience. After 15 years of existence, the expected hazard for dissolution remains relatively consistent through subsequent years.

Hypotheses

We propose an empirical model based on prioritization for predicting the dissolution of motorsports teams reliant on sponsorship resources for survival. To test our hypotheses, we start with a basic model (Model 1 in Table 2) inclusive of the primary variables representing three sponsorship categories—performance, financial, and operational—as well as most control variables (i.e., sponsors' experience, team points, drivers' championships, team sold, and global GDP growth). Next, we insert quadratic terms to examine the possibility of diminishing returns to each resource category—both with (Model 3) and without (Model 2) a measure quantifying team experience. Finally, we insert the dichotomous indicator of the institutional change that followed the 1995 season—first, in a model without the quadratic resource terms (Model 4) and then in a full comprehensive model (Model 5). All five models outperform a constant-only model at a highly significant level ($p < .001$). The third and fourth models also outperform nested Model 1, and the final model outperforms nested Model 4 at a marginally significant level ($p < .10$). Results for each model are displayed in Table 2, and discussion of findings is based on the statistically preferred comprehensive model (Model 5) unless stated otherwise.

H1 is the first of three hypotheses through which we examine the effects of sponsorships that vary in the resources offered to competing teams. Keep in mind that a negative coefficient to an independent variable signifies a reduced hazard of dissolution or, alternatively, an increased probability of survival. As we generally predicted in H1 and H2, access to both performance and financial resources enhanced the likelihood of

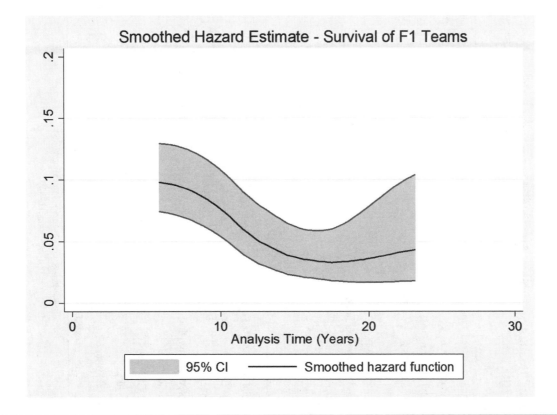

Figure 1 — Plot of smoothed hazard estimate of survival of Formula One (F1) teams over time. CI = confidence interval.

Table 2   Results of Survival Analysis of Team Dissolution

Variable	Hypothesis (effect)	Model 1	Model 2	Model 3	Model 4	Model 5
Performance-based sponsors	1a (−)	−0.64*** (0.17)	−0.77*** (0.18)	−0.81*** (0.18)	−0.89*** (0.19)	−1.11*** (0.25)
Performance sponsors squared	4a (+)		0.03*** (0.01)	0.03*** (0.01)	0.03*** (0.01)	0.04 (0.03)
Team experience		0.09 (0.09)		0.11 (0.10)	0.08 (0.11)	0.11 (0.11)
Performance Sponsors × Team Experience	1b (+)	0.03** (0.01)		0.01 (0.01)	0.05** (0.02)	0.04* (0.02)
Financial sponsors	2 (−)	−0.28† (0.15)	−0.71** (0.25)	−0.65** (0.25)	−0.47* (0.20)	−1.20** (0.37)
Financial sponsors squared	4b (+)		0.08* (0.03)	0.07† (0.03)		0.23* (0.10)
Operational sponsors	3 (−)	0.14 (0.19)	0.17 (0.29)	0.15 (0.29)	0.10 (0.28)	−0.17 (0.47)
Operational sponsors squared	4c (+)		−0.02 (0.03)	−0.02 (0.03)		0.10 (0.20)
Team sponsors' experience	control (−)	0.02 (0.02)	0.03 (0.02)	0.03 (0.02)	0.02 (0.02)	0.03 (0.02)
Post-1995 dummy	control				−1.02 (2.67)	6.16 (4.26)
Financial Sponsors × Post-1995	control (+)				1.71** (0.62)	−0.89 (1.15)
Team points	control (−)	−0.09** (0.03)	−0.07** (0.03)	−0.08** (0.03)	−0.08** (0.03)	−0.08** (0.03)
Team Points × Post-1995	control (−)				−2.93** (1.04)	−3.64** (1.32)
Drivers' championships	control (−)	−0.38 (0.33)	−0.21 (0.30)	−0.42 (0.40)	−0.74† (0.43)	−0.80† (0.45)
Team sold	control	−16.12 (1489)	−26.44 (998)	−24.18 (1040)	−37.05 (1427)	−76.17 (1157)
Global GDP growth	control	−0.02 (0.11)	−0.03 (0.11)	−0.03 (0.11)	−0.02 (0.12)	−0.01 (0.12)
−2 log-likelihood		241.83	235.43	232.85	218.26	211.47
Likelihood ratio $\chi^2(df)$		73.76*** (10)	80.16*** (11)	82.74*** (13)	97.33*** (13)	104.12*** (16)
Change vs. prior nested model (1, 4)				8.975*	23.572***	6.785†

Note. Standard errors are in parentheses. GDP = gross domestic product.

†$p < .10$. *$p < .05$. **$p < .01$. ***$p < .001$ (two-tailed tests).

survival by negatively influencing team dissolution to a significant degree ($p < .01$). For each additional performance-based sponsor, the team's odds of dissolving the following season fell by 67% (or a factor of 0.33).[7] We further hypothesized based on organizational learning theory that the effect of performance-based sponsorships would weaken as the team gained experience (H1b). Indeed, this interaction with team experience is empirically supported ($p < .05$). As a team gained a year of experience, the marginal contribution to team survival of an additional performance-based sponsor was reduced by 4.2%. However, results did not match the expectation that financial sponsors are less influential to survival than performance-based sponsors (H2b). Instead, sponsors primarily offering financial resources had a slightly greater impact on team survival—reducing the odds of team dissolution by 70% for each additional financial sponsor—though the difference in effect compared with performance-based sponsors was not statistically significant ($Z = 0.10$, $p > .05$). The results also fail to provide significant support for the hypothesis (H3a) that access to operational resources enhances the likelihood of team survival, but this finding follows the hypothesized prioritization of sponsorship resource categories in that operational sponsorships appear to be least influential (H3b).

Given that sponsorships offering either performance or financial resources enhance the likelihood of team survival, we offer a test of diminishing returns to these effects in H4. Initially, we examined this hypothesis in a base model (Model 2) that included the associated quadratic terms in addition to the linear terms for each sponsorship category, and the control variables, but did not control for the effects of team experience or the institutional change after 1995. This model specification maintained the main effects of the number of performance and financial sponsors as significant negative influencers of the odds of dissolution (i.e., enhancing survival) while also revealing significant positive quadratic terms for both resource types ($p < .05$). The positive coefficients on the quadratic terms signify diminishing returns to both sponsorship types. That is, as the number of sponsorships offering performance or financial resources reaches a certain level, incremental sponsorships of each type positively influence the odds of team dissolution (i.e., reduce the likelihood of survival). Although H4a and H4b are supported by these results, neither the main effect nor the quadratic term for operational sponsorships (H4c) was significant.

Control Variables

In subsequent models, we enter the variable of team experience (Model 3) and control for the institutional change after the 1995 season in the full model (Model 5). The quadratic effects for sponsorships offering performance or financial resources remain at least marginally significant when simultaneously considered with team experience. However, the effect of diminishing returns to performance-based sponsorships (H4a) loses statistical significance when modeled with the post-1995 dummy variable in the full model. Because greater numbers of sponsorships occur in the modern era, the binary variable signifying the institutional change after 1995 appears to also capture the effect of diminishing returns to performance-based sponsorships.

Further concerning the post-1995 control variable, which marked the increase in prize money allocated to teams, we speculated that enhanced access to institutional financial resources might reduce teams' survival dependence on financial resources via sponsorship and marginally increase the importance of race results (i.e., team points). As expected (and displayed in Model 4), the interaction of the dichotomous variable indicating the more recent era (i.e., post-1995) and the variable quantifying a team's financial sponsorships does significantly influence team dissolution in the positive direction ($p < .01$), thereby signaling a reduced impact of sponsorships offering financial resources after 1995. Simultaneously, the negative relationship between team points and team dissolution has indeed been enhanced in the modern era ($p < .01$). Before the change, each 1-point rise in the 5-year average reduced a team's odds of dissolution by just 7.7%. After the change in the Concorde Agreement, a 1-point rise in the 5-year average of team points scored reduced a team's odds of dissolution by almost 95%.[8] When evaluated in the presence of the quadratic terms in the full model (Model 5), however, the reduced effect of financial sponsors after 1995 is no longer statistically significant. The sign of the coefficient on the interaction term actually changes, which implies correlation with the quadratic term—most likely as an indicator of the greater number of sponsorships in the modern era. As a result, any conclusions regarding the longitudinal effect of financial resources via sponsorship in the context of institutional changes (here post-1995) should be considered tentative and the subject of further future research that also allows for diminishing returns to sponsorship resources.

The control variables quantifying sponsors' experience, sales of teams, and annual global GDP growth did not achieve significance in any model specifications. However, both control terms measuring team performance (points and drivers' championships) show at least marginal significance in the most comprehensive models, and team points is a significant deterrent to team dissolution in all models ($p < .01$).

In summary, the broad findings across hypotheses indicate that sponsorships offering access to certain resources contribute to the survival of sponsored teams even when controlling for teams' competitive performance. Specifically, sponsorships that offer either performance or financial resources exhibit a significant negative relationship to team dissolution in every application of the model. We also uncover evidence that suggests the relationship to team dissolution may be subject to diminishing returns and institutional dynamics such as changes in prize money distribution.

Discussion: Implications, Limitations, and Future Research

The development of the RBV of the firm refocused the search for a competitive advantage from external industry factors to internal organizational resources (Barney, 1995). Since then, scholars have migrated back toward a middle ground where external elements such as institutional norms, regulations and governance, and even other firms impose limits, offer provisions, or present access to useful resources (Auh & Menguc, 2009). The latter of these perspectives frames the context of this study, where we address with our primary research question how access to various resources through corporate sponsorship influences the survival of F1 teams in their highly competitive environment. To address this question, we studied teams competing in F1 motor racing over 40 years as entrepreneurial enterprises that rely on their alliances with sponsoring firms to access different types of organizational resources. Though a team's offering to its sponsoring firms may be relatively consistent (i.e., promotional and hospitality services), the reciprocal resources accessed from sponsors are not necessarily equivalent and their impact on team outcomes differs.

By accessing either performance or financial resources through sponsors, F1 teams were able to reduce their odds of dissolution by over 65%. However, sponsorships offering operational resources had no effect on the team's survival. Though contrary to the third hypothesis, this finding did confirm the anticipated lower priority of operational resources. Such divergent effects based on resource type supports Grant's (1991) theory of heterogeneous resources and challenges organizational scholars to closely examine the type of sponsorship and other alliance contributions. Future researchers should be mindful of the utility of alliance categorization based on the exchanged resources' strategic application in the relevant institutional environment. This contribution supports Skilton's (2009) claim that segmenting resources should be "supplemented by an understanding of the functions of different resources in a production system" (p. 840).

While this study's findings provide evidence to support the contention that sponsorships offering access to performance-based resources are effective survival tools in this context, the impact of such sponsorships appears to weaken as teams gain experience. The interaction effect between sponsor-based performance resources and organizational experience arises because F1 teams become more self-sufficient and less reliant on external sources for a competitive performance advantage as maturing teams develop internal performance competencies over time (Levitt & March, 1988). Accordingly, researchers must consider organizational experience or life stage in future studies of resource utility. Managers of a new or young team would be wise to prioritize sponsorships offering resources directly related to competitive performance. After teams establish internal performance expertise, managers may wish to reallocate their focus to more financially oriented sponsorships while being cognizant of the potential for diminishing returns.

The influence of the quadratic terms in this investigation provides support for the argument that sponsorships offering access to performance or financial resources contribute to team survival but are not unlimited in their capacity to ward off dissolution. At a certain threshold, adding incremental sponsorships fails to discourage team dissolution, thereby suggesting an inverted U-shaped relationship. This finding further substantiates the theory that organizations possess an alliance management capability (Ireland et al., 2002), which is not without restrictions. Though Deeds and Hill (1996) uncovered a similar effect when examining the influence of alliances on rates of new product development, the idea of diminishing returns to alliance engagement has yet to be widely adopted in interorganizational research or questioned in a sponsorship context (Rothaermel & Deeds, 2006). At the very least, future studies quantifying sponsorship propensity as related to team performance should consider curvilinear possibilities. Meanwhile, scholars must also recognize that a single dependent variable (e.g., team survival) does not capture the complete utility of sponsorship resources.

Future researchers should recall the potential for diminishing returns in light of the study's limitations. Although we quantify the number of sponsorships offering access to different resources, a weighting of each sponsorship by the quantity of resources exchanged would be a more accurate measure of each sponsorship's meaning. However, the magnitude of resources exchanged within each sponsorship is unknown here. This research compromise confines the scope of conclusions drawn since some sponsorships likely contribute a greater magnitude of resources than other sponsorships. To demonstrate such disparity, a team could access resources worth US$50 million annually from just one sponsor, while other teams may be dependent on five sponsorships providing US$10 million each to access equivalent resources. Presumably, managing five sponsorships to access the same magnitude of resources that competitors acquire in a single sponsorship would strain a team's sponsorship management capacity, but comparing the magnitude of resources across teams in this longitudinal study was not feasible because of data restrictions.

Likewise, this study represents a test of sponsorship resource prioritization in just one sporting context that admittedly entertains some unique institutional qualities (e.g., global market, barriers to entry/exit, competitive rules, and team operating structure [Concorde Agreement]). Still, the empirical evidence offered for the varying influence on survival of different sponsorship resources in combination with diminishing returns represents relevant consideration for ongoing research in this domain. Future researchers might test the prioritization of performance and financially based sponsorships versus operational sponsorships in other sporting domains. Of particular interest may be sporting events that rely on sponsorship for continued operation and situations of team promotion and relegation. Beyond motorsports, events in golf, tennis, athletics, and other sports depend on corporate sponsor engagement to survive. Is there a sponsorship prioritization relevant to these types of events? Might operational sponsors be a higher priority in such instances where the dependent organization is an event operator as opposed to a competing team (as in this study)?

Where team sponsorship is the focus, circumstances of promotion and relegation provide an interesting context to study whether certain types of sponsors provide greater assistance in avoiding relegation or achieving promotion to a more competitive league. Accordingly, what distinctions in sponsorship resource prioritization might be necessary between sports that heavily rely on equipment in combination with human performance (e.g., motor racing, sailing) and those that minimize the use of equipment external to the athlete (e.g., soccer, athletics, basketball)? For instance, when compared with business operations sponsors such as Staples or Accenture, do human performance-oriented sponsors such as nutritional, training, or specialized apparel and equipment firms (e.g., AdvoCare, Cybex, Under Armour) contribute disproportionally to the success of soccer, basketball, or baseball teams? Finally, as related to diminishing returns, is there a consistent relationship between the number of sponsors and sporting success or organizational longevity in various sporting contexts? Each of these questions challenges researchers to extend the results of this study more broadly.

Furthermore, analysis of the control variable for institutional era illustrates the potential for a governing force (i.e., league) to change the competitive environment and influence the resource dependency of teams operating within that environment. Within this study's F1 racing context, evidence of a major alteration in institutional governance emerged after 1995, when the flow of resources from the regulatory institution was adapted to provide enhanced financial reward for race performance. Consequently, sponsor-based financial resources became less influential in staving off team dissolution after the institutional change (though this finding is tentative given nonsignificance in the full model), and team points increased in importance. Such fluctuation in sponsor resource utility emphasizes the peril in neglecting dynamic institutional forces present within an investigative context (Miller & Shamsie, 1996). Though many interorganizational studies do not take a longitudinal approach, recognition of the institutional conditions and their influence on the current reality as well as their potential for change is a necessary contemplation toward achieving relevance in organizational research (Koza & Lewin, 1998). Failure to consider the institutional dynamics within this particular context would have not only overlooked the changing influence of financially based sponsorships but also left hidden the increasing reward for earning team points through positive race results.

Conclusion

By analyzing over 4 decades of sponsorships between F1 teams and their corporate partners, this study has taken the perspective of sponsored sport organizations that offer promotional services to sponsoring firms in exchange for various other resources. The relationship between this exchange process and the team's propensity to survive was explicated, and certain resources were identified as more crucial than others. For sport managers, the results offer empirical evidence to consider in the prioritization of sponsorship resources subject to team experience and institutional dynamics. Sponsorships based on operational resources, such as those providing logistical or office services, should receive the lowest priority. Teams early in their history should seek to engage sponsors that can offer performance-related resources relative to the teams' competitive environment, while mature teams are wise to focus on sponsorships that maximize financial resources.

For scholars, the findings advance the broadening scope of the RBV (Auh & Menguc, 2009), where the strategic value of organizational resources is a function of both internal capacities and competitive influences. Sponsorship may be the most popular interorganizational exchange mechanism in sports, but the resources available through sponsoring firms are heterogeneous in their utility. Consequently, further theoretical development in sponsorship management strategy must account for such disparity and incorporate a prioritized delineation of the potential resources accessed. Methodologically, this paper provides an empirical framework for conducting longitudinal studies via organizational survival analysis, which are rare to date in sport management scholarship despite their enhanced efficacy in drawing causal inferences (Jensen & Turner, 2016).

Acknowledgment

The authors would like to thank Jonathan Davies at ChicaneF1 for assistance in data collection, and Jay Gladden, Neil Longley, Robert Faulkner, and Mark Groza for their helpful guidance and useful suggestions regarding an earlier version of this manuscript.

Notes

[1]Before 1967, corporate sponsorship was prohibited by F1 regulations; thus sponsorship data begins in 1967.

[2]In addressing the sale of teams (represented by name changes) within the collection of 124 teams, we recognized the team as continuing to exist as a consistent organization when the name changes. This data treatment is consistent with the fact that corporate sponsorships, team personnel, and even previous season team results (for the purposes of grid and pit positioning) are typically transferred as a condition of the sale.

[3]Of the total 776 team years, 570 occurred after 1967 when the institutional regulations first permitted corporate sponsorships.

This latter time frame serves as the context of the investigation here, though drivers' championships and team experience accumulated before 1967 are represented in the analyzed data (i.e., control variables).

[4]Given the historical nature of the data set, a primary industry classification for the sponsoring firm was only feasible for 91.75% of the team–sponsor alliance years in the raw data set. For example, even after consulting various sources, we could make no solid determination as to what sponsoring firm was referenced by "LBT" in relationship to the 1982 March racing team. As a result, the analysis and data descriptions are inclusive of solely the sponsoring firm data with verifiable industry designations.

[5]FOA awards points to teams at the conclusion of each race based on the finish of their cars in that race. More points are awarded for better finishes. FOA then maintains a running tally of points throughout the season, which is deemed the Constructors' Championship. FOA also tracks individual drivers' earned points throughout the race season for the awarding of the Drivers' Championship, which has traditionally been the more prestigious of the F1 Championship awards.

[6]VIF statistics ranged from 1.074 to 7.349 (drivers' championships). Even though VIF values less than 10 indicate inconsequential collinearity (O'Brien, 2007), several alternate models were analyzed that isolated, excluded, and transformed variables that were correlated above .70 (Van den Poel & Larivière, 2004). Coefficient values and model significance did not change substantially between models compared with the primary specification. Therefore, we judged estimates within the primary model to be generally robust to collinearity concerns.

[7]In the Cox regression model, the antilog of the variable's coefficient produces the hazard ratio, which is the dissolution rate for an enterprise with 1 more unit of the variable in comparison with the dissolution rate for another enterprise without that additional variable unit. As it concerns performance-based sponsors, the antilog of the estimated coefficient ($e^{-1.11}$) produces a ratio of 0.33, which indicates that a 1-unit increase in performance-based alliances yields a 67% reduction in the odds of the team's dissolving in the following season.

[8]This interaction effect is calculated by antilogging the aggregated coefficients of the team points term and its associated interaction with the post-1995 binary variable, which is coded as 1 after 1995. The resulting statistic is the hazard ratio for a unit (point) increase after 1995, which we calculate from Model 4 as $e^{(-0.08-2.93)} = 0.05$. The interpretation is that a team with 1 more average point scored over the previous 5 seasons enjoys a probability of dissolution the following season that is reduced by a factor of 0.05 or 95% (1–0.05) compared with a team without the additional average point.

References

Amis, J., Pant, N., & Slack, T. (1997). Achieving a sustainable competitive advantage: A resource-based view of sport sponsorship. *Journal of Sport Management, 11,* 80–96. doi:10.1123/jsm.11.1.80

Anand, B.N., & Khanna, T. (2000). Do firms learn to create value? The case of alliances. *Strategic Management Journal, 21,* 295–315. doi:10.1002/(SICI)1097-0266(200003)21:3<295::AID-SMJ91>3.0.CO;2-O

Audretsch, D.B., & Mahmood, T. (1995). New firm survival: New results using a hazard function. *The Review of Economics and Statistics, 77,* 97–103. doi:10.2307/2109995

Auh, S., & Menguc, B. (2009). Broadening the scope of the resource-based view in marketing: The contingency role of institutional factors. *Industrial Marketing Management, 38,* 757–768. doi:10.1016/j.indmarman.2008.02.011

Barney, J.B. (1991). Firm resources and sustained competitive advantage. *Journal of Management, 17,* 99–120. doi:10.1177/014920639101700108

Barney, J.B. (1995). Looking inside for competitive advantage. *The Academy of Management Executive, 9*(4), 49–61.

Bergmann Lichtenstein, B.M., & Brush, C.G. (2001). How do 'resource bundles' develop and change in new ventures? A dynamic model and longitudinal exploration. *Entrepreneurship Theory and Practice, 25*(3), 37–58.

Brett, J.A., Olekalns, M., Friedman, R., Goates, N., Anderson, C., & Lisco, C.C. (2007). Sticks and stones: Language, face, and online dispute resolution. *Academy of Management Journal, 50,* 85–99. doi:10.5465/AMJ.2007.24161853

Brush, C.G., Greene, P.G., & Hart, M.M. (2001). From initial idea to unique advantage: The entrepreneurial challenge of constructing a resource base. *The Academy of Management Executive, 15*(1), 64–78. doi:10.5465/AME.2001.4251394

Chan, S.H., Kensinger, J.W., Keown, A.J., & Martin, J.D. (1997). Do strategic alliances create value? *Journal of Financial Economics, 46,* 199–221. doi:10.1016/S0304-405X(97)00029-9

Chung, S.A., Singh, H., & Lee, K. (2000). Complementarity, status similarity and social capital as drivers of alliance formation. *Strategic Management Journal, 21,* 1–22. doi:10.1002/(SICI)1097-0266(200001)21:1<1::AID-SMJ63>3.0.CO;2-P

Cobbs, J., Groza, M., & Pruitt, S. (2012). Warning flags on the race track: The global markets' verdict on F1 sponsorship. *Journal of Advertising Research, 52,* 74–86. doi:10.2501/JAR-52-1-074-086

Collings, T. (2004). *The Piranha Club.* London, UK: Virgin.

Cornwell, T.B. (2008). State of the art and science in sponsorship-linked marketing. *Journal of Advertising, 37*(3), 41–55. doi:10.2753/JOA0091-3367370304

Cox, D.R. (1972). Regression models and life-tables. *Journal of the Royal Statistical Society. Series B. Methodological, 34,* 187–220.

Crowley, M. (1991). Prioritising the sponsorship audience. *European Journal of Marketing, 25*(11), 11–21. doi:10.1108/EUM0000000000628

Cui, A.S. (2013). Portfolio Dynamics and alliance termination: The contingent role of resource dissimilarity. *Journal of Marketing, 77*(3), 15–32. doi:10.1509/jm.11.0164

Cui, A.S., Calantone, R.J., & Griffith, D.A. (2011). Strategic change and termination of interfirm partnerships. *Strategic Management Journal, 32,* 402–423. doi:10.1002/smj.881

Cui, A.S., & O'Connor, G. (2012). Alliance portfolio resource diversity and firm innovation. *Journal of Marketing, 76*(4), 24–43. doi:10.1509/jm.11.0130

Das, S., Sen, P.K., & Sengupta, S. (1998). Impact of strategic alliances on firm valuation. *Academy of Management Journal, 41,* 27–41. doi:10.2307/256895

Davies, J., & Lawrence, B. (n.d.). Sponsors [data file]. *ChicaneF1*. Retrieved February 19, 2009, from http://www.chicanef1.com/list.pl?who=s

Deeds, D.L., & Hill, C.W.L. (1996). Strategic alliances and the rate of new product development: An empirical study of entrepreneurial biotechnology firms. *Journal of Business Venturing, 11,* 41–55. doi:10.1016/0883-9026(95)00087-9

Donaldson, G. (2002). *Formula 1: The autobiography*. London, UK: Weidenfeld & Nicolson.

Dyer, J.H., & Singh, H. (1998). The relational view: Cooperative strategy and sources of interorganizational competitive advantage. *Academy of Management Review, 23,* 660–679.

Fahy, J., Farrelly, F., & Quester, P. (2004). Competitive advantage through sponsorship: A conceptual model and research propositions. *European Journal of Marketing, 38*(8), 1013–1030. doi:10.1108/03090560410539140

Fleck, N.D., & Quester, P. (2007). Birds of a feather flock together . . . Definition, role and measure of congruence: An application to sponsorship. *Psychology and Marketing, 24*(11), 975–1000. doi:10.1002/mar.20192

Formula One Administration. (n.d.). Season results [data file]. Retrieved March 3, 2014, from http://www.formula1.com/results/season/

Freeman, J., Carroll, G.R., & Hannan, M.T. (1983). The liability of newness: Age dependence in organizational death rates. *American Sociological Review, 48,* 692–710. doi:10.2307/2094928

Grant, R.M. (1991). The resource-based theory of competitive advantage: Implications for strategy formulation. *California Management Review, 33*(3), 114–135. doi:10.2307/41166664

Hoang, H., & Rothaermel, F.T. (2005). The effect of general and partner-specific alliance experience on joint R&D project performance. *Academy of Management Journal, 48,* 332–345. doi:10.5465/AMJ.2005.16928417

International Events Group. (2015, January 26). Sponsorship spending report: Where the dollars are going and trends for 2015. Retrieved from http://www.sponsorship.com/Resources/Sponsorship-Spending-Report–Where-The-Dollars-Are.aspx

Ireland, R.D., Hitt, M.A., & Vaidyanath, D. (2002). Alliance management as a source of competitive advantage. *Journal of Management, 28,* 413–446. doi:10.1177/014920630202800308

Jensen, J.A., & Cobbs, J.B. (2014). Predicting return on investment in sport sponsorship: Modeling brand exposure, price, and ROI in Formula One automotive competition. *Journal of Advertising Research, 54,* 435–447. doi:10.2501/JAR-54-4-435-447

Jensen, J.A., Cobbs, J.B., & Turner, B.A. (2016). Evaluating sponsorship through the lens of the resource-based view: The potential for sustained competitive advantage. *Business Horizons, 59,* 163–173. doi:10.1016/j.bushor.2015.11.001

Jensen, J.A., & Turner, B.A. (2016). Event history analysis of longitudinal data: A methodological application to sport sponsorship. *Sport in Society, 19*(6), 1–18. doi:10.1080/17430437.2016.1179728

Koza, M.P., & Lewin, A.Y. (1998). The co-evolution of strategic alliances. *Organization Science, 9,* 255–264. doi:10.1287/orsc.9.3.255

Lee, C., Lee, K., & Pennings, J.M. (2001). Internal capabilities, external networks, and performance: A study on technology-based ventures. *Strategic Management Journal, 22*(6-7), 615–640. doi: 10.1002/smj.181

Levitt, B., & March, J.G. (1988). Organizational learning. *Annual Review of Sociology, 14,* 319–338. doi:10.1146/annurev.so.14.080188.001535

Magretta, J. (2002). Why business models matter. *Harvard Business Review, 80*(5), 86–93.

McFadyen, M.A., & Cannella, A.A., Jr. (2004). Social capital and knowledge creation: Diminishing returns of the number and strength of exchange relationships. *Academy of Management Journal, 47,* 735–746. doi:10.2307/20159615

Meenaghan, T. (2001). Understanding sponsorship effects. *Psychology and Marketing, 18*(2), 95–122. doi:10.1002/1520-6793(200102)18:2<95::AID-MAR1001>3.0.CO;2-H

Miller, D., & Shamsie, J. (1996). The resource-based view of the firm in two environments: The Hollywood film studios from 1936 to 1965. *Academy of Management Journal, 39,* 519–543. doi:10.2307/256654

O'Brien, R.M. (2007). A caution regarding rules of thumb for variance inflation factors. *Quality & Quantity, 41,* 673–690. doi:10.1007/s11135-006-9018-6

Olson, E.L., & Thjømøe, H.M. (2011). Explaining and articulating the fit construct in sponsorship. *Journal of Advertising, 40*(1), 57–70. doi:10.2753/JOA0091-3367400104

Papadimitriou, D., & Apostolopoulou, A. (2009). Olympic sponsorship activation and the creation of competitive advantage. *Journal of Promotion Management, 15*(1–2), 90–117. doi:10.1080/10496490902892754

Pfeffer, J., & Nowak, P. (1976). Joint ventures and interorganizational interdependence. *Administrative Science Quarterly, 21,* 398–418. doi:10.2307/2391851

Rao, H. (1994). The social construction of reputation: Certification contests, legitimation, and the survival of organizations in the American automobile industry: 1895–1912. *Strategic Management Journal, 15*(S1), 29–44. doi:10.1002/smj.4250150904

Rothaermel, F.T., & Deeds, D.L. (2006). Alliance type, alliance experience and alliance management capability in high-technology ventures. *Journal of Business Venturing, 21,* 429–460. doi:10.1016/j.jbusvent.2005.02.006

Sarkar, M.B., Echambadi, R., Cavusgil, S.T., & Aulakh, P.S. (2001). The influence of complementarity, compatibility, and relationship capital on alliance performance. *Journal of the Academy of Marketing Science, 29,* 358–373. doi:10.1177/03079450094216

Schlegelmilch, R.W., & Lehbrink, H. (2004). *Formula 1, 1950–present*. Berlin, Germany: Feierabend Verlag OHG.

Singer, J.D., & Willett, J.B. (2003). *Applied longitudinal data analysis: Modeling change and event occurrence*. New York, NY: Oxford University Press. doi:10.1093/acprof:oso/9780195152968.001.0001

Skilton, P.F. (2009). Knowledge based resources, property based resources and supplier bargaining power in Hollywood motion picture projects. *Journal of Business Research, 62,* 834–840. doi:10.1016/j.jbusres.2008.05.001

Smith, L. (2015, February 5). As Caterham's F1 story ends, will Marussia live on? *NBCSports.com.* Retrieved December 11, 2015, from http://motorsportstalk.nbcsports.com/2015/02/05/as-caterhams-f1-story-ends-will-marussia-live-on/

SportsPro Media. (2007). *Black Book Formula One.* London, UK: SportsPro Media.

Stuart, T.E. (1998). Network positions and propensities to collaborate: An investigation of strategic alliance formation in a high-technology industry. *Administrative Science Quarterly, 43,* 668–698. doi:10.2307/2393679

Sylt, C. (2015, January 4). Marussia F1 Team Lost $45,000 in Bid to Race at Final Grand Prix. *Forbes.* Retrieved December 11, 2015, from http://www.forbes.com/sites/csylt/2015/01/04/marussia-f1-team-lost-45000-in-bid-to-race-at-final-grand-prix/

Sylt, C., & Reid, C. (2008, May 20). Keeping the wheels turning. *Financial Times.* Retrieved June 12, 2008, from http://www.ft.com/cms/s/2/333268be-25c4-11dd-b510-000077b07658.html#axzz1hyABN6cD

Truyens, J., De Bosscher, V., Heyndels, B., & Westerbeek, H. (2014). A resource-based perspective on countries' competitive advantage in elite athletics. *International Journal of Sport Policy and Politics, 6,* 459–489. doi:10.1080/19406940.2013.839954

Tsai, W. (2000). Social capital, strategic relatedness and the formation of intraorganizational linkages. *Strategic Management Journal, 21,* 925–939. doi:10.1002/1097-0266(200009)21:9<925::AID-SMJ129>3.0.CO;2-I

U.S. Department of Agriculture Economic Research Service. (2016). Real GDP historical data set. Retrieved January 9, 2016, from http://www.ers.usda.gov/Data/Macroeconomics/

Van den Poel, D., & Larivière, B. (2004). Customer attrition analysis for financial services using proportional hazards models. *European Journal of Operational Research, 157,* 196–217. doi:10.1016/S0377-2217(03)00069-9

Varadarajan, P.R., & Cunningham, M.H. (1995). Strategic alliances: A synthesis of conceptual foundations. *Journal of the Academy of Marketing Science, 23,* 282–296. doi:10.1177/009207039502300408

Verity, J. (2002). Maximising the marketing potential of sponsorship for global brands. *European Business Journal, 14,* 161–173.

Wernerfelt, B. (1984). A resource-based view of the firm. *Strategic Management Journal, 5,* 171–180. doi:10.1002/smj.4250050207

Journal of Sport Management, 2017, 31, 111-112
https://doi.org/10.1123/jsm.2017-0014
© 2017 Human Kinetics, Inc.

Human Kinetics

OFF THE PRESS

The Secret Lives of Sports Fans: The Science of Sports Obsession

By Eric Simons. Published in 2013 by Overlook Duckworth. (320 pages)

Reviewed by Young Do Kim, PhD, University of Nebraska Kearney, and Hyun-Woo Lee, PhD, Georgia Southern University

The Secret Lives of Sports Fans: The Science of Sports Obsession by journalist Eric Simons is a welcome contribution to the vibrant field of sport fan behavior. Simons' primary goal was to explain the blended areas of science behind the motives of complex fan behaviors and nature of sport fans. His findings are presented through a reflection of his own physical and psychological responses; weaving interviews with well-known professionals and scholarly experts; and a vast range of literature, theories and research in the fields of anthropology, biology, neuroscience, philosophy, psychology, and sociology. In investigating sport fans, Simons underpins his findings on topics ranging from biological responses to psychological motives and social influences.

This book is organized into three parts: "Reflex", "Control," and "Consequence" and each part includes multiple sections. In part one ("Reflex"), Simons explains sport fan behaviors by reviewing numerous scientific studies about the influence of hormones and neurons. In the first section, "The Edge of Your Seat," Simons challenges the premise that sport fans undergo unconscious hormonal changes that affect their attitude, personality, and a variety of physical reactions. For instance, he takes the reader through the study of testosterone involving aggression, dominance, and effects of winning and losing in a variety of contexts. Through investigating numerous experimental studies and conducting his own experiments, however, Simons argues that humans "adulterate our reflexes" (p. 49). That is, the hormonal responses could be influenced or even overwhelmed by an individual's neuronal reflex (e.g., reaction with empathy).

In the second section, "Sports as Empathy," Simons explores another reflex response happening in the sport fan's brain—the mirror neuron system. The fundamental premise of the mirror neuron $_{system}$ is the eye-brain-action interface. When a sport fan sees a motion, mirror neurons activate to copy such experience. Mirror neurons carry signals to the brain's center of emotions (i.e., the limbic system), which then brings up an emotion to match the action. The more a sport fan has experiences with the sports and its plays/actions, the more he or she intends to mirror (or mimic) the plays/actions as if they were the athletes on the field. Therefore, sport fans exert emotions

in the grandstands by imitating their favorite team athletes' joy in victory or pain in defeat while watching sporting events. While the mirror neuron and hormone systems in a human body together shape sport fans' reflex responses, Simons notes that what motivates passionate and sometimes irrational behaviors of sport fans is more complex and beyond the biological system. He further explicates that such fan behavior depends on psychological capacities that often overpower biological reflexes.

In part two, Simons identifies sport fans' psychological drivers to address the reasons why fans find and retain, expand, obsess, and regulate their commitments to sport teams. Part two consists of four sections. In the first section, "A Case of Identity," Simons explains the important concepts of personal identity and pride in framing the psychological and emotional commitments of sport fans. The process by which pride turns into self-esteem is highlighted as imperative in motivating sport fans to exert a persistent behavior. In the second section, "Relationships," Simons highlights that sport fans are inherently motivated to build relationships with a team offering platforms to self-expand values such as camaraderie and tradition. Those platforms bolster the energy, meaning, memory, and emotional support; and thereby enforce fans' psychological commitment. In the third section, "Love," Simons insists that sport fans tend to overwhelm their self-control due to a deeply expanded relationship with their favorite sport team. Fans at this stage conceivably promote emotional bias, prejudice, or obsession and relinquish their self-control to what they would normally respond. In the final section of part two, "Addiction," Simons provides relevant scientific and vital ethnographic evidence to identify international Bay Area Arsenal fans—who watch matches five thousand miles away in a local bar with requirements of thirty-eight predawn wake-ups a year with no guaranteed rewards—as addicted fans. Consequently, Simons argues that most sport fans who keep returning to a team in spite of inconsistent rewards always exert self-control and can *stop* being a fan for a while if they want to. Yet, fans choose to *stay* without rewards due to individual psychological drivers (i.e., motivation), as well as the powerful draw of belonging to and fitting in with a group of like-minded supporters.

In the final part of the book, Simons scrutinizes the stereotypes of sport fans commonly depicted through media. Based on social science literature and theories, Simons lays out that the stereotypical male sport fan behaviors in our society are over exaggerated due to the commodification of sport and the notion of masculinity. This is contrasted with the inherent behaviors within in the male sport fan culture that drives men to behave collectively and care about their fellow fans to form and maintain groups. This insight leads the reader to comprehend the roles and consequences of group behavior in fandom. In the end of the book, Simons emphasizes that, despite all the biological reflexes, psychological motivations, and societal influences, sport fans still retain and can exercise the power to choose and control obsessive drivers: "We sports fan are glorious expressions of all the wondrous quirks and oddities in human nature" (p. 312).

In summation, Simons earnestly and enthusiastically investigated the varying values, attitudes, and behaviors of sport fans. One of the book's strengths lies in Simons' effort to build a coherent taxonomy of sport fandom based on biological, psychological, and sociological aspects of sport fan behaviors. This makes it not only a great starting line for a reader to better understand a big picture of antecedents and consequences of sport fan behaviors but also a supplemental reading for a reader studying sport consumer behavior. Nonetheless, although the chapters covered in this book are presented with clear depiction of sport fandom, the intended narrative of the book solely reads as male sport fans. Other sport fan behaviors, particularly female sport fan behaviors, still remain an undisclosed inquiry in this book. In addition, in spite of scientific underpinnings addressed in the book, neither proper citations nor a specific list of references were provided to corroborate the statements and encourage future studies. Overall, filled with vivid and rich evidences of sport fan behaviors, various perspectives and multiple voices about the nature of sport fandom are synthesized in this book. *The Secret Lives of Sports Fans: The Science of Sports Obsession* by Eric Simons would be suitable for as a supplemental book for graduate level courses on sport consumer behavior. It is a worthwhile read and welcome contribution to sport consumer behavior literature.

Journal of Sport Management, 2017, 31, 113-114
https://doi.org/10.1123/jsm.2017-0013
© 2017 Human Kinetics, Inc.

This Is Your Brain on Sports: The Science of Underdogs, the Value of Rivalry, and What We Can Learn From the T-shirt Cannon

By Jon Wertheim and Sam Sommers. Published in 2016 by Crown Archetype. (279 pages)

Reviewed by Jonathan A. Jensen, PhD, University of North Carolina at Chapel Hill

This is Your Brain on Sports examines the psychology of the sport consumer. Authors Jon Wertheim, an editor for *Sports Illustrated*, and Sam Sommers, a professor of social psychology at Tufts University, team up in the latest work that attempts to introduce academic research to the masses. Readers may expect the work to provide a nuanced look at what makes sport consumers, or fans, uniquely different from typical consumers. However, the prevailing theme throughout the work is the exact opposite. Wertheim and Sommers suggest time and again that sport consumers are exceedingly rational, and no matter how astonishing their actions in support of their favorite teams, each has an easily explainable foundation in theories from the psychology and consumer behavior literature. They state, "That is, that 'your brain on sports' is really just your regular brain acting as it does in other contexts" (p. 247).

Each individual chapter focuses on one psychological phenomenon that helps to explain the behavior of sport consumers. For example, one chapter focuses on the power of free stuff and how sport consumers are not alone in their affinity to a great deal. As Wertheim and Sommers (2016) explain, just as we scream at the top of our lungs to receive a free t-shirt shot from a cannon at a sporting event, shoppers are likely to purchase more at a grocery store after receiving a free sample thanks to the principle of reciprocity. "Reciprocity is a very, very strong instinct," noted psychologist Dan Ariely in the book (p. 8). "If somebody does something for you, you really feel a rather surprisingly strong obligation to do something back for them." Wertheim and Sommers describe Ariely's recounting of his own experience going to the car dealership, ostensibly to pick out a new minivan. He departed with an Audi, solely due to the fact that the salesman offered free oil changes. Similarly, in one of Ariely's famous experiments described in the book, participants were just as likely to purchase a Hershey's Kiss for a penny as a Lindt chocolate, priced at 26 cents. However, as soon as the price for the Kiss was reduced by one cent, to free, 90% of the participants chose the Hershey's Kiss chocolate. This was despite the fact that the price differential for both products was exactly the same in both scenarios, 25 cents. The same forces were at work when more than a dozen consumers volunteered to have a theater's logo tattooed on them when offered free movies for one year, as well as when a tennis star was being wooed to participate in a tennis tournament in Japan. No amount of money could convince her to participate, until the moment the tournament organizer offered free transportation to the event for her and all of her family. The allure of "free" was the tipping point. She agreed to appear and won the tournament.

Another chapter describes why our propensity to root for the underdog is not limited to the March Madness tournament. In one study spotlighted in the book, researchers created an animated game in which circles either struggled or zipped up a hill. Participants in the study not only rooted more for the struggling circle, they had higher levels of sympathy for it and even reported higher feelings of personal identification with the circle. Similarly, the underdog effect was also apparent in a study utilizing the context of politics, which found that voters on both sides of the aisle were more likely to perceive their preferred candidate as an underdog, even the sitting president who was a considerable favorite. Participants who were told a candidate was an underdog also perceived that candidate as warmer and more competent than the frontrunner. Plus, they reported they were more likely to vote for the underdog candidate as well. As noted by Wertheim and Sommers, the effect has been leveraged in the business world as well.

The principle of effort justification (also known as cognitive dissonance or dissonance theory) helps explain why long-suffering fans of the New York Mets and the Chicago Cubs, continue their support despite a lack of any rational explanation for their efforts. The authors point out that it's the same principle that helps explain why we purchase the right to spend hours constructing a desk or bookcase purchased at Ikea. The authors describe an experiment in which the researchers subjected women to an embarrassing initiation in order for them to gain access to a discussion group. However, after being told they had passed the initiation, the discussion group turned out to be nothing more than a boring, clinical dialogue focused on bird plumage and migration patterns. Still, the participants who had undergone the embarrassing initiation said they thoroughly enjoyed the discussion, reporting that it was far more interesting than another group that had not been forced to survive the initiation. When asked by the authors whether the study and dissonance theory echoed the actions of the suffering sport consumers we all know, they enthusiastically replied in the affirmative.

In the end, what these and other theories spotlighted in the book explain is not what the sport context can teach us about the rest of the world, but the opposite. The authors provide countless examples of theories and associated studies utilizing the fertile context of sport that help to explain irrational behavior among seemingly normal humans. "Sports and athletic competition are fertile ground for scientists across disciplines to test their hypotheses about basic aspects of human life," explain Wertheim and Sommers (p. 247). In a chapter focusing on the power of rivalries, Werthheim and Somers cite researchers who used the context of the Yankees-Red Sox rivalry to examine how human brains react to stimuli. In the experiment, functional magnetic resonance imaging (fMRI) was used to investigate how participants' reactions to their teams losing to each other's hated rival revealed activity in the anterior cingulate cortex, the region of the brain associated with an emotional response to pain. The same effect was not found when watching poor play or losses to other non-rivals, such as the Baltimore Orioles or Toronto Blue Jays. The study

has implications far beyond sport, and helps to better understand how to assuage global conflicts between rival tribes and associated human aggression.

Wertheim and Sommers' work serves as a perfect companion to an introductory social psychology course, a course focused on sport consumer behavior, or a sport marketing course that seeks to be rooted in psychology and/or consumer behavior. The parallels to fandom and the sport context may assist students in grasping such concepts as cognitive dissonance or reciprocity, using real world examples. Though the authors have provided complete citations to every study referenced in the text, some scholars may find the absence of figures or models make it challenging to fully comprehend some of the more advanced concepts. Therefore, the book is recommended as a companion to a text on consumer behavior or social psychology, designed to aid understanding of the concepts, rather than the course's key text. However, any sport fan or scholar of sport seeking a more nuanced understanding of the psychology of the sport consumer will undoubtedly enjoy the experience.

Journal of Sport Management, 2017, 31, 115-118
https://doi.org/10.1123/jsm.2017-0015
© 2017 Human Kinetics, Inc.

Support of Politicians for the 2016 Olympic Games in Rio de Janeiro

The bulk of the research evaluating the perceived legacy impact of mega events (e.g., Olympics and FIFA World Cup) centered on investigating resident and non-resident perceptions. However, the author argues this method of inquiry is limited because of the lack of awareness/knowledge that residents and non-residents have to make an informed stance on the potential long-term impact of the event. Therefore, this study surveyed Brazilian politicians at the city, state, and country levels four years prior to hosting the 2016 Summer Olympic Games. While the response rate was low (8.95%), the results of the study were very informative and outline some potential areas for future investigation. For example, the results indicated the politicians support the Olympic Games regardless of political affiliation or place of representation. Alternatively, political affiliates of the current government evaluated the work of the government significantly better than those in the opposing party. Finally, the results indicated the politicians believe tourism legacy was more likely to occur post event, while concerns about the environmental impact and safety and security were raised. Thus, further investigation into groups with substantial information of planning major events is warranted to further support the conclusions of this investigation.

Rocha, C.M. (2016). Support of politicians for the 2016 Olympic Games in Rio de Janeiro. *Leisure Studies, 35*, 487–504. doi:10.1080/02614367.2015.1042508

The Essential Role of Sense of Community in a Youth Sport Program

Previous research has indicated parents want their children involved in youth sport programs that offer several learning opportunities, which may include coaches providing a supportive environment, learning sport skills, and developing social abilities to interact with peers. The authors argued the ability to develop social skills and interact with others may enhance participants' sense of community. Furthermore, they proposed parents would desire a sense of community for both themselves and their children. This study centered on examining parents overall satisfaction of their child's competitive swim team and the likelihood of reenrollment. In a two-part study, Phase 1 utilized a focus group approach to develop an understanding of parents' desired outcomes associated with the swim club. Phase 2 collected parents' assessment of the program via an online questionnaire post-season. Phase 1 and Phase II both concluded parents place sense of community as a priority before and after the season. Phase 1 also indicated parents felt coaching was essential, but not the determining factor for their child to learn the necessary swimming skills. Both phases illustrated the value of good coaching involves more than teaching correct skills and techniques, but also impacts the sense of community. Developing an encouraging social environment is also equally important to the perceived sense of community. Finally, path analysis indicated sense of community was the key driver of satisfaction and repeat purchase intentions with coaching quality, friendships, organizational communication, and sport and life skills included in the model.

Lin, Y., Chalip, L. & Green, B.C. (2016). The essential role of sense of community in a youth sport program. *Leisure Sciences, 38*, 461–481. doi:10.1080/01490400.2015.1093973

How to Select Sponsorships That Benefit the Sponsor's CSR Image

Most of the research on Corporate Social Responsibility (CSR) strategies focus on whether CSR activities are advantageous for firms, yet few studies are dedicated to perhaps an even more poignant issue: *Which type* of CSR activities are most advantageous for firms? Thus, the purpose of this study was to compare two forms of sponsorship to examine which one is more effective to the CSR image of the sponsor. The two attributes that were used to categorize sponsorship were community engagement and community proximity (the scope of the property as national versus grassroots sports). The authors used a between-subjects 2×2 experimental design with community engagement measured as yes or no, and community proximity measured as grassroots or national. Each group contained 100 respondents, contributing to an overall sample of 400 respondents. The analysis revealed that a pro-active community engagement of the sport property is beneficial for enhancing the sponsor's CSR image, particularly if the sport was at a national rather than grassroots level. On the other hand, organizations supporting grassroots properties benefit from their sponsorship because they support a sports property in close proximity to the community.

Plewa, C., Carrillat, F.A., Mazodier, M., & Quester, P.G. (2016). Which sport sponsorships most impact sponsor CSR image? *European Journal of Marketing, 50*, 796–815.

How Should Sport Teams Pursue a CSR Agenda?

In his research, Kent (2016) discussed the efforts of sport entities (leagues, teams, athletes) to initiate corporate social responsibility (CSR) activities. Based on the work he has done over the years with different sport organizations, he proposed three guidelines that managers should keep in mind when initiating CSR programs. First, he advises them to be strategic, which means they need to prioritize those social issues that are closely related to their own activities, which for sport teams often means focusing on health and wellness, youth, and general philanthropy. Second, he advises organizations to be efficient about their CSR efforts. It is not always about spending more money or resources, but figuring out how you can maximize the returns on your investments. With poignant examples, he shows that some organizations do much better in this than others. Third, he advises organizations to be realistic. A major challenge within the CSR world is to oversell the merits of their programming, which creates expectations for the program that are unachievable. Sport can be good, but is not necessarily the best solution to all societal issues. While sport organizations often have high profiles which allows them to create awareness for many issues, they need to understand that simply engaging with the community or a social cause does not guarantee long term success and sustainable social impact, particularly if it does not follow the above guidelines.

Kent, A. (2016). CSR in sport: Doing it right. *Sport & Entertainment Review, 2,* 31–37.

MLB Teams Undervalue Young and Relatively Young High School Players

For over 30 years, researchers have been studying the impact of the relative age effect (RAE) on elite sport participation. The RAE has to do with when athletes are born relative to others within an age-defined cohort. Research across a number of different sports has generally demonstrated that athletes born earlier in the selection year are over-represented on elite teams. However, there is some evidence to suggest that relatively younger athletes who persevere in sport systems that are biased against them tend to outperform their relatively older counterparts. Thus, the purpose of this article was to examine the impact of both age and relative age on MLB performance among players drafted out of high school from 1987 through 2011. Using a series of regression models, the authors determined that both age and relative age had a significantly negative impact on high school players making it to the majors; that is, despite a larger number of relatively older high school athletes being drafted, relatively younger players had a greater chance of playing at the MLB level. Nevertheless, subsequent analyses demonstrate that once a player reached the MLB level, there were no significant differences in the performances of relatively older and younger athletes. Based on these findings, the authors concluded that MLB teams have undervalued both young and relatively young high school players.

Sims, J., & Addona, V. (2016). Hurdle models and age effects in the Major League Baseball draft. *Journal of Sports Economics, 17,* 672–687. doi:10.1177/1527002514539516

University Degrees in Sport Sciences Positively Impact Coaching Salaries

Human capital theory posits that an individual's income will be commensurate with her/his human capital investment. For coaches, human capital investments may come in a variety of forms including, but not limited to, on-the-job training (i.e., years of experience), formal education (i.e., academic degrees), and the acquisition of licenses or certificates that serve to increase coaches' sport-specific knowledge base. To date, most of the research examining the effect of human capital on coaching salaries has been conducted in the context of intercollegiate sport due to the public availability of salary data. The purpose of this study was to examine the relationship between coaching qualifications and income based on survey data collected from elite German national team coaches in less commercialized sports (i.e., excluding soccer, tennis, and boxing). In sum, the 186 coaches who completed the survey identified 65 different types of formal qualifications, which were grouped into 11 categories. Based on the results of the log-linear regression analyses, a university degree in sport sciences was the only formal qualification that had a significantly positive effect on income; all other formal qualifications were found to be insignificant. Thus, possessing a degree in sport sciences provides German coaches with a competitive advantage in the labor market. In light of these results, sport officials and policy makers may wish to reconsider the value of providing, promoting, and requiring licenses and certifications to be completed by elite coaches since they are not being compensated for these human capital investments.

Wicker, P., Orlowski, J., & Breuer, C. (2016). Human capital, formal qualifications, and income of elite sport coaches. *International Journal of Sport Finance, 11,* 204–220. doi:10.1177/1527002516641168

Continued Underrepresentation of Females in the Sport Industry

Using an autoethnographic approach, the researcher detailed and analyzed her experiences as a female basketball official over the span of a year. The results were analyzed and compared to other sport-specific feminist autoethnographic work. In doing so, this study highlighted the lack of females in officiating and the gendered discourse experienced. Specifically, the author detailed the importance of self-acceptance, being confident and effectively communicating in her work as a female official. This work emphasizes the importance of auothethnographic work in sport and the need to further address the underrepresentation of females in the sport industry.

Schaeperkoetter, C.C. (in press). Basketball officiating as a gendered arena: An autoethnography. *Sport Management Review*. doi:10.1016/j.smr.2016.05.001

Finding a Balance of Support for Parents of College Athletes

As students-athletes transition to intercollegiate sports, it is important to understand the role of parents in this transition. In this study, the researcher analyzed the perceptions of parent involvement from key stakeholders, including coaches, administrators, and directors in athletics of two NCAA Division I programs. Using a grounded theory approach, the results suggested consistent positive parent involvement can contribute to the success of the athletes. The findings also suggest it is important to educate parents of athletes in a manner that emphasizes how to support and encourage their child and some of the barriers that need to be overcome and addressed. Recommendations on an effective method for providing this educational information to the parents of student-athletes is provided.

Dorsch, T.E., Lowe, K., Dotterer, A.M., Lyons, L., & Barker, A. (2016). Stakeholders' perceptions of parent involvement in young adults' intercollegiate athletic careers: Policy, education, and desired outcomes. *Journal of Issues in Intercollegiate Athletics*, *9*, 124–141.

Sport Management Internships

Many sport organizations often require that job candidates include work experience in the field among their qualifications. To assist in fulfilling this expectation, many sport organizations offer internships, often unpaid, to students. This study concentrated on the pedagogical, ethical, legal implications of unpaid internships by focusing on the Fair Labor Standards Act of 1938 (FLSA) and its minimum wage requirements. The FLSA mandates that unpaid internships are similar to training in an educational environment and primarily benefit the intern. The authors report that such authorizations can be achieved with proper pedagogical structure and appropriate oversight by the educational institution. Ultimately, the authors indicate that it is the credit-granting, tuition-receiving college or university that must accept responsibility as the third-party intermediary for the pedagogical, legal, and ethical legitimacy of the internship experience.

Burke, D.D, & Carton, R. (2013). The pedagogical, legal, and ethical implications of unpaid internships. *Journal of Legal Studies Education*, *30*, 99–130.

Using Social Networking Sites to Increase Intercollegiate Football Fans

College athletics is a significant revenue producer in the United States. However, universities in urban settings often struggle to attract student fans to their athletic contests. Thus, this study analyzed the role social networking sites (SNS) play in increasing student game attendance and school spirit. Results indicated that many of the fans are interested in two main areas: a) the pageantry of the game such as university band, cheerleaders, and the energy of the crowd, and b) refreshments which included eating, drinking, and tailgating at the game. As a result, the authors recommend that SNS should be used to create hype and excitement about attending the game. In this way, practitioners should communicate factors that influence pageantry and refreshments, such as fan enthusiasm and fan involvement. For example, SNS could be employed to convey the "gameday experience" with real-time snapshots of students involved with pageantry and refreshments. Additionally, student fans should be inspired to involve other fans. Results also indicated that fans conveyed attention in single players rather than the whole team. Communication practitioners should leverage SNS as a communication strategy by providing information about individual athletes. As a result, SNS content related to individual athletes could bridge students with the university and generate social capital. Sport marketers can use these strategies so audiences will see the opportunities and networking benefits SNS provides.

Haught, M.J., Willis, E., Furrow, A., Morris III, D.L. Freberg, K. (2016). From tweets to seats: How does social networking site use affect commuter university students' football fandom? *Journal of Issues in Intercollegiate Athletics*, *9*, 17–38.

Keeping Up With the Joneses, University Edition: Understanding Determinants of University Branding Strategies

Universities face increasing competition for students, alumni donations, and grant funding. As a result, many institutions have undertaken strategic branding initiatives. In this research, the authors used dyadic event history to identify the determinants of branding strategies used by research extensive institutions. The authors found evidence of institutional isomorphism at the state and national level. Additionally, they found that branding efforts are used by universities to promote organizational successes. This research is relevant for sport management research related to both marketing and strategic management. It provides a foundation for understanding the importance of collegiate athletics programs in university branding efforts as well as in university's attempts to establish competitive advantage through the promotion of their athletic teams.

Fay, D.L., & Zavattaro, S.M. (2016). Branding and isomorphism: The case of higher education. *Public Administration Review, 76,* 80–815.

Denial, Distancing, and the Blame Game: Crisis Response in the 2010 Delhi Commonwealth Games

The communities that host major sport events commonly cite image benefits as a justification for hosting events. However, when a sport event (or the event's host community) experiences a crisis, the response of event stakeholders and their efforts to influence media coverage can determine the extent to which the community image is enhanced or diminished. In this article, the authors used a crisis management framework to examine how event organizers managed negative media coverage of the 2010 Delhi Commonwealth Games. The authors conducted a content analysis of English-language media, including news articles, photos, and videos from 2006 to 2010. In this case, the authors applied five frames to the media coverage of the event, including four frames which are established in the literature (i.e., attribution of responsibility, conflict, consequences, and human interest) and one new frame identified through this research (i.e., the savior frame, which refers to positive representations of elites responding to the crisis). The results of this research can provide guidance for researchers interested in optimizing the benefits realized by event hosts and those interested in the public policy implications for event hosts in the developing world.

Carey, K.M., & Mason, D.S. (2016). Damage control: Media framing of sport event crises and the response strategies of organizers. *Event Management, 20,* 119–133.

Call for Papers
Special Issue of the *Journal of Sport Management*
Sport Leadership: A New Generation of Thinking

Guest Editors: Associate Professor Lesley Ferkins (Auckland University of Technology)
Professor James Skinner, Dr Ben Corbett, Dr Steve Swanson (Loughborough University London)

While we consider leadership theory and research to be constantly evolving, over the past 10 years we see a significant shift away from a pre-occupation with formal, assigned leaders (e.g., CEOs) toward greater emphasis on (what has been variously described as) the **social construction of leadership** (Grint, 2005). This perspective views leadership as a social, collaborative, relational experience focusing on the idea that leadership emerges from the interactions and constructions of people in a particular context (Grint, 2011; Kihl, Leberman, & Schull, 2010; Ospina & Foldy, 2009). In this, leadership is viewed as a **collective achievement**, not something that belongs to an individual (Cullen-Lester & Yammarino, 2016).

This is an example of an innovative turn in leadership thinking that we consider has important implications for the study of leadership in sport management, organisations and systems, (or 'sport leadership'). In what way have we kept pace with this new generation of leadership thinking? While our field of sport management is perhaps too small to limit a special issue on sport leadership to submissions orientated toward the social construction of leadership, we do propose to encourage approaches that consider **multilevel analysis** (Burton, 2015; Fink, 2008; Welty Peachey, Damon, Zhou, & Burton, 2015) and fresh approaches to leadership. As explained by Welty Peachey et al (2015) in their 40 year review of leadership research in sport management, multilevel analysis of leadership research includes individuals, dyads, teams, groups, and organisations. We would also add systems. We agree that, "There is a critical need to incorporate multilevel investigations into our work to develop sport-focused leadership theory …" (p. 578) in a way that appreciates the diverse contexts and ways within which leadership occurs within our sector.

A multilevel approach to leadership expands on a foundational bias in the literature toward researching traits and characteristics of individual leaders (often white, male (Burton, 2015)) where **leader-centred perspectives** and theories such as transformational, transactional and charismatic, have taken prominence (Welty Peachey et al., 2015). A response to concerns about the leader-centric focus (sometimes referred to as the hero leader – often propagated by the sports media) has been the emergence of **follower-centred perspectives on leadership** (Uhl-Bien, Riggio, Lowe, & Carsten, 2014). Still relatively new to the leadership theory debate, this more expansive view of leadership aligns with the social construction of leadership, and has also helped to advance a resurgence of alternative theories such as emergent and servant leadership (Greenleaf, 1997; Parris & Welty Peachey, 2013). Such approaches have extended mainstream leadership research and practice but need more exploration in sport settings (O'Boyle, Murray, & Cummins, 2015). We also point to the emergence of **self leadership** and **emotional intelligence** as a central aspect of new leadership thinking that complements a more expansive view of leadership theory (Schneider, 2012). As Pearce and Manz (2005) offer, "In contrast to the traditional approach to leadership development, we argue that followers should also be included in leadership development efforts in order to prepare them to exercise responsible self-leadership and to effectively utilise shared leadership" (p. 130).

We consider there to be immediate relevance of this broader view of leadership for a special issue on sport leadership for the *Journal of Sport Management*. Most notably, a focus on informal/emergent leadership and followership would be valued alongside assigned leaders, in combination with the encouragement of leadership research at multiple levels. A special issue orientated in this way would serve as an innovative, thought provoking resource for sport management academics and those in practice seeking to understand new ways of leadership within sport organisations and sport systems around the globe.

Theme and topics of the special issue:

The overall theme for this special issue is: **Sport Leadership: A New Generation of Thinking.** Papers adopting either a theoretical, conceptual, or empirical approach to the study of sport leadership that embrace new leadership thinking would be especially encouraged. In this way, the special issue would bring together a collection of papers that demonstrate the variety of approaches to sport leadership in order to map out future directions for research on sport leadership. Suggested topics of focus include (but are not limited to):

- **Collective sport leadership -** Cullen-Lester and Yammarino's (2016) exploration of collective and network approaches to leadership establishes leadership as a collective behaviour where leadership in organisations and other collectives is considered to "reside in the interactions between people thereby constituting a network of relationships that emerges and shifts over time" (p. 1). We contend that sport organisations and sport systems (leadership within and across organisations) would greatly benefit from empirical and conceptual work that explores leadership as a collective phenomenon.

- **Social construction of sport leadership –** as with the above, this view stresses the importance of context in the leadership dynamic. This matters because, as a body of scholars, we argue that the sport context has special characteristics that combine often competing elements of high performance and community interests, not-for-profit and commercial sensibilities, and a professional workforce alongside voluntary contribution (Ferkins, Shilbury & McDonald, 2009). Renewed investigations of the social construction of leadership grounded in the sport context is likely to yield new insights.

- **Multilevel analysis of sport leadership –** encouraging the investigation of multilevel analysis of leadership within the sport setting/system(s) is also likely to yield new insights and create future research and theory development opportunities (Welty Peachey et al., 2015).

- **Sport leadership and diversity –** leadership studies in sport management that have focused on elements such as gender, age, sexuality, race and ethnicity have offered rich insights about the leadership dynamic (Cunningham, 2010; Fink, Pastore, & Riemer, 2001; also see Ospina & Foldy, 2009). To date, we have not fully embraced the exploration of diversity in sport leadership.

- **Women in sport leadership -** the social construction theory has been widely used in understanding gender, and as noted above, the theory is increasingly used to understand leadership. At the nexus is the construction of leadership roles between men and women. The highly masculine, uber-competitive, and hierarchal nature of the sport industry offers a particularly meaningful context for understanding how leadership roles differ and, more importantly, understand how to manipulate follower perceptions to equalize the representation of women in sport leadership roles.

- **Leadership in sport governance –** surprisingly, governance and leadership (in any context) have rarely been explored as complementary of each other and little is known about the impact of one's theoretical frameworks on the other's field (Erakovic & Jackson, 2012; Pye,

2002). We propose that much insight could be gained from further exploring these two areas concurrently within the sport context.

- **Self and emotional intelligence in sport leadership** – as Schneider (2012) notes, this is one of the missing elements of leadership within the sport management literature. The idea that leadership begins with self and self awareness followed by social and emotional intelligence (Goleman, 2005; Pearce & Manz, 2005) is potentially a major gap of investigation within our context that has grown significantly in literature beyond sport management.

- **The dark side of sport leadership** – understanding the characteristics of unhealthy and dysfunctional leadership can enlighten future sport leaders of the dangers they could confront. Case studies identifying the traits and behavioural practices of these leaders could promote constructive debate for innovative solutions to deter and restrict corrupt leadership practices (Tomlinson, 2014).

- **Ethical sport leadership** – given the FIFA, IAAF and IOC scandals and regular indiscretions by players and coaches, there is a need for further exploration in this area. This also still appears to be a salient topic in business schools as they are criticized for developing leaders without any exposure to ethical leadership perspectives while at the university and who, subsequently, make poor decisions in practice. There is also scope to explore how ethical leadership is/should be intertwined with sport governance (Sherry & Shilbury, 2007).

- **Leadership background** - to what degree do managers in sport organisations need to have sporting backgrounds to be effective leaders? This is an interesting topic in relation to entry and advancement into leadership positions in sport and worthy of further consideration (Swanson & Kent, 2014).

Submission guidelines:

Manuscripts should follow the guidelines in the *Publication Manual of the American Psychological Association* (www.apa.org), and should be prepared in accordance with the *Journal of Sport Management* "Instructions to Authors" (www.humankinetics.com/JSM/journalAbout.cfm). Manuscripts must not be submitted to another journal while they are under review by the *Journal of Sport Management*, nor should they have been previously published.

Manuscripts should be submitted **no later than April 30, 2017** using ScholarOne. Authors should indicate in their cover letter that the submission is to be considered for the Special Issue 'Sport Leadership: A New Generation of Thinking'.

Guest editors – contact information:

Associate Professor Lesley Ferkins | Sport Leadership & Governance|
Auckland University Technology, New Zealand
Sports Performance Research Institute, New Zealand (SPRINZ)
Private Bag 92006 | Auckland 1142 | New Zealand
lesley.ferkins@aut.ac.nz
 Mobile + 64 (0) 22 072 9787

Dr Ben Corbett
Loughborough University, London
3 Lesney Avenue, The Broadcast Centre, Here East
Queen Elizabeth Olympic Park
Stratford, London, E15 2GZ
B.D.Corbett@lboro.ac.uk
Mobile: +44 7824 546278

Professor James Skinner
Loughborough University, London
3 Lesney Avenue, The Broadcast Centre, Here East
Queen Elizabeth Olympic Park
Stratford, London, E15 2GZ
J.L.Skinner@lboro.ac.uk
Mobile: +44 7775 502818

Dr Steve Swanson
Loughborough University, London
3 Lesney Avenue, The Broadcast Centre, Here East
Queen Elizabeth Olympic Park
Stratford, London, E15 2GZ
S.Swanson@lboro.ac.uk
Mobile: +44 07785 593098

Learn the skills to become a successful sport facility manager

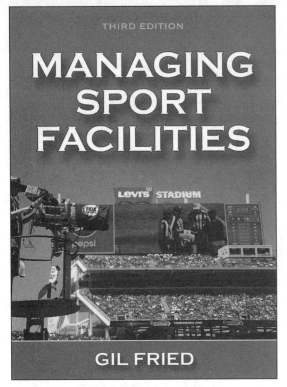

Managing Sport Facilities, Third Edition
Gil Fried, JD
©2015 • Hardback • 440 pp
Print: 978-1-4504-6811-4
E-book: 978-1-4925-1205-9

College Instructors: To request an exam copy, please visit our website at **www.HumanKinetics.com/Higher-Education.**

Audiences: *Text for students in sport facility management or sport facility and event management courses. A reference for sport facility managers and industry professionals.*

Managing Sport Facilities, Third Edition, provides future and current sport facility managers with the knowledge they need in order to make the proper decisions in all areas of facility management. This text engages readers with extensive real-world examples and information on managing a range of facilities, from smaller health clubs, colleges, and recreational environments to professional sport stadiums. This edition has been updated to include the following:

- A new chapter on implementing and maintaining green facilities
- Updated Sport Facility Management Profile sections featuring industry experts introducing applied connections for each chapter
- Expanded Facility Focus sidebars presenting facts and strategies used by real facilities

In *Managing Sport Facilities, Third Edition,* students will learn the primary goals and objectives of facility managers; how to build and finance a facility; facility operation; administration of marketing and finance; and event administration and management.

A complete ancillary package is free to course adopters, and includes instructor videos that feature professionals in the field offering advice and insight. Ancillaries are available at **www.HumanKinetics.com/ManagingSportFacilities.**

For more information or to order, visit **www.HumanKinetics.com** or call:
(800) 747-4457 US • (800) 465-7301 CDN • 44 (0) 113-255-5665 UK
(08) 8372-0999 AUS • 0800 222 062 NZ • (217) 351-5076 International

 HUMAN KINETICS
The Information Leader in Physical Activity & Health

1219   4/15

Build a foundation for working in collegiate athletics administration

Administration of Intercollegiate Athletics

Erianne A. Weight | Robert H. Zullo

Editors

Administration of Intercollegiate Athletics
Erianne A. Weight, PhD, and Robert H. Zullo, PhD, Editors
©2015 • Hardback, e-book • 320 pp
Print: ISBN 978-1-4504-6815-2
E-book: ISBN 978-1-4925-0349-1

For more information or to order,
visit **www.HumanKinetics.com**
or call: (800) 747-4457 US
(800) 465-7301 CDN
44 (0) 113-255-5665 UK
(08) 8372-0999 AUS
0800 222 062 NZ
(217) 351-5076 International

Audiences: *Textbook for undergraduate and graduate students in upper-level sport management courses; reference for athletics administrators or anyone interested in the complex dynamics of intercollegiate athletics.*

In *Administration of Intercollegiate Athletics,* some of the most knowledgeable professionals in athletics administration have come together to create an essential resource for all who aspire to work in this exciting field. This compilation is the most comprehensive textbook available on the subject.

Through this text, students will be able to access ideas and research to incorporate into their evolving professional philosophy. Coverage of media relations, marketing, corporate sponsorship, event management, alumni relations, and athlete services is unparalleled to coverage in any other text in the industry.

The following learning tools in *Administration of Intercollegiate Athletics* will enrich students' understanding:

- Leadership Lessons provide key points, inspiring a leadership mind-set critical to success in today's world of collegiate athletics administration.

- Opening scenarios, chapter objectives, and learning activities provide a framework for learning, highlighting critical points and translating material to a real-world setting.

- Sidebars and case studies call out important concepts from readings.

- Industry Profile Q&As offer students a chance to see how working administrators reached their present roles.

College Instructors: To request an exam copy, please visit our website at
www.HumanKinetics.com/Higher-Education.

Ancillary materials, including a test package and an image bank, are available to course adopters at
www.HumanKinetics.com/AdministrationOfIntercollegiateAthletics.

HUMAN KINETICS
The Information Leader in Physical Activity & Health